Tynnwyd

FOR
REFERENCE ONLY
Withdrawn

D1759592

Equality and Anti-Discrimination Law

The Equality Act 2010 and other anti-discrimination protections

Dr Mark Butler

University of Lancaster

Tynnwyd yn ôl
SWANSEA LIBRARIES
Withdrawn

0001382595

First published January 2016

by

Spiramus Press Ltd
102 Blandford Street
London W1U 8AG
United Kingdom

www.spiramus.com

© Spiramus Press Ltd, 2016

ISBN
Paperback   978 1907444470
Ebook   978 1907444562

This publication is based upon the law as at 1 November 2015.

The right of Mark Butler to be identified as the author of this work has been asserted by him in accordance with the Copyright, Designs and Patents Act, 1988.

All rights reserved. No part of this publication may be reproduced in any material form (including photocopying or storing it in any medium by electronic means and whether or not transiently or incidental to some other use of this publication) without the prior written permission of the copyright owner except in accordance with the provisions of the Copyright, Designs and Patents Act 1988 or under the terms of a licence issued by the Copyright Licensing Agency Ltd, 90 Tottenham Court Road, London W1P 4LP.

Printed and bound in Great Britain by

Grosvenor Group (Print Services) Ltd, UK

In memory of Rachel Agnew (2015), never to be forgotten.

Contents

EQUALITY AND ANTI-DISCRIMINATION LAW

CONTENTS

EQUALITY AND ANTI-DISCRIMINATION LAW

List of abbreviations

AML	Additional maternity leave
CAP	Community Action Programme
CJEU	Court of Justice of the EU
CoE	Council of Europe
DDA	Disability Discrimination Act 1995
DDA 2005	Disability Discrimination Act 2005
EAT	Employment Appeal Tribunal
ECHR	European Convention on Human Rights
ECJ	European Court of Justice
ECtHR	European Court of Human Rights
EPD	Equal Pay Directive
EqA	Equality Act 2010
EqPA	Equal Pay Act 1970
ERA	Employment Rights Act 1996
ET	Employment Tribunal
ETD	Equal Treatment Directive
FTER	Fixed-Term Employees (Prevention of Less Favourable Treatment) Regulations 2002
GMF	genuine material factor
GOR	genuine occupational requirement
IGO	inter-governmental organisation
ILO	International Labour Organisation
ITEPA	Income Tax (Earnings and Pensions) Act 2003
JES	job evaluation study
OML	Ordinary maternity leave
PCP	provision criterion or practice
PHA	Protection from Harassment Act 1997
PSED	public sector equality duty
PTWR	Part-Time Workers (Prevention of Less Favourable Treatment) Regulations 2000
RRA	Race Relations Act 1976
SAP	Statutory adoption pay
SDA	Sex Discrimination Act 1975
ShPP	Statutory Shared Parental Pay
SMP	Statutory maternity pay

SPL   Shared Parental Leave
SPP   Statutory Paternity Pay
TFEU   Treaty on the Functioning of the European Union

Tables of authorities

Cases

　　　EQUALITY AND ANTI-DISCRIMINATION LAW

EQUALITY AND ANTI-DISCRIMINATION LAW

TABLES OF AUTHORITIES

Regulations

Other Authorities

EQUALITY AND ANTI-DISCRIMINATION LAW

1. Introduction to Equality Law

1.1. The legal landscape

Since 1965 and the introduction of the initial Race Relations Act the UK has had some form of statutory protection against discrimination, although this was significantly limited. However, the protection in this area has expanded immensely over the past half a century, with a number of national and European initiatives being key drivers in this respect. It is notable that since the first piece of legislation was introduced, which solely focussed on race, equality law has expanded and now covers a wide range of different characteristics and different circumstances. It is a work in progress which has recognised that there are certain characteristics or situations that should not be used to drive a decision, or to influence the treatment of a person; to do so would be to make arbitrary work decisions. Instead, the development of equality law seeks to ensure, to some extent, that the work place is determined by meritocracy: an individual should be provided with appropriate terms and conditions that reflect their worth to an employer, and every individual should have an equal opportunity to work, with appointments and opportunities based on skill set rather than on their gender, sexual orientation, race, or some other arbitrary reason.

It cannot be underestimated the role that the European Economic Community, now the European Union, has played in the development of protection on equality grounds, with aspects of equal treatment being a prominent goal since the inception of the European model under the Treaty of Rome in 1957. Not only has equality been considered a key principle that operates across the four fundamental freedoms of the supranational state and beyond, but it has also been recognised as a fundamental constitutional principle of the Union. It is the recognition of non-discrimination and equality as being central to the European model that has inevitably led to numerous European initiatives enshrining this principle as a necessity for Member States in a number of their transposing obligations. As a consequence of Europe the UK, and the other States that make up EU28, have been obliged to introduce a number of legislative protections that can be categorised as non-discrimination or equality initiatives. The influence of Europe is ongoing (and hopefully will be after any UK referendum in 2017…) and as such is a key area that practitioners and academics dealing with equality issues must keep on top of. Reference to key European developments will be made throughout this text where necessary.

The current UK legal landscape that seeks to protect on non-discrimination grounds and provide some form of equal treatment to the workforce can be complicated to navigate (although it is accepted it is a lot easier than the pre-Equality Act 2010 position), especially given that it is not as straightforward as going to an all-encompassing self-evident document, and indeed is read across a number of different pieces of legislation, and supplemented and developed through key case law decisions. In addition, there are non-legal documents such as Codes of Practices and guidance notes that offer useful practical advice. They are worth keeping up to date with, as these help with contextualising the legal provisions, and offer much needed practical explanations as to how the legal provisions were intended to operate. Having such interaction between such a range of sources can cause some difficulties, especially to those that are not too familiar with how law develops as a living and breathing instrument, and how the legal and non-legal interact. Further difficulties in understanding the protections can be caused by the choice of language which is used in legislation, which is not always user friendly, and often slips into legalese, which in itself can cause confusion.

Although the majority of protections on discrimination grounds can be read from the Equality Act 2010 and supporting case law and documents, there are other areas which the reader should also be aware of. Crucial protection that seeks to provide workers with equality of opportunity and equality of treatment can be witnessed in the regulatory initiatives termed as 'family friendly' policies, as well as those that seek to introduce parity of treatment for those who are engaged on atypical work contracts. All of these are equally important and, in their own way, add to the equality laws of the UK. Each of these areas will be discussed independently.

1.2. Purpose of this text

It is not the intention of this text to provide a heavyweight academic read, as there are a number of other texts on the market that can quite easily be considered to satisfy this desire should it arise; however, this text has a number of purposes:

1. provide an interesting an up-to-date guide through the necessary legal areas that make up equality law in the UK;
2. highlight relative strengths and weaknesses of the protections that are currently in force;
3. offer useful and thought-provoking analysis which introduces the reader to some of the contemporary academic debates without getting too bogged down with it; and

4. try to explain the different focusses of the relevant legislation with a view to explaining whether this has impacted upon the approach adopted.

Hopefully each of these aims will be achieved and will help in developing the readers understanding of the equality laws of the UK.

1.3.   Structure

The structure of the book has been kept quite simple, and is aimed at building up an understanding of equality law by laying down foundations of understanding against which the current position can be developed and considered. It has already been suggested that Europe has been a huge influence on the development of the UK's equality laws. It is this development where the text commences. In considering this development of equality law, **Chapter 2** will focus on both the development at international level as well as that at national level, to identify the sources and potential interactions that each system has and to highlight where the journey began. The book then moves on to consider the concept of equality itself in **Chapter 3**. It is important to first understand what is meant by equality before one can move on to consider the approaches adopted under the relevant legislation. Often equality is viewed through a single lens, with focus being on whether like is being treated alike; however, this does not tell the full story. If one was solely to consider the equality laws of the UK through such a limited viewpoint then many aspects of the regulatory framework could be open to criticism, in particular those aspects that go beyond treating people alike (i.e. formal equality) and seek to take account of differences when seeking equality of outcome (i.e. substantive equality). It is only after these building blocks have been put in place that the text then moves on to consider substantive areas of UK equality laws, focussing on the Equality Act 2010 in **Chapters 4 – 10**, advancements in family friendly policy in **Chapter 11** and atypical worker protection in **Chapter 12**.

EQUALITY AND ANTI-DISCRIMINATION LAW

2. Development of Non-Discrimination/Equality Protection

It is important to note from the outset that this text will be using equality law and non-discrimination law interchangeably, although there is a difference if one was to trace the development of each concept: the most notable difference is that the word 'discrimination' tends to suggest a focus on differences of treatment, whereas equality is a much broader concept and can include much more than this. An important point, without looking at the micro-differences between the concepts, is that the development of non-discrimination protection can be said to make up a huge portion of what is referred to as equality law.

Although the introduction to this text only referred to the development of the European Economic Communities in terms of an international influence, this is not strictly true, as there have been other influences too including the International Labour Organisation ('ILO') as well as from international jurisdicions, most notably the US. However, it is safe to say that two of the key sources of development are the European Convention on Human Rights (the 'ECHR') and European Union Law ('EU Law'). It is not the intention of this book to fully develop a discussion of these two systems, but to introduce them initially here, before alluding to developments in these respective systems that have influenced the shape of UK protections in appropriate places throughout the text.

2.1. European Union Level

The supranational body of the EU currently consists of 28 Member States. It has developed significantly from its initial purpose of stimulating economic growth across its members, and now quite visibly takes into account other important contexts such as social rights and human rights in the development of its protections. However, the initial focus on economic growth led to the introduction of various protections which sought to ensure that Member States could compete on a level playing field, many of which were predicated on the non-discrimination principle; none more so than the development of the four fundamental freedoms of free movement of goods, capital, people and services. The idea is a simple one: an individual would not be able to move freely across Europe as a worker or as a citizen if once they moved they were subject to discriminatory treatment, and as such it is easy to appreciate why this principle is central to this freedom.[1] Furthermore, being able to employ individuals in a discriminatory way would enable an employer to assemble a cheaper workforce and be at a competitive advantage when compared to employers that are located in a member state that had to offer equal treatment of such workers. Equality laws and the principle of non-discrimination is a means of levelling such unequal competitive advantages, which was a crucial requirement as the internal market was being completed. The same rationale can be attached to other important European protections that are primarily concerned with non-discrimination. For example, equal pay protection has clear roots set in the European ideology of creating a level playing field: Member states which allowed a cheaper female workforce would be at a competitive advantage if compared to workforces where both males and females were subject to the equal pay principle. The shift away from being solely an economic unity, with social protection and protection on human rights grounds has simply acted to strengthen Europe's focus on non-discrimination and equality. The focus is no longer solely on the economic position that such less favourable treatment introduces, but there is an increased focus that such treatment has on the person.

2.1.1. Early developments of European non-discrimination Protection

One of the earliest EU initiatives in this field was that of equal pay, with the initial Treaties providing that member states were tasked with ensuring and maintaining 'the application of the principle that men and women should receive equal pay for equal work'[2], which was described as forming 'part of the social objectives of the Community, which is not merely an economic union, but is at the same time intended, by common action, to ensure social progress and reach the constant improvement of the living and working conditions of their peoples'.[3] Equal pay as a Treaty principle was largely ineffective before the series of cases brought by Defrenne against the Belgian national airline in the early 1970s. It was the second of the cases brought by Defrenne that really advanced the protective aspect of the principle when the ECJ held that Article 119 EC was directly applicable in the Member States as regards 'direct and overt' discrimination, and

---

[1] The principle of non-discrimination is equally important across the other fundamental freedoms, but these are not the subject of this discussion.

[2] This was introduced at Article 119 of the EC Treaty, and has been maintained throughout Treaty Amendments. Currently equal pay protection can be found at Article 157 of the TFEU.

[3] *Défrenne v. Sabena* [1971] E.C.R. 445, para 10 (Case C-80/70)

further that the principle 'forms part of the social objectives of the Community, which is not merely an economic union, but is at the same time intended, by common action, to ensure social progress and reach the constant improvement of the living and working conditions of their peoples.'[4]

The equal pay principle contained within the founding treaty was later supplemented by the Equal Pay Directive[5], which provided flesh to the bones of the principle in terms of how it worked, but also expanded the concept of equal pay by providing that the concept 'means for the same work or for work to which equal value is attributed, the elimination of all discrimination on grounds of sex, with regard to all aspects of remuneration'[6]. This in effect meant that all aspects of remuneration were covered, and that work did not have to be identical for the principle of equal pay to apply, but that work which was of equal value was also included within the protection. The Equal Pay Directive was introduced following the Council Resolution of 21 January 1974. This introduced a social action programme, which listed as a priority the need for 'action for the purpose of achieving equality between men and women as regards access to employment and vocational training and promotion and as regards working conditions, including pay'.[7]

Alongside the Equal Pay Directive the Equal Treatment Directive[8] also developed, which sought to introduce protection against discrimination on the grounds of sex in matters that were not covered by the Equal Pay Directive. The Equal Treatment Directive, common with the Equal Pay Directive was as a consequence of the 1974 Council Resolution. The Equal Treatment Directive was amended and updated in 2002[9] in order to ensure

---

[4] *Defrenne v Sabena (No 2)* [1976], para 10; (Case C-43/75)

[5] The Equal Pay Directive saw the Union adopt the ILO's standard in relation to equal pay, which is contained at Art.2(1) of ILO Convention No.100 (1951), and has also formed part of the ILO Constitution since 1919, that men and women workers should be paid "equal remuneration … for work of equal value.".

[6] This closely followed the approach to equal pay contained within Art 2(1) of ILO Convention No.100 (1951).

[7] This can be read in Recital 1 of the Preamble to the Directive.

[8] Directive 76/207.

[9] Directive 2002/73.

that it was consistent with more recent European developments, such as the Race Directive[10] and the Framework Directive.[11]

2.1.2. Development of Non-discrimination Protections at European Level: Article 13 Treaty of Amsterdam

Although non-discrimination had long been acknowledged as a fundamental right that needed protection at European level, Community action was originally severely limited. This was because initially the Community only had competence in the areas of EU nationality and sex discrimination. This position was dramatically changed during the 1996 Intergovernmental Conferences,[12] which led to renegotiation of the European Community (EC) Treaties. The new EC Treaty that was concluded at Amsterdam included a new Article 13,[13] which placed anti-discrimination as a basic founding principle of the Union. Article 13 stated:

> Without prejudice to the other provisions of this Treaty, and within the limits of the powers conferred by it upon the Community, the Council, acting unanimously on a proposal from the Commission, and after consulting the European Parliament, may take appropriate action to combat discrimination based on sex, racial or ethnic origin, religion or belief, disability, age or sexual orientation.

This provided the EU with a new legal basis to take action to combat discrimination on a wide range of issues, including age, sexual orientation and disability.[14]

Despite Article 13 at the time it was introduced being criticized for both its lack of direct effect[15,] and the requirement of proposals based upon it

---

[10] Directive 2000/43.

[11] Directive 2000/78.

[12] The key meeting that led to the introduction of Article 13 (which was originally Article 6a before renumbering) was the European Council meeting in Dublin in December 1996, as this was where the proposed new competences were first committed to paper. Insertion of Article 13 was due to all member states expressing a desire to expand Community powers beyond the then legislative limits of gender discrimination; these negotiations although crystallizing in Dublin commenced at the Intergovernmental Conference that took place in Turin on 29-30 March 1996.

[13] Following renumbering under the Treaty of Lisbon this provision is now contained at Article 19 of the Treaty on the Functioning of the European Union (TFEU).

[14] Although this ground was already protected against discrimination in a number of member states of the EU, including the UK.

requiring unanimity in voting before the EU's Council, the amendment was a considerable step in the right direction toward removing discrimination more comprehensively. Furthermore, Article 13 signalled a move towards a new method of dealing with discrimination; namely dealing with different grounds of discrimination by common measures in the same instrument (horizontal legislation). Bell[16] suggested this to be a positive advance, as from the perspective of fundamental rights and equality before the law 'it is difficult to justify why any ground of discrimination is more or less deserving of legal protection'.

Introducing the basis for horizontal discrimination legislation had the potential to enhance equal treatment and give strength and substance to EU citizenship. The argument is that citizens of the EU need to feel as part of the same group and as equals, and not part of a lower sub-group, to truly foster the idea of citizenship. Once this equality is achieved, European integration will have solid foundations from which to build upon. Equal protection of every individual is therefore to be considered an essential element in establishing and upholding this sense of inter-citizen solidarity. This is highlighted by Bell,[17] recognising that 'the full realisation of the right to free movement depends on individuals and businesses being able to exercise these rights on a non-discriminatory basis, and more generally in a context of 'freedom and dignity'.[18]

---

[15] When a Community instrument is considered to have direct effect it enables direct reliance on the provisions of that instrument by an individual. The concept of direct effect was first introduced by the ECJ in *Van Gend en Loos v. Nederlandse Administratie der Belastingen* [1963] ECR 1 (Case 26/62). The criteria for determining whether an instrument had direct effect was developed by Advocate General Mayras in *Reyners v. Belgium* [1974] ECR 631 (Case 2/74), and required that: (i) the provision must be clear and unambiguous; (ii) it must be unconditional (iii) its operation must not be dependent on further action being taken. It is accepted that Article 13 is merely an enabling clause, which is to say that the Council is merely offered the opportunity to take action in this area consequently not satisfying the third limb of the *Reyners* requirements.

[16] Bell, M. (2000), 'Article 13 EC: The European Commission's Anti-discrimination Proposals', *Industrial Law Journal*, Volume 29(1), pp.79-84, at p.81.

[17] Bell, M. (2002), *Anti-Discrimination Law and the European Union*, Oxford University Press: Oxford, at p.161.

[18] This idea was first introduced by the European Commission in its 1994 White Paper on European social policy, stating that: 'the Union must act to provide a guarantee for all people against the fear of discrimination if it is to make a reality of free movement'; European Commission (1994), *European Social Policy – A Way Forward For the Union*, COM (94) 333.

The positive advances through this new approach can be appreciated by considering a general weakness of the vertical strategy, namely, the inability to deal with multiple discriminatory grounds which overlap.[19] A major limitation with the previous vertical approach followed in member states,[20] occurs when there is an instance of 'multiple discrimination'.[21] This is not expressly dealt with by the majority of member states , but rather each discriminatory ground is dealt with in separate legislation.[22] Case law across the EU suggests that in such circumstances each ground is dealt with separately in separate proceedings, which means that vulnerability to discrimination due to a combination of grounds is not dealt with;[23] a problem exacerbated when one considers the general need for a comparable worker in order to bring a claim. If one takes, for example, an elderly female worker being discriminated in the UK, the legislation regulating gender discrimination will only allow a comparison with a male

---

[19] This expected advantage of a horizontal approach is reflected through the Commission's explanatory memorandum to the general framework directive: 'the scope of the present proposal covers all discriminatory grounds referred to in Article 13 except sex and does not rank them in any way. This absence of a qualitative hierarchy among the discriminatory grounds is of particular importance in cases of multiple discrimination'; European Commission (1999), *Proposal for a Council Directive Establishing a General Framework for Equal Treatment in Employment and Occupation*, COM (1999) 565, at p.6.

[20] Which included the UK, and to some extent this approach is still evident under the Equality Act; this will be touched upon again later.

[21] Multiple discrimination is taken to occur when discrimination occurs on two or more grounds simultaneously, and where these grounds are inseparable.

[22] This was the case in the UK prior to the introduction of the Equality Act, with protected characteristics being the subject of the their own individual regulatory approach: for example sex discrimination was dealt with under the Sex Discrimination Act 1975, race discrimination under the Race Relations Act 1976 and disability discrimination under the Disability Discrimination Act 1995. If there was a complaint based on less favourable treatment based on an individual being disabled Muslim female then the claim would have had to have been broken up and considered under each of the three statutes, rather than accumulating the three characteristics.

[23] A study carried out by the Danish Institute for Human Rights initiated by the European Commission highlighted, for example, that groups including disabled women, elderly women, and young ethnic minority men amongst others were vulnerable to multiple discrimination. The study highlights that individuals can and do 'belong to several disadvantaged groups […] the focus of both governmental and non-governmental institutions is placed mainly on one ground of discrimination, often due to strategic litigation reasons'. The study can be found at:
http://ec.europa.eu/employment_social/fundamental_rights/pdf/pubst/stud/multdis_en.pdf.

who is employed in a similar position, the only variable being a change in gender. A second and equally valid claim may arise with a comparison between the elderly worker and a younger worker under the UK age discrimination laws; however, neither piece of legislation provides for a comparison between the elderly female and a young male so as to take into account the cumulative effect of the multiple grounds.[24] Adopting a horizontal approach[25] has the potential to resolve this problem, and could encourage member states to introduce similarly worded horizontal initiatives, and would have the consequence of advancing equality to fill a gap that has existed across the EU in a number of member states .

In 1999, Anna Diamantopoulou, the then EU Social Affairs Commissioner, wasted little time in utilising these newly extended competencies, issuing an extensive anti-discrimination package on 25 November 1999, which is a mix of both the horizontal and vertical approaches. This package consisted of:

1. a Commission Communication;[26]
2. a proposal for a Council Directive establishing a general framework for equal treatment in employment and occupation;
3. a proposal for a Council Directive implementing the principle of equal treatment between persons irrespective of racial or ethnic origin; and
4. a proposal for a Council Decision establishing a Community Action Programme (CAP), 2001-2006.[27]

---

[24] For a fuller account of the inability of vertical legislation to deal effectively with instances of multiple discrimination can be seen in: (i) Moon, G. (2008), 'Multi-Dimensional discrimination: justice for the whole person', *Equal Opportunities Review*, Issue 173, pp.14-17, and (ii) Zarrehparvar, M. (2008), 'Multiple Discrimination in the EU', *Equal Opportunities Review*, Issue 173, pp.18-19.

[25] However, not all academics view the proposals based on Article 13 as truly horizontal. For example, Waddington, L. (2000), 'Article 13 EC: Setting Priorities in the Proposal for a Horizontal Employment Directive', *Industrial Law Journal*, Volume 29(2), pp.176-181, at p.176, highlights that the proposal based on Article 13 gives special attention in the text to four of the seven covered grounds. This is certainly a proposition that is difficult to disagree with in light of reviewing the Article 13 proposals; although, it is accepted that there are varying degrees of protection afforded to each ground, it can be defended in being out of necessity for attaining political support rather than being predetermined.

[26] This introduced the proposals and explained the necessity of action in this area.

[27] The CAP was passed in 2000 and was designed to support activities that would actively involve discriminated groups

The Council Directive establishing a general framework for equal treatment in employment and occupation is an example of a horizontal Directive. This placed all the grounds stated in Article 13 on an equal footing with EU anti-discrimination legislation that already existed, namely that relating to nationality and sex. In contrast, the anti-racism Directive was purely vertical in nature, and offered greater protections to those falling within its ambit. This extensive programme exemplified non-discrimination measures as a priority in European Social policy, and provided a great step forward in the EU's approach to non-discrimination and equality.

2.1.3. Development of Family Friendly Protections at European Level

The EU protections discussed above are often viewed as the traditional non-discrimination instruments, where the focus is on a protected characteristic, with a familiar framework constructed in order to offer some level of protection. However, there have been other developments at EU level which also go some way to protecting against discrimination with a view to ensuring equality. Of particular importance have been the developments in the area of family friendly rights alongside the protections developed for atypical workers.

The suite of family friendly policies at EU level is often viewed as vital to ensuring equality of opportunity and career progression,[28] as without any such protections employers may be dissuaded from employing particular persons due to associated costs of losing members of their workforce for various periods of time; consequently, this would potentially impact upon those of an age where having a family is a realistic possibility, and females, with whom the primary responsibility for childcare in most Western societies still rests. Furthermore, it is an inevitable consequence that a pregnant female will take various periods away from the workplace in relation to their pregnancy, whether that be for antenatal classes, scans, or at the very least, for child birth. It is thus easy to conceive why there was a need for protection in this area, and why the Commission reached a conclusion that without measures that "enable men and women to reconcile their occupational and family obligations"[29] then full equality of opportunity will not be achieved. In order to further equality of opportunity two EU directives with a view towards reconciling work with family life were introduced:

---

[28] In particular on gender grounds.

[29] Social Charter of 1989, para 3(16).

EQUALITY AND ANTI-DISCRIMINATION LAW

- Directive 92/85 on Pregnant Workers
- Directive 96/34 on Parental Leave

The development of protections that are termed family friendly is certainly an important step in the context of equality. It suffices at this point to note that these legislative initiatives act to ensure that individuals are not precluded from the labour market due to having less flexibility in their family life. This ensures that parents or, more particularly, mothers[30] do not have to make a choice between a career and a family. However, it does go further than this in that through ensuring family life does not impede the career continuance then it highlights to employers that parents and those with caring responsibilities do not necessarily become a burden to the employer, and can continue to be an asset to the business: this ability to impact upon mindsets and potential misconceived prejudices is key to ensuring equality.

2.1.4. Development of Atypical Worker Protection at European Level family friendly policies

Regulation of certain types of atypical working was first mooted at European level in 1981, when a draft Directive on voluntary part-time working was submitted to the Council. A further draft Directive on temporary work was submitted in 1982. The major stumbling block for both of these was the legal base which the initiatives had to be forwarded upon. Both were based on Article 100, which brought with it the requirement of unanimity. On both occasions discussions were fruitless and no progress was made. In fact these were not the only failures of attempted regulation in this area, with the period of 1982 to 1990 witnessing a staggering eight failures in comparison to only one initiative being adopted as a Directive.

It was the 1989 Social Charter Action Programme which gave a new impetus to the potential of introducing regulation of atypical work, promising new action in this area,[31] and in 1990, the Commission adopted three draft Directives, using different legal bases, on:

---

[30] Mothers still appear to shoulder the greater burden in terms of time and responsibility within a family setup. Although this is not the case in all families, since this is the most common, it can be perceived as being the norm.

[31] The desire can be identified on the basis of expressly identifying that there was a need for action to ensure the improvement in living and working conditions as regards 'forms of employment other than open-ended contracts, such as fixed-term contracts, part-time working, temporary work and seasonal work'.

1. the improvement of living and working conditions, based on Article 100 and facing the requirement of unanimous agreement;
2. the elimination of distortions of competition, based on Article 100A and so being subject to qualified majority voting; and
3. the protection of health and safety for part-time, temporary and seasonal workers, based on Article 118A, also subject to qualified majority voting.

It was this legislative push that witnessed Europe's first success in this area, although being quite limited in its scope. The draft Directive based on Article 118A was subsequently adopted in June 1991, and required implementation by 31 December 1992. However, debates on the other two were inconclusive, with the UK and Danish Governments in particular opposing such measures.

The issue then lay untouched until 1993 when under the Belgian Presidency an attempt was made to breathe new life into the proposals by merging the Article 100 and Article 100A drafts in 1993. Once more this was unsuccessful in achieving a breakthrough.

The desire to regulate these areas then emerged to the forefront of the plans of the German Presidency in the second half of 1994, when a new text was issued, based on Article 100[32] for "the promotion of employment and the protection of part-time and fixed-term employment relationships". This was considered to be the final opportunity for a whole-community proposal to be discussed in this area as, by this time, the Maastricht Treaty had entered into force, which brought with it an alternative route which social policy initiatives could be progressed. Once more due to a stubborn UK Government refusing to accept such proposals, Social Affairs Council meetings were unproductive. This was the final straw for the Commission who consequently launched consultation of management and labour at European level on this issue under the social policy Agreement route,[33] on 27 September 1995. The European social partners decided that they would like to try to negotiate an agreement, and formal talks began on 21 October 1996. In 1997 they concluded a formal agreement covering part-time work. This agreement was then adopted as a Directive, which, following the British signature of the Social Chapter, was applied to the UK as well.

---

[32] The importance of Article 100 being the legal bases was that introduced a requirement of unanimous agreement among the member states, which was obviously going to be difficult in light of certain member states' long opposing action in this area.

[33] At the time the social policy agreement route excluded the UK.

EQUALITY AND ANTI-DISCRIMINATION LAW

The Commission's attempts at regulation in this area have frequently ended in failure, and as a consequence their proposals have consistently been weakened over the years in an attempt to secure Member State acceptance. Early attempts insisted on a broad definition of 'atypical work', but when this became apparent as not acceptable this was soon substituted for a more restrictive definition with narrower scope. This watering down of the proposals can best be seen through the period of the German Presidency highlighted above. In order to appease the strongly contesting UK Government a number of changes were introduced:

- a non-discrimination general principle was introduced to replace the previous specific requirements;
- the inclusion of social security was dropped; a wide range of express exceptions were introduced; and
- and the scope of the proposals were limited to part-time work only.

The resulting proposal was reluctantly accepted by the Commission as representing, in the words of Commissioner Flynn:

> ...the minimum of the minimum, below which nothing is conceivable in social protection.

However, even this very much weakened attempt failed, and the Commission turned to the new procedure that was available under the Protocol and Agreement on Social Policy. The Commission stressed that the whole question of European regulation on 'atypical work' would start from the beginning without taking into account earlier attempts as its starting point, a wise move considering the degree to which the legislation had weakened.

It is worth noting here that although this first agreement only concerned regulation of part-time work, the preamble to the agreement contained reference to similar agreements for other forms of flexible work in the future. On the basis that the Commissions intentions were always to include other forms of atypical work, it was of no surprise when a similar agreement on fixed-term contracts was announced.[34]

As highlighted above, there is evidence that there had long been a desire on behalf of the European Union to regulate 'atypical work' before anything was finally introduced, and this impetus did not appear to be waining, with further evidence being witnessed in the actions of other EU institutions. Although the Commission has regularly been at the forefront

---

[34] 28 June 1999.

of this, other EU bodies, for example, the Council in 1979[35] and the Parliament in 1990[36] have also pushed for action in this area. Furthermore, the jurisprudence of the ECJ can equally be interpreted as calling for an equalisation of the rights of part-time and full-time workers. The case of *Jenkins v. Kinsgate*[37] is a good place to start. In this case the ECJ held that differences in the rate of pay between full-time and part-time workers must be based on objectively justifiable factors which are in no way related to discrimination based on sex. The Court has also shown an interest in equalizing the so-called 'fringe' benefits, such as sick pay schemes in *Nimz v. Freie und Hansestadt Hamburg*,[38] severance payments in *Kowalska v. Freie und Hansestadt Hamburg*,[39] the right to be paid for attendance at work-related training courses in *Arbeiterwohlfahrt der Stadt Berlin v. Botel*[40] and access to opportunities for career progression in *Kording v. Senator fur Finanzen*.[41] A further example includes *Preston and Others v. Wolverhampton Healthcare NHS Trust and Others [2000]*,[42] where the Court held that the UK's application of a two year limitation on a part-time worker's entitlement to retroactive membership of an occupational pension scheme to be contrary to European law. These cases highlight that even before the introduction of specific legislation dealing with the position of atypical workers the ECJ saw adopted a protective approach.

2.2.   European Convention of Human Rights

Alongside the EU's initiatives, there are also the initiatives to deal with non-discrimination and equality introduced by the Council of Europe (CoE). The CoE is an inter-governmental organisation (IGO) that was created following the end of the Second World War. The core aim of the CoE is expressed within the preamble and Article 1 of the Statute of the Council of Europe as being to promote, amongst other things, the rule of law, democracy, human rights and social development. As a means of helping achieve these aims members of the CoE became signatories to the European Convention on Human Rights (ECHR), a document which

---

[35] OJ C 2/1 (4 January 1980).

[36] EP Document A 3-134/90 (1 June 1990).

[37] *Jenkins v. Kinsgate* [1981] ECR 911 (Case 96/80)

[38] *Nimz v. Freie und Hansestadt Hamburg* [1991] ECR I-297(Case C-184/89)

[39] *Kowalska v. Freie und Hansestadt Hamburg*[1990] ECR I-2591 (Case C-33/89)

[40] *Arbeiterwohlfahrt der Stadt Berlin v. Botel* [1992] IRLR 423.

[41] *Kording v. Senator fur Finanzen* [1997] ECR I-5289 (Case C-100/95).

[42] *Preston and Others v. Wolverhampton Healthcare NHS Trust and Others [2000]* (Case C-78/98).

provides all citizens within the jurisdiction of the signatory state[43] a list of human rights that are guaranteed. As with many legal documents the ECHR is subject to development and amendment as needs require; however, the principle of non-discrimination has remained central to the ECHR, as well as other important CoE documents, and can be seen, for example, at:

- Article 14 of the ECHR provides a guarantee of equal treatment in the enjoyment of the other rights contained within it;[44]
- Protocol 12 to the ECHR is wider than Article 14 and guarantees equal treatment in the enjoyment of any right. An important distinction between Article 14 and Protocol 12 is the ground in which the guarantee is provided: Article 14 is limited to matters that fall within the material jurisdiction of one of the other Convention rights, whereas Protocol 12 provides for a general guarantee that is not limited, and thus covers rights that are provided from other sources;
- The European Social Charter provides a right to equal opportunities and treatment in employment and occupation, as well as protecting against sex discrimination;[45]
- the Framework Convention for the Protection of National Minorities;[46] and
- Convention on Action Against Trafficking in Human Beings.[47]

There are numerous other examples across the range of CoE documents which protect on the principle of non-discrimination; this highlights that from a CoE perspective, consistent with the EU vision, that non-discrimination and equality is a central fundamental right that needs protected.

---

[43] It is important to note that the protections under the ECHR extends beyond citizenship and focusses on jurisdictional boundaries.

[44] Article 14 ECHR is a good example of a CoE protection that is horizontal in nature, as is s.26 of the International Covenant on Civil and Political Rights, which provides a useful comparison to the horizontal nature of what was Article 13 of the TEU. This can be contrasted with the vertical approach in other CoE conventions, including the Convention on the Elimination of All Forms of Discrimination against Women.

[45] For example, see Article 20 and Article E in Part V of the European Social Charter.

[46] See Articles 4, 6(2) and 9 in the Framework Convention for the Protection of National Minorities.

[47] See Article 2(1) in the Convention on Action Against Trafficking in Human Beings.

2.3.   National Level

2.3.1. Early developments

Although membership to the European Union[48] is often viewed as the key source of equality and non-discrimination laws in the UK, the history of such protection predates this membership, with common law developments being evident for many years before accession. Additionally statutory developments in this area can be traced back to at least the Race Relations Acts of 1965 and 1968; however, statutory developments since these initial intrusions have been varied and, to some extent, incoherent; it is evident that the statutory developments since the first 1965 Race Relations Act introduced inconsistent approaches to similar concepts. This made it very difficult to understand how the protections worked and interacted with one another.

Once the UK acceded to the Europe they were faced with having to introduce legislation to give effect to funademental European principles of non-discrimination. And as a result the UK introduced various pieces of legislation, which included primary legislation such as the the Sex Discrimination Act of 1975, the Race Relations Act 1976 and the Disability Discrimination Act 1995, and secondary legislation including the Employment Equality (Sexual Orienation) Regulations 2003, the Employment Equality (Religion or Belief) Regulations 2003 and the Employment Equality (Age) Discrimination Regulations 2006. These instruments were further supported by various non-legislative instruments, in particular Codes of Practices that were developed and published by the equality bodies that were set up in order to assist with the administration of the relevant laws. These bodies included the Equal Opportunities Commission, the Commission for Racial Equality and the Disability Rights Commission, all of which were combined to form the Commission for Equality and Human Rights.

It is important to appreciate the impact of EU developments on each of these instruments, with protection against discrimination being substantially amended over the years, partly due to European Directives such as Directive 2000/43/EC (the Race Directive) and 2000/78/EC (the employment framework Directive) and partly due to developments through the jurisprudence of the European Court of Justice. With key developments to core concepts, which stretched across the breadth of the non-discrimination protections, maintaining separate instruments pertaining to individual grounds of discrimination was becoming

---

[48] As it is now.

cumbersome and complex. It appeared somewhat odd to have different approaches to the same concept depending on what area of equality law one was considering. There was a need for consolidation, and that came in the form of the Equality Act 2010.

2.3.2. The Equality Act 2010

The Equality Act 2010 replaces the raft of legal instruments that had been introduced over the years to deal with a number of issues pertaining to discrimination and/or equality.

According to the Explanatory Notes issued with the Act, it was intended 'to harmonize discrimination law, and to strengthen the law to support progress on equality'. In other words its primary purpose was not simply to enhance equality protection, but it also had the aim of harmonization, which was considered a key aim at simplifying what had become an overly-complex area of regulation.

The Act is mainly a consolidating statute, bringing together the previous national legislation, the previous EU legislation as well as the relevant case law, and as such is heavily influenced by the previous approaches witnessed under each of the respective statutes dealing with an individual characteristic. As a consequence of a lack of perceived progress the Equality Act has been described as a damp squib by some legal commentators. However, as the Explanatory Notes point out, and as is clear through case law, there has been some substantive changes to the law which have been effected by this Act which have seen equality law strengthened in the UK.

2.3.3. Family Friendly Policies

The area of family friendly rights has seen a great range of development in recent years. The UK has gone from a position of having very few rights in this area in the mid-1990s to the development of rights, which include protection from dismissal and detriment, through to more positive rights. The impetus for development in this area came from the Labour Government under Tony Blair, with his 1997 government committing itself to undertake a thorough review of family friendly rights, with a view to enhancing a better balance between home and work. Since 1997 the rights have continuously developed and been enhanced in a number of different ways. Not only is there now a suite of rights that include protection for pregnant workers along with maternity leave rights, as well as rights for others with parental responsibilities, but there are other rights which includes the right to request flexible working amongst others and the right for parental leave to be taken.

Although many of these developments can be viewed throught the eyes of providing a stronger work/life balance, they can also be viewed through the eyes of equality, especially given that much of the burden of family life has traditionally rested with the mother, which in turn can lead to less favourable treatment in the labour market. Such protections have potential to redress this issue.

2.3.4. Atypical Worker Protections

As a direct result of the introduction of atypical worker protection at European level in the form of Directives, the UK was obliged to transpose protections into national law that provided equivalent protections. This ties in quite nicely with the family friendly policies, with a high proportion of part-time work being filled with females, in particular those that are requiring a lesser working time obligation due to circumstances within their lives, which can include family and caring responsibilities. Introducing protection for persons on such contracts thus has the potential to offer further protection on the grounds of equality to those with a family.

However, atypical worker protection goes beyond this and ensures that there is equality in treatment between the different types of contracts.

The introduction of protection for particular contracts is relatively new in the UK regulatory landscape. This can be explained quite simply: UK employment law has traditionally and historically been developed against the backdrop of a *laissez faire* approach, with the consequence that individuals were free to agree to different forms of contract with little or no interference. As a result those that entered into a contract that was either part-time or for a fixed term were free to do so, and their relationship would be governed on the terms that they negotiated. However, this position is clearly open to abuse, especially when one bears in mind the unequal bargaining power that exists within the employment relationship. Argubaly those seeking, or willing, to enter employment on an atypical arrangement are in an even weaker negotiating position that those seeing the norm, as they may be in a position whereby they have no other choice: this shifts the power even further toward the employer. Regulation of this area was inevitable.

It became even more inevitable that action was going to be taken in this areas when certain indirect sex discrimination cases are considered: there are a number of examples where female atypical workers contested an approach that caused them less favourable treatment through indirect sex discrimination, on the basis of the proportions of females on such contracts when compared to males. Due to these proportions anything that impacted upon such a contract could easily be suggested to cause an impact because of the protected charateristic of sex. Case law including *R v Secretary of State for Employment, ex parte Seymour Smith,*[49] where fixed-term workers challenged the requirement of two years' continuous service to qualify for unfair dismissal protection, and *R v Secretary of State for Employment, ex parte Equal Opportunities Commission,*[50] where part-time workers challenged the need for five years continuous service to qualify for unfair dismissal where the worker was part-time and worked between 8 and 16 hours per week. In both cases statistics were used to show that such measures impacted disproportionately on the female workforce.

Other than this indirect protection for atypical workers through indirect sex discrimination there was little in terms of protection for such workers in the UK in advance of the current approach contained within the Part-Time Workers (Prevention of Less Favourable Treatment) Regulations 2000 and the Fixed-Term Employees (Prevention of Less Favourable Treatment) Regulations 2002, which is the subject of **Chapter 12**.

---

[49] *R v Secretary of State for Employment, ex parte Seymour Smith* [2000] ICR 244.

[50] *R v Secretary of State for Employment, ex parte Equal Opportunities Commission* [1995] 1 AC 1.

3.   Defining Equality

3.1.   Introduction

We have all heard of the concepts of discrimination and equality, but understanding what they actually mean is not straightforward. Often these concepts are taken down to their basic meaning, with a focus on treating everybody the same, or avoiding treating somebody differently. Although this is true, this does not explain the full ambit of these concepts. For example, this narrow understanding would justify dismissing a new mother for taking 39 weeks off work (or for taking ordinary maternity leave to give it its proper title) if that same employer would take the same action if a male worker missed the same period of work. However, there is a clear difference between the treatments of the two: the action is failing to understand the different needs of persons with different characteristics; there are certain characteristics that require different treatment in order to achieve the same equal outcome. It is such situations that a basic interpretation of discrimination and equality misses.

This chapter will provide a brief introduction to the concept of discrimination, before giving consideration to some of the different faces of the overarching term 'equality'. This will provide sufficient explanation that will enable the reader to identify the different forms of equality in play when this text turns to consider the relevant statutory protections that make up the equality laws of the UK, as what will be seen is that the UK laws are not predicated on a singular form of equality, but is made up of a variety of different forms.

3.1.1. The Non-Discrimination Principle

It ought to be noted from the outset that the notion of discrimination does differ depending on the discipline of the scrutinizer. For example, the economic definition differs somewhat in focus than that of the sociological and legal view. The economic approach focuses on the issue of productivity of an individual; if differential treatment is due to a personal characteristic that does not affect productivity then discrimination is said to have occurred. According to Baumle and Fossett[1], this means that where there is a legitimate base that has a direct impact on productivity, for example education and work experience, then differential treatment will

---

[1] Baumle, A.K. and Fossett, M. (2005), 'Statistical Discrimination in Employment: Its Practice, Conceptualization, and Implications for Public Policy', *American Behavioural Scientist*, Volume 48(9), pp.1250-1274, at p.1258.

not be deemed to be an act of discrimination. Burstein[2] suggests that a clear implication of this accepted definition is that discrimination from the economic perspective can occur in a vast array of circumstances due to a number of personal characteristics that do not directly impact on an individual's productivity. Baumle and Fossett express that as this definition has such wide scope it includes situations such as kinship, friendship and social network with which there is no societal consensus to offer protection, at least in the same manner as issues such as gender, race and disability.[3]

Whereas the economic definition of discrimination places emphasis on productivity, a sociological approach focuses on negative attitudes due to belonging to a particular group. Thompson[4] has defined discrimination as being:

> Unfair or unequal treatment of individuals or groups; prejudicial behaviour acting against the interest of those people who characteristically tend to belong to relatively powerless groups within the social structure (women, ethnic minorities, old or disabled people and members of the working class in general). Discrimination is therefore a matter of social formation as well as individual/group behaviour or praxis.

Thompson[5] further highlights that negative discrimination occurs through attaching a 'negative or detrimental label or connotation to the person, group or entity concerned', which leads generally to experiencing some form of oppression. Thompson defines oppression as:

> Inhuman or degrading treatment of individuals or groups; hardship and injustice brought about by the dominance of one group over another; the negative and demeaning exercise of power. Oppression often involves disregarding the rights of an individual or group and is thus a denial of citizenship.[6]

---

[2] Burstein, P. (1990), 'Intergroup conflict, law, and the concept of labour market discrimination', *Sociological Forum*, Volume 5(3), pp.459-476, at p.463.

[3] Baumle, A.K. and Fossett, M. (2005) at p.1258.

[4] Thompson, N. (2001), *Anti-Discriminatory Practice*, 3rd Ed., Palgrave Macmillan: Basingstoke, at p. 33.

[5] Thompson, N. (2003), *Promoting Equality: challenging discrimination and oppression*, 2nd Ed., Palgrave Macmillan: Basingstoke, at p.10.

[6] Thompson, N. (2001) at p.34.

This approach appears consistent with Sunstein's earlier work.[7] Sunstein argued that discrimination was essentially made up of three fallacies:

(i) an incorrect view that groups possess particular characteristics;

(ii) that the vast majority of persons within that group have these characteristics, when in reality only a few of them do; and

(iii) a reliance on fairly accurate group-based generalisations coupled with a failure to utilise more accurate classifying devices that are available.

It is clear that discrimination, in a general sense, is the application of a generalisation to a group of individuals, with each member of the group being held to possess the aforementioned generalisation. This sociological line of definition has greatly influenced the legal definition of discrimination which is aptly summarised through the simple definition provided by Connolly[8], that '...an easily-received legal definition of discrimination is different treatment motivated by prejudice or hostility'. According to Jaret[9], the major difference between the sociological definition and the legal definition is that the legal definition tends to be limited to particular grounds, whereas the sociological definition remains unfettered, and as such is not limited to specific groups or categories. The legal definition according to Burstein[10] was born from the failure of early discrimination legislation, such as the US Title VII of the Civil Rights Act of 1964, to provide a substantive definition of the term discrimination, but instead identified specific group characteristics on which employment decisions could not be made.

For the purposes of this work discrimination is defined as differential treatment based on prejudices that are attached to particular group.

3.1.2. The Equality Principle

There a number of different concepts of equality that makes up the overarching umbrella term, each of which has a different focus. It is difficult, and it would be incorrect, to place all of the equality laws under one particular type of equality. Indeed the equality laws of the UK can quite easily be seen as encapsulating a number of the different forms that equality takes. In particular, the equality laws can be seen to take account

---

[7] Sunstein, C. (1991), 'Three Civil Rights Fallacies', *California Law Review*, Volume 79(3), pp.751-774.

[8] Connolly, M. (2006), *Discrimination Law*, Thomson Sweet and Maxwell: London, at p.1.

[9] Jaret, C. (1995), *Contemporary racial and ethnic relations*, Harper Collins: New York, at p.254.

[10] Burstein, P. (1990) at p.459.

of the different concepts of formal equality, substantive equality and transformative equality. Each of these will be discussed briefly below.

(i) Formal Equality

Formal equality is often referred to as the non-discrimination principle, as this is essentially what it is, and is often viewed as the narrowest form of equality. The idea behind formal equality is that an applicant will be judged solely on their merits. All individuals start from the same starting point and the person who is judged and evaluated as being the most suitable candidate is appointed. This effectively ensures that the most qualified or suitable candidate is offered a job or promotion, or whatever it is they have applied for. This is the standard 'like compared with like' approach. This is probably the most understood method of equality.

Early attempts at equality and non-discrimination protection in the UK were grounded in formal equality, and this is evident through the early regulation, such as the Equal Pay Act 1970 and the Sex Discrimination Act 1975. Both of these pieces of legislation simply sought to draw comparisons between a male worker and a suitable comparable female worker when determining whether unequal or discriminatory treatment had taken place.

One of the clear weaknesses to formal equality is the comparison that it inevitably introduces. Formal equality only has application when you can identify two persons who are alike (unless a hypothetical comparator is allowed). This is not always an easy task, as when are two people ever sufficiently similar for these purposes; it is a difficult question to answer. Any differences would make it easy for an employer to justify the difference in treatment, as if there is something unique about one individual inevitably the employer would be able to express that it was that difference, rather than a protected characteristic such as sex, that led to the different treatment. This suggests that the selection of a comparator is crucial to formal equality.

Formal equality still has a key role to play in the UK's equality laws, and can be seen through the concept of direct discrimination in the Equality Act 2010, or through the non-discrimination principle contained within the atypical worker protection legislation.

(ii) Substantive Equality

The development of the idea of substantive equality can be traced back to the criticisms that enveloped formal equality. It was clear that formal equality alone would not be able to achieve what the EU termed 'full equality in practice', whereas a system developed on substantive equality could. Substantive equality is not as limited as formal equality, and has greater scope.

Unlike formal equality, which focusses on treatment of an individual, substantive equality focusses on the impact on an individual. In other words, the focus is shifted away from the individual to focus on barriers that may have a negative impact on the person. If there is a requirement or practice which negatively impacts upon an individual's ability to work due to a particular characteristic that that individual has, then substantive equality seeks to alleviate that barrier.

Two of the common substantive equality tools that will be discussed in this text are indirect discrimination and the duty to make reasonable adjustments.

(iii) Transformative Equality

The idea of transformative equality is closely linked to that of substantive equality. Transformative equality, as the name suggests, is the placing of a positive obligation to transform approaches that are being adopted with a view towards equality. This effectively requires a focus on measures that are to be introduced, and consideration given to whether they impede access to any particular group, and if so, to transform the measure to ensure that this impediment is removed.

Understanding transformative equality is probably done best through a comparison with substantive equality, and Hepple explains it best when he states that:

> substantive equality affords opportunities to people who have in the past been disproportionately excluded, without disturbing the underlying social framework that denies them genuine choice and generates inequitable outcomes, transformative equality is aimed at the dismantling of systemic inequalities and the eradication of poverty and disadvantage.[11]

This requires institutions to adopt a positive role to remove barriers and provide appropriate resources where needed. Too often inequality is perpetuated by systemic failings, and transformative equality is a means of tackling this.

One of the most obvious transformative equality approaches evident in UK equality law is the public sector equality duty contained within the Equality Act.

---

[11] Hepple, B. (2014), *Equality: the Legal Framework*, Hart Publishing, p.28.

3.1.3. Conclusion

This chapter has outlined the different facets of equality, and considered the tools that have been adopted with a view to achieving it. It is important to understand these concepts when one considers that the equality laws of the UK are made up of a subtle mix of approaches, with different protections being based on different ideas of equality. This becomes even more important when one wishes to consider how things could be done differently; although this question is not one that this text will address, it is certainly worth bearing in mind.

It is clear, once one considers the UK laws on equality, that formal equality is still very much the driving force. It is easy to appreciate why, given that this form of equality is much easier to put to paper and much easier to apply in practice. Substantive equality, although having its clear advantages over formal equality, especially given its potential to impact upon a much wider range of inequality, is much more difficult to achieve in practice. Substantive equality is a spectrum, and there will always be debating points over the the most effective way to achieve it, and there will always be question marks over how far the approach can be stretched, especially as stretching it too far will start to look like unequal treatment for the comparator group. It is for this reason that much of substantive equality provisions are couched in quite general terms, simply because it is not as black and white as formal equality, and the same can be said for transformative equality.

4.   The Equality Act 2010

This book now turns to the key piece of legislation when once considers equality law in the UK, the Equality Act. This chapter will consider the key protections contained within the Act and give consideration to how this legislation operates.

The primary purpose of this chapter is to give a practical understanding as to how the Act operates to provide, to some extent, equality for workers. However, the discussion will also look beyond the practical operation to highlight where the Act has been innovative in its approach and introduced new approaches to achieving equality, as well as also highlighting where it possibly falls short in this pursuit. Although some of the approaches under the Act will be criticised for not going far enough there will, where appropriate, be some attempt to explain as to why the protections have developed the way in which they have.

The Equality Act is the most influential piece of legislation in the UK with regards equality and non-discrimination, and is where the majority of the laws that pertained to such protection was centralised. On the whole, the approach contained within the Act is one which many will be familiar with – breaking protection against discrimination into four distinct concepts:

- Direct discrimination
- Indirect discrimination
- Harassment
- Victimisation

Each of these concepts is vitally important, and as such understanding their operation is crucial. However, alongside these concepts there are other important aspects of the Equality Act that needs assessed in order to evaluate the system as a whole: important provisions relating to the burden of proof, remedies and time limits will also be considered.

However, it is not on these well-rehearsed areas of equality law that this chapter will commence with. There are some interesting developments contained within the Equality Act purely from an equality point of view, such as introducing (to some extent) a wider range of positive duties.

These innovative approaches include a widened and consistent public sector equality duty and an expansion of the principle of positive action. These introduce, in part, a shift of focus under the Equality Act, no longer solely focussing on the actions of the discriminator but enables focus to be had on the body or bodies who are capable of implementing and achieving reform in pursuit of equality, or more specifically, the introduction of transformative equality. In essence, focussing on transforming the approach to the labour market is almost, as suggested by Fiss, introducing a form of structural reform rather than the traditional approach of dispute resolution[1]; this transformative equality certainly has a significant advantage when compared to the standard formal equality approach to protection in that it seeks to prevent injustices at their source, rather than punishing a wrongdoer and compensating a victim, which may not have the desired outcome of altering practices in the future.

Before turning to consider the traditional concepts of discrimination which make up the bulk of the protections contained within the Equality Act, this chapter will first consider two of the newer developments that were originally contained within it, namely the Public Sector Equality Duty and the insertion of a provision protecting against discrimination on combined grounds. This discussion provides an insight into how the Equality Act is moving away from the standard non-discrimination model in an attempt to modernise the protections and provide a greater level of substantive equality.

4.1. Public Sector Equality Duty

Although public bodies have long been required to positively promote equality, this was not consistent across the legislative initiatives. The Equality Act expanded the public sector equality duty ('PSED')[2] and introduced a single uniform duty, which operates across the full range of protected characteristics. Section 149 of the Equality Act thus requires public bodies and private bodies that exercise public functions, in the exercise of its functions:

- to have 'due regard'[3] to the need to eliminate conduct prohibited under the Equality Act;
- to advance equality of opportunity across the protected characteristics; and
- to 'foster good relations'.[4]

---

[1] Fiss, O. (1979), 'The Forms of Justice' *Harvard Law Review*, 32. Similar views can be seen in the context of the Public Sector Equality Duty by O'Brien: O'Brien, N. (2013) 'Positive about Equality: The Public Sector Duty under Threat' *The Political Quarterly* 486, at p.489.

[2] It is suggested by Fredman that the equality duty within the 2010 Act has been 'both deepened and expanded since its original introduction: Fredman, S. (2011), 'The Public Sector Equality Duty', *Industrial Law Journal*, pp405-427.

[3] Fredman argues that this could have been further strengthened if there was a requirement to take all proportionate steps towards achieving the equality goals rather than simply 'having regard' to them.

Arguably the duty expands the role that public bodies will have in ensuring equality. In a sense this moves the role of a public body from simply promoting equality as the previous duty required, and will now require them to advance and make progress in achieving it. It was suggested by Fredman that introducing such a wide duty was "one of the key ways in which the [2010 Act] aims to strengthen the law to support progress on equality".[5] Importantly, the strength of the provision is such that it will require public bodies to consider the inherent differences that disadvantage members of a particular group with a view to accommodating those differences in order to enhance and facilitate participation in the workplace. By requiring such a review and analysis to take place before and during the exercise of such functions at least the Equality Act is introducing the potential for the Act to make strides towards dealing with barriers to equality, which is often the root cause of the problem, rather than merely reacting to negative treatment post-impact, which does not always prevent the problem from perpetuating.

However, despite the PSED being initially viewed as a potentially great leap forward in terms of advancing equality, it is certainly questionable whether it will have the impact that may have been intended. The weakness of the duty lies with the express wording of s.149; the standard required is merely to have 'due regard', but is not as high as requiring a public body to take active steps, which in practice is a low threshold that needs to be achieved[6]. As the Court of Appeal stressed, the standard is not "a duty to achieve a result... it is to have due regard to the need to achieve the goals".[7] It does not impose a duty to achieve equality, but simply the need to consider it. This leaves a great deal of discretion to the public officer. It is very much a cautious approach adopted in this respect. Interestingly, it can be argued that the weak approach to the duty may actually be a blessing in disguise, as requiring to active a role may have had the unintended consequence of placing greater focus on particular groups, including religious groups, which have had a detrimental impact.[8]

---

[4] EqA s.149.

[5] See Fredman, S. (2011), 'The Public Sector Equality Duty', *Industrial Law Journal*, pp405-427.

[6] O'Brien (2013) argues that this is a 'relatively low and quite easily surmounted threshold'.

[7] *R (on the application of Baker & Ors) v Secretary of State for Communities and Local Government, London Borough of Bromley* [2008] EWCA Civ 141.

[8] Vickers, L. (2011), 'Promoting Equality or Fostering Resentment? The Public Sector Equality Duty and Religion and Belief', *Legal Studies*, pp135-158, at p.145.

The PSED certainly represents a positive development in terms of progressing the UK's approach to equality on paper. It has great potential in dealing with the source of unequal treatment, and in that respect is positive. Although the provision can be considered weak and over-cautious it is a step in the right direction. This places equality at the forefront of the minds of public officers when making decisions, and as such will have some positive impact, but moreso, it provides a useful platform from which the duty can be enhanced.

4.2.   Combined Discrimination

What appeared to be a useful provision that had the potential to advance the protection against discrimination in the UK was also one of the final provisions to be added to the Equality Act before it received royal assent, that being s.14 of the Equality Act, which sought to introduce protection against combined or intersectional discrimination.[9] Section 14 was aimed at situations where the interaction of two protected characteristics produced "a condition more terrible than the sum of their two constituent parts".[10] Whilst the Coalition Government announced in 2011 that it would not be bringing s.14 into force, expressing that this decision was part of its approach to 'minimise regulatory burdens'[11] on business and would save businesses an estimated £3 million per year,[12] and with the current Conservative Government looking unlikely reverse this decision,[13] it still warrants discussion insofar as it could be considered that this decision constitutes a sacrifice of greater equality at the expense of monetary considerations and as a consequence may imply that 'equality is regarded as a vehicle for increasing economic efficiency rather than as a goal in its own right'.[14] Interestingly, and suggesting that this may have been an incorrect decision from an equality perspective, a pre-Equality Act study in

---

[9] This has already been mentioned as problem introduced through the need for a comparable worker that is in materially the same circumstances as the complainant.

[10] Burton B. (2014), 'Neoliberalism and the Equality Act 2010: A Missed Opportunity for Gender Justice?' *Industrial Law Journal* 122, 132

[11] HM Treasury/BIS (2011) *The Plan for Growth*, p.23, available at: http://cdn.hm-treasury.gov.uk/2011budget_growth.pdf (last accessed 19/04/2015)

[12] This was the estimated cost to business of introducing the provision: HM Treasury/BIS (2011), p.53.

[13] The initial decision appeared to intend only to 'delay commencement'[13] of the provision. However, it later became clear from the Home office website that section 14 will not be coming into force at all.

[14] Burton B. (2014) at p.139

2009 suggested that s.14 had the potential to address 90% of cases concerning dual combination discrimination.[15] The section would have 'challenged the fiction that each discrimination has a single, direct and independent effect on status'.[16] Furthermore, like the extension of indirect discrimination to disability, it would have challenged judicial reluctances to engage with the complexity.[17]

Section 14 was primarily drafted in response to the Court of Appeal's decision in *Bahl v The Law Society*[18] where 'black women' were not a recognised group despite the claimant being unable to produce adequate evidence to demonstrate discrimination in relation to the separate attributes of race and gender.[19] It is clear to see, especially using the *Bahl* case as an indicative example, that not introducing this provision introduced a gap in the protections that an individual may fall between.[20] As a consequence of this decision, the success of a claim brought involving two or more protected characteristics wholly depended on the evidence a complainant had that would distinguish and satisfy the tribunal that discrimination had taken place on one of the protected characteristics over the other(s). Without s.14, the Equality Act may arguably no longer be able to protect against the mischief that was intended by the provision: protecting 'minorities within minorities'[21].

Despite the obvious potential of s.14, it is debatable whether, in practice, it would have gone far enough in the pursuit of equality. By definition it is limited to *dual* characteristic claims of direct discrimination. The argument was once again based on monetary and business concerns and the results of a CAB study into direct discrimination showing that only 20% of cases involved three or more characteristics.[22] Once again, such an approach not

---

[15] GEO, *Peers Briefing* (HMSO, 2009)

[16] Solanke, I. (2011) 'Infusing the Silos in the Equality Act 2010 with Synergy' *Industrial Law Journal* 336, 339

[17] Solanke, I. (2011) at p.340

[18] *Bahl v The Law Society* [2004] EWCA Civ 1070.

[19] This overturned the approach that was adopted in the lower tribunals; in particular the employment tribunal considered that they could accommodate such a claim using a white male as the suitable comparator.

[20] McColgan went as far as suggesting that the *Bahl* decision was "protect[ing] intersectional discrimination from challenge under domestic discrimination law": McColgan A. (2007) "Reconfiguring discrimination law", *Public Law Journal* 74, 81

[21] Ashtiany, S. (2010) 'The Equality Act 2010: Main Concepts', *Equal Rights Review* 25, 26

[22] Citizens Advice Research for the GEO (2009), *Potential Intersectional Discrimination Cases,* 12

only carries the Orwellian posit that 'some are more equal than others', but undermines its very existence as a constituent part of *equality* legislation. This latter point is reinforced when one considers that during the committee stage of the Equality Bill in the House of Lords, Lord Lester remarked "[i]f two grounds are not enough, there is nothing to stop you adding others, as is the case at the moment".[23] The introduction of s.14 would therefore unfortunately appear to work on a utilitarian basis of equality for the masses as opposed to equality for all.

A further limitation of section 14 that one must bear in mind, and one that drew further criticism, is that the wording of it acted so as to preclude both indirect discrimination and harassment claims from its remit, and thus was criticised for ignoring the fact that people may be both directly discriminated against and indirectly discriminated against or harassed within the same situation.[24] One notable critic who acknowledged such a point was Lord Ouseley who described the omission of indirect discrimination and harassment as "a ludicrous oversight [which] requires addressing."[25] Despite such stern criticism, some deem this limitation unsurprising given that one of the Government's key objectives was to design an understandable provision applicable by businesses and public authorities in 'everyday situations' so as to avoid "disproportionate burdens on those who have responsibilities under the law".[26] However, the same CAB study also revealed that over 20% of cases studies involved a combination of direct and indirect discrimination and over 33% involved harassment as a composite element.[27] Whilst the CAB admittedly used a comparatively small sample size the proportions are not insignificant, thereby indicating that framing claims under the Act is "ripe for confusion with different contextual arguments necessary for the connected claims".[28]

Additionally, under s.14(2) of the Equality Act, Hand notes a further idiosyncrasy in that the grounds of marriage/civil partnership and pregnancy/maternity are not included within the list of which the

---

[23] HL Deb 13 January 2010, vol 716, col 543

[24] See *Azmi v Kirklees BC* [2007] I.C.R. 1154; [2007] IRLR 484.

[25] *Hansard* HL Vol.715 col.1492 (December 15, 2009) (Lord Ouseley)

[26] Solanke, I. (2011), at p.346

[27] Citizens Advice Research for the GEO, (2009) at p.12.

[28] J Hand, J. (2011), 'Combined Discrimination - section 14 of the Equality Act 2010: a partial and redundant provision?' PL 482, p.486

provision would have applied.[29] Lastly, it has been hinted that s.14 would be to some extent a remedy of last resort insofar as 'it is not intended that this provision should be a panacea for all forms of discrimination'[30]. Therefore, the much anticipated 'compensatory change' in terms of bridging the gap between fiction and reality[31] would not appear to be achievable on the off chance that s.14 is actually introduced.

The criticism that exists of s.14 appears to concern what can be considered a single-dimension approach to the Equality Act; however, such an approach should not always be viewed in the negative, as in some ways it at least introduces legal certainty, which arguably may be needed to make a provision work in practice. A similar suggestion can be seen in AG Sharpston's Opinion in *Ruiz Zambrano v Office National de l'emploi*[32], where she highlighted that there is a need for boundaries to every rule granting entitlement because otherwise the rule becomes undecipherable and no one can tell with certainty who will, and who will not, enjoy the benefit it confers.[33] Yet, no matter how persuasive the arguments in favour of legal certainty or saving business costs (raised by the Government) may be, one cannot overlook the fact that a single-dimension stance creates the potential of a blind spot in the Equality Act; the most important being that of intersectionality.[34]

Although, on the face of it, it appears that the decision to not bring s.14 into effect may have a severe impact upon achieving equality in the UK through providing a lacuna in the Equality Act in which a number of claimants may find themselves, to state that it does so may be overplaying the potential of the provision. Even had s.14 been given effect its relative potential would have been lower than first anticipated given its numerous limitations. Furthermore, there is evidence to suggest that, even without this provision, the tribunals will adopt a purposive approach to the non-discrimination protections to avoid a submission that discrimination was because of two characteristics as opposed to one from succeeding in defending against a claim for discrimination. An illustrative approach can be seen in the high

---

[29] Hand, J., Davis, B. & Feast, P. (2012), 'Unification, simplification, amplification? An analysis of aspects of the British Equality Act 2010' CLB 509, p.516

[30] CAB Research.

[31] Solanke, I. (2011), at p.346

[32] *Ruiz Zambrano v. Office National de l'emploi* [2012] QB 265, 300G-H

[33] See Cabrelli D. (2014) *Employment Law in Context: Text and Materials Employment Law in Context: Text and Materials,* Oxford University Press

[34] See Solanke I. (2011).

profile case involving Miriam O'Reilly, when she claimed discrimination by the BBC based on her age and sex, with the ET, when concluding, accepting that a characteristic need not be "the sole reason, or even the principal reason, why a person suffers detrimental treatment."[35] This certainly appears to be a more relaxed approach to causation,[36] which will assist claimants who cannot differentiate between two or more characteristics in relation to that which led to the less favourable treatment being complained of, and is certainly a welcome approach that goes some way to achieving the purpose of the Equality Act, in spite of section 14 not coming in to force.

4.3.   Direct Discrimination

This chapter now turns to give consideration to the concepts that have been developed that make up this overarching term: direct discrimination, indirect discrimination, harassment and victimisation.

Direct discrimination is defined in the Equality Act at s.13 as covering situations where:

(1) A person (A) discriminates against another (B) if, because of a protected characteristic, A treats B less favourably than A treats or would treat others.

(2) If the protected characteristic is age, A does not discriminate against B if A can show A's treatment of B to be a proportionate means of achieving a legitimate aim.

(3) If the protected characteristic is disability, and B is not a disabled person, A does not discriminate against B only because A treats or would treat disabled persons more favourably than A treats B.

(4) If the protected characteristic is marriage and civil partnership, this section applies to a contravention of Part 5 (work) only if the treatment is because it is B who is married or a civil partner.

(5) If the protected characteristic is race, less favourable treatment includes segregating B from others.

(6) If the protected characteristic is sex—

(a) less favourable treatment of a woman includes less favourable treatment of her because she is breast-feeding;

(b) in a case where B is a man, no account is to be taken of special treatment afforded to a woman in connection with pregnancy or childbirth.

---

[35] *O'Reilly v BBC & Anor* 2200423/2010 (ET), para 245.

[36] The employment tribunal appears to have borrowed this approach to causation from the developments to factual causation in negligence claims involving claimants injured by working with asbestos.

The concept of direct discrimination essentially can be viewed as requiring two things to be established:

1. Less favourable treatment
2. 'because of' a protected characteristic.

The first of these two requirements is essentially looking for some form of detrimental treatment. As it is focussing on less favourable treatment then there will need to be a comparison with somebody who is not of that particular characteristic, as this is the only way of establishing that treatment is indeed less favourable. The second aspect is focussing more on causation and the link between the less favourable treatment and the protected characteristic. Each of these will be discussed in detail below.

4.3.1. Less favourable treatment

Direct discrimination rests on the notion that alike must be treated alike, and as a consequence is usually viewed through comparing the treatment of a person with a particular protected characteristic against the treatment of a person without that same protected characteristic. Examples would include:

- a female being compared with a non-female (a male);
- a homosexual being compared with a non-homosexual; or
- a catholic being compared with a non-catholic.

It is this comparative approach which will form the investigation into whether less favourable treatment because of a protected characteristic has taken place. However, there is scope for the tribunal to use a hypothetical comparator where there is no actual comparator available, giving consideration as to how a comparator in similar circumstances would have been treated.

Irrespective of the protected ground in question there is the additional requirement, by virtue of s.23 of the Equality Act, that there is no 'material difference' between the circumstances of the comparable workers. This thus requires that the only material difference between the comparable workers must be the protected characteristic itself, otherwise it is not suitable. So, for example, if the complaint concerns an application for a vacant position a suitable comparator will need to have similar experiences or qualifications, otherwise the reason behind the selection may be due to some other reason indissociable from the protected characteristic, which may then be used to explain the difference in treatment. The idea behind this approach is to isolate the protected characteristic from other reasons that may explain the differential treatment. The case of *Hurley v. Mustoe*[37] provides an illustrative example where the EAT considered the issue of a suitable comparable worker in circumstances where the Mrs Hurley was dismissed by her employer for being a mother with a young family, which her employer considered to make her an unreliable worker. The accepted suitable comparator in these circumstances was a male worker with dependent children, and thus in similar circumstances to the complainant, with the only material difference being sex. This highlights that when looking for a suitable comparable worker the task is to identify an individual who is in similar circumstances, with the only material difference being the protected characteristic on which a claim is being brought. If there are any other differences within the circumstances of the complainant and the chosen comparator that is not in any way linked to the protected characteristic in question then the employer can easily submit that the difference in treatment is due to that other difference, in which case any less favourable treatment will not be caused in any way by the protected characteristic, and consequently discrimination will not be established.

The idea of 'less favourable treatment' itself has received much judicial consideration. It covers any treatment that the individual concerned considers to be treating them to a detriment, so long as it is not an unreasonable conclusion to reach; it is very much decided using a subjective approach, at least initially, with an element of objective analysis to ensure that the wholly unreasonable subjective view of a treatment does not lead to such an action.

A few examples to illustrate the breadth of a detriment include:

- In *Ministry of Defence v. Jeremiah*[38] male employees in the respondent's factory were contracted and thus obliged, as a condition of doing overtime, to undertake particular dirty work which the women refused to do as they did not wish to take shared showers afterwards. Despite receiving extra pay for the dirty work the courts still held that this was being subjected to a detriment. The courts appear to be suggesting that an employer cannot buy the right to discriminate.

- In the case of *Calder v. James Finlay Corporation*[39], the detriment was that all males were being given a benefit and Mrs Calder was not. The

---

[37] *Hurley v. Mustoe* [1981] IRLR 208.

[38] *Ministry of Defence v. Jeremiah* [1980] QB 87.

[39] *Calder v. James Finlay Corporation* [1989] IRLR 55.

detriment in that case being that female workers did not have access to the same mortgage subsidies that were provided to male workers

- In the case of *De Souza v. Automobile Association*[40] the detriment was found to be a racial insult, which was considered enough of a detriment if the employee felt disadvantaged by it.

- In the case of *Burton v. De Vere Hotels*[41] the meaning of the phrase 'subjecting to a detriment' was given a broad interpretation. In this case two waitresses were working at a function which had Bernard Manning as a guest act. Having been subject to racist jokes and comments directly about them, the waitresses made a complaint. Both waitresses argued that the employer had subjected them to a detriment, in this case racial harassment by a third party. The EAT accepted this argument and found that the employer had subjected his employee to a detriment if he caused or allowed harassment to happen in circumstances where he could control whether it happened or not.

- The detriment in *Chief Constable of West Yorkshire Police v. Khan*[42] was the refusal to provide a reference on the reason that Mr Khan was pursuing a race discrimination claim against his employer.

As expressed above, determining whether an individual has been treated less favourably is a mix between a subjective and objective approach, and the leading authority in this respect is the House of Lords decision in to *Shamoon v. Chief Constable of Royal Ulster Constabulary.*[43] In *Shamoon* the detriment was that Ms Shamoon, who was a female chief inspector, was stopped from doing staff appraisals after there were some complaints about the manner in which she carried them out. On complaining of sex discrimination, the House of Lords, Lord Rodgers giving the leading judgment, came to the view that a detriment occurs if a reasonable worker would or might take the view that they had been disadvantaged in the circumstances in which they had to work. This was further explained by Lord Scott, explaining that the test must be applied "by considering the issue from the point of view of the victim. If the victim's opinion that the treatment was to his or her detriment is a reasonable one to hold, that ought ... to suffice".[44] The House of Lords also made it clear that there was

---

[40] *De Souza v. Automobile Association* [1986] IRLR 103.

[41] *Burton v. De Vere Hotels* [1996] IRLR 596.

[42] *Chief Constable of West Yorkshire Police v. Khan* [2001] UKHL 48; [2001] ICR 1065.

[43] *Shamoon v. Chief Constable of Royal Ulster Constabulary* [2003] IRLR 285.

[44] *Ibid* at 301.

not a need to show some physical or economic consequence, this was not a requirement when looking for a detriment. In other words, instead of simply focussing on the views of the complainant, or imposing their own view, a tribunal or court is required to first consider the views of the complainant in the circumstances that they are complaining and whether they consider that their treatment is a detriment, before considering whether holding such a view was something that a reasonable worker might view as such. This appears a fairly easy test to satisfy, and from that point of view extends the scope of the protection through opting not to introduce a technically and legally complex test for detriment.

4.3.2....'because of' the protected characteristic...

The Equality Act advanced the concept of direct discrimination in relation to a number of the protected characteristics[45] by altering the need to show that there was less favourable treatment 'on the grounds'[46] of a protected characteristic to the requirement to establish that the less favourable treatment was 'because of' a protected characteristic. This does not make the case law under the old approach redundant as the 'on the grounds of' approach still forms part of the 'because of' approach. Indeed 'because of' can be viewed as being an umbrella term that covers four different approaches, each of which will now form part of direct discrimination:

1. The traditional 'on the grounds' approach to direct discrimination
2. Associative discrimination
3. Perceived discrimination
4. Deterred Discrimination

On the grounds of...

The approach to 'on the grounds of' direct discrimination is something that lawyers will all be familiar with as it essentially follows the approach that is adopted in relation to factual causation in a number of different legal areas, such as in negligence claims. An instructive case in this area is *James v. Eastleigh BC*[47]. Mrs James was entitled to free admission to the local swimming pool because she had reached the state pension age for women, at the time it was 60 and Mrs James was age 61. However, Mr James, her husband, who was also 61 years of age, was not entitled to free admission as the state retirement age for men was set at 65. There was no intention to

---

[45] Although what it has done in reality is that it has introduced the approach that was adopted to direct discrimination in relation to protected characteristics such as disability to ensure that there is a consistent and equal approach adopted across all of the characteristics.

[46] This was the approach evident in both the SDA and the RRA.

[47] *James v. Eastleigh BC* [1990] 2 AC 751.

discriminate on the part of the council; all it was doing was offering a concession to pensioners in order to encourage them to remain active. In this case the House of Lords discussed the interpretation of the words 'on the grounds of…'. And on this issue the House of Lords introduced the 'but for' test. The question that one asks, according to the House of Lords is: 'Would the complainant have received the same treatment from the defendant but for his or her sex?' If the answer is "yes" then the treatment is not on the grounds of the complainant's sex and thus no discriminatory act for the purposes of the legislation. However, if the answer is "no" then the differential treatment must have been down to the gender of the individual. As this case suggests, and also evident in the case of *R v. Birmingham City Council, ex parte Equal Opportunities Commission*[48] the motive of the discriminator is irrelevant[49], but it is the impact that is important and relevant to direct discrimination: it is never a defence to direct discrimination to submit and evidence that the aim was to introduce a benefit with no discriminatory motive. In this case the local authority offered more places in selective secondary education to boys than to girls. This was held to be treating those girls less favourably on the grounds of their sex, but for being a female they would have been treated more favourably, the fact that there was no intention to discriminate was irrelevant.

The application of the 'but for' test is a simple but well-rehearsed approach to establishing a causative link between the less favourable treatment and the protected characteristic.

Associative Discrimination

The Sex Discrimination Act 1975 ('SDA') provided no protection for the idea of associative discrimination; however, it was previously protected under the RRA. An early example of this protection in practice is the case of *Showboat Entertainment Centre v. Owens*[50] where a claim was brought under section 1 of the RRA following Mr Owens's dismissal when he refused to carry out a racially discriminatory instruction from his employer which required him to stop young blacks from entering the amusement centre. In these circumstances the EAT held that the RRA covered

> all cases of discrimination on racial grounds when the racial characteristics in question are those of the person treated less favourably or of some other person. The only question in each case is whether the

---

[48] *R v. Birmingham City Council, ex parte Equal Opportunities Commission* [1989] AC 1155.

[49] This is discussed in more detail below.

[50] *Showboat Entertainment Centre v. Owens* [1984] IRLR 7

unfavourable treatment afforded to the claimant was caused by racial consideration.

This evidenced a purposive approach to the protection in order to offer some protection to those who were treated less favourably not because of their race, but because of the race of another.

A similar approach was witnessed in relation to the DDA following the judgment in *Coleman v. Attridge Law*.[51] Initially it was unclear whether direct discrimination under the DDA was broad enough to also cover associative discrimination, which led to the EAT referring the matter to the European Court of Justice[52]. Interestingly Advocate General Maduro made some general sweeping statements in his Opinion rather than focussing on the protected characteristic of disability, of particular note he stated that:

> One way of undermining the dignity and autonomy of people who belong to a certain group is to target not them, but third persons who are closely associated with them and do not themselves belong to the group. (para. 12)

It is clear that he envisaged that associative discrimination is something which is implicit within the European framework of non-discrimination protection. At least in relation to disability discrimination the European Court of Justice agreed, when its judgment was released on 31 July 2008, indicating that

> ...the purpose of the Directive, as regards employment and occupation, is to combat all forms of discrimination on grounds of disability. The principle of equal treatment enshrined in the Directive in that area applies not to a particular category of person but by reference to the grounds mentioned in Article 1.

In other words, the protection extends beyond the the charateristic of the complainant, and will cover less favourable treatment that is caused by the characteristic of an associative. This judgment was accepted and given force when the matter returned to the EAT.[53]

Adopting a single definition to direct discrimination predicated on the concept of 'because of' brings all the protected characteristics in line with the approach adopted in Framework Directive 2000/78, which was the Directive referred to in the *Coleman* case, and as such provides protection against associative discrimination across all of the protected characteristics.

---

[51] *Coleman v. Attridge Law* [2007] IRLR 88; C- 303/06.

[52] As it then was.

[53] *EBR Attridge Law LLP & Anor v Coleman* [2009] UKEAT 0071 09 3010

Perceived discrimination

The move to 'because of' also had the impact of introducing protection for individuals against perceived discrimination across the protected characteristics, again bringing the UK approach in line with the approach that is required by Framework Directive 2000/78. The issue of perceived discrimination arose in *English v. Thomas Sanderson Blinds Ltd*[54] following a claim by Mr English under the Employment Equality (Sexual Orientation) Regulations 2003 that he was subject to homophobic harassment despite not being homosexual. He claimed that the harassment he suffered stemmed from the fact that he had attended boarding school and was living in Brighton. It was accepted that none of his work colleagues actually considered him to be gay.[55] The majority[56] of the Court of Appeal on these facts considered that the Directive protections could be applied directly to Mr English's situation with a finding that he has been harassed on the grounds of sexual orientation. Sedley LJ giving the leading judgment stated that:

> In my judgment it did not matter whether he was gay or not. The calculated insult to his dignity, which depended not at all on his actual sexuality, and the consequently intolerable working environment were sufficient to bring his case both within Regulation 5 and within the 1976 Directive. The incessant mockery ("banter" trivialises it) created a degrading and hostile working environment, and it did so on grounds of sexual orientation. That is the way I would prefer to put it. Alternatively, however, it can be properly said that the fact that the appellant is not gay, and that his tormentors know it, has just as much to do with sexual orientation – his own, as it happens – as if he were gay.
>
> If, as is common ground, tormenting a man who is believed to be gay but is not amounts to unlawful harassment, the distance from there to tormenting a man who is being treated as if he were gay when he is not is barely perceptible. In both cases the man's sexual orientation, in both cases imaginary, is the basis – that is to say, the ground – of the harassment. There is no Pandora's box here: simply a consistent application of the principle that, while you cannot legislate against prejudice, you can set out in specified circumstances to stop people's lives being made a misery by it.

---

[54] *English v. Thomas Sanderson Blinds Ltd* [2008] EWCA Civ 1421.

[55] This fact, according to Burton in the EAT, meant that his claim could not succeed. Burton J considered that as there was no suggestion that his work colleagues thought he was gay then the harassment could not be said to be on grounds of sexual orientation.

[56] Laws LJ dissented.

This certainly is a logical conclusion given that irrespective of whether an individual actually has a characteristic or not does not prevent them from being subject to intolerable treatment which makes their working life difficult. This is especially the case where comments are used in a negative derogative manner; in such circumstances an individual can feel intimidated, humiliated or degraded irrespective of whether they have the characteristic that is being used to oppress them.

As with associative discrimination, this approach has now been adopted across all of the protected characteristics.

Deterred discrimination

The decision of the ECJ in *Firma Feryn*[57] further expanded the concept of direct discrimination to cover situations where there is deterred discrimination, even where there is no identifiable complainant. This case concerned a Belgian company that specialised in the sale and installation of doors. When advertising to recruit fitters and installers, a Belgian newspaper interview with one of the comnpany's directors recorded that none of the positions would be offered to persons of a Moroccan origin, as the company's client base did not want them in their homes. Before the Belgian courts there was no finding of discrimination as there was no evidence to show that any applicant had been refused on this basis; however, it was appealed to the ECJ.

Both the Advocate General's Opinion and the decision of the ECJ found that the scope of the Race Directive was not limited to situations where there was an identifiable complainant, and that Member States, including the UK must ensure that public bodies can bring judicial proceedings in the absence of such an identifiable victim.

This decision enables the Equality and Human Rights Commission in the UK to bring procedings against employers that make such statements, or hold such a discriminatory position, in circumstances where there is nobody who has actually able to show that they have suffered as a result. Obviously, much of this will depend on the finances that the EHRC has to pursue such matters.

The idea of deterred discrimination applies across all the protected characteristics and is not limited to race discrimination issues.

---

[57] *Centrum voor Gelijkheid van Kansen en voor Racismebestrijding v Firma Feryn NV* [2008] ECR I-5187.

4.3.3. Justifying direct age discrimination

Age discrimination, unlike the other protected characteristics, is the *only* form of direct discrimination where justification is possible. This is possible where the treatment being complained of is a proportionate means of achieving a legitimate aim.

Justification of direct age discrimination was provided for by Article 6 of Framework Directive 2000/78/EC, which states that:

> differences of treatment on grounds of age shall not constitute discrimination, if, within the context of national law, they are objectively and reasonably justified by a legitimate aim, including legitimate employment policy, labour market and vocational training objectives, and if the means of achieving that aim are appropriate and necessary.
>
> Such differences of treatment may include, among others:
> (a) the setting of special conditions on access to employment and vocational training, employment and occupation, including dismissal and remuneration conditions, for young people, older workers and persons with caring responsibilities in order to promote their vocational integration or ensure their protection;
> (b) the fixing of minimum conditions of age, professional experience or seniority in service for access to employment or to certain advantages linked to employment;
> (c) the fixing of a maximum age for recruitment which is based on the training requirements of the post in question or the need for a reasonable period of employment before retirement.

Although the express wording in the Equality Act does not adopt the language of the Framework Directive, most notably through not providing an explicit list of specific justification, the approach is compatable and consistent with it, as was explained by the ECJ in the *Heyday*.[58]

Although worded similarly to that justification which is available for indirect discrimination (which is discussed at p.47, the justification for direct age discrimination works slightly differently. The key difference is that direct age discrimination will only be capable of justification where the aim behind any such measure is in the public interest.[59] Bearing this in

---

[58] *R (on the application of The Incorporated Trustees of the National Council for Ageing (Age Concern England)) v. Secretary of State for Business, Enterprise and Regulatory Reform*, [2009] IRLR 373 (Case C-388/07).

[59] This is clearly expressed in a number of important CJEU decisions, including *Age Concern England (The Incorporated Trustees of the National Council on Ageing (Age Concern England)) v Secretary of State for Business, Enterprise and Regulatory Reform*[2009] IRLR 373 (Case C-388/07)

mind there are three requirements that need to be established in order for direct discrimination to be justified:

1. a need to establish a legitimate public interest aim;
2. the measure adopted is appropriate to achieve the aim; and
3. the measure is necessary to achieve the aim.

The focus of the discussion here will be solely on the need for a legitimate public interest aim, because the other two requirements form part of the indirect discrimination justification and, as such, will be discussed there.

It has regularly been accepted before the CJEU that not having the legitimate aim in mind when developing the measure in question will not automatically exclude the finding of justification, as in such circumstances the national courts will be able to look at the underlying aim of the measure taken from the general context of the aim concerned.[60] This enables the tribunals and courts to look behind a measure which fails to be expressly linked to a legitimate aim to see whether it can be implicitly linked in some way. Obviously, from a practical point of view, this opens up the possibility of justification in circumstances perhaps where an employer had a different aim in mind, but can convince the tribunal in submissions that it is indeed for a public interest reason.

Case law since the introduction of age discrimination protection has seen the acceptance of a number of different legitimate aims, including:

*   creating jobs;
*   intergenerational workforce;
*   avoiding humiliation;
*   protection of health;
*   operational capacity;
*   proper functioning of the profession; and
*   securing agreement for change.

Reasons such as creating jobs, intergenerational workforce, and proper functioning of the profession all appear to have a similar focus that is treating people of one age to a detriment (usually older workers in the form of dismissal) for the benefit of the those of another age (usually younger workers). On the face of it these legitimate aims appear to defeat the

---

and, *Fuchs und Köhler v. Land Hessen* [2011] ECR I-000 (Cases C-159 & 160/10). This approach differs from the approach evident in indirect discrimination cases, which focusses on business reasons.

[60] See *Palacios de la Villa* [2007] E.C.R. I-8531, paras 56 and 57 (Case C-411/05); *Petersen* [2010] ECR I-0000, para.40 (Case C-341/08); and *Rosenbladt* [2010] E.C.R. I-0000, para.58, (Case C-45/09)

purpose of the protection in that they allow an employer to treat an older work less favourably in order to open up positions to younger workers; however, Hepple explains that this justification operates in this way as age discrimination is viewed from a societal equality perspective rather than an individual equality view, which is the approach applied in relation to the other protected characteristics. The argument is that through adopting this approach then society as a whole benefits: by enabling employer's to remove older workers positions will be opened up to be filled by younger workers.[61]

What is clear is that the courts have effectively provided employers with almost an express list of accepted aims, leaving it to them to make the link between the measure adopted and one of the accepted justifications. Argubaly the breadth of the justifications makes such a justification easy to establish.[62]

4.4.   Indirect Discrimination

Indirect discrimination differs from direct discrimination in that it focusses on the impact a measure has on a group of individuals with a shared protected characteristic, rather than focusing on the treatment of an individual. Indirect discrimination is defined in the Equality Act at s.19, and is defined as covering situations where:

(1) A person (A) discriminates against another (B) if A applies to B a provision, criterion or practice which is discriminatory in relation to a relevant protected characteristic of B's.

(2) For the purposes of subsection (1), a provision, criterion or practice is discriminatory in relation to a relevant protected characteristic of B's if—

(a) A applies, or would apply, it to persons with whom B does not share the characteristic,

(b) it puts, or would put, persons with whom B shares the characteristic at a particular disadvantage when compared with persons with whom B does not share it,

(c) it puts, or would put, B at that disadvantage, and

(d) A cannot show it to be a proportionate means of achieving a legitimate aim.

(3) The relevant protected characteristics are—

age;

disability;

---

[61] Hepple, B. (2014), at pp.38-39.

[62] For further discussion on this see Butler, M. (2011), 'Marginalising the objective justification defence in retirement cases?', International Journal of Law and Management, pp.375 – 388.

> gender reassignment;
> marriage and civil partnership;
> race;
> religion or belief;
> sex;
> sexual orientation.

When the statutory definition of indirect discrimination is broken down it can be seen that there are three things that need to be considered and understood before it can be established whether such discrimination has taken place or not:

1. the concept of a 'provision, criterion or practice' needs to be considered;
2. the matter of putting a group at 'a particular disadvantage'; and
3. the phrase 'a proportionate means of achieving a legitimate aim' needs to be understood.

4.4.1.Provision, Criterion or Practice

Unfortunately, there is no statutory definition of 'provision criterion or practice' ('PCP') despite the existence of a PCP being crucial to the operation of indirect discrimination, amongst other protections within the Equality Act. A PCP will be determined by tribunals and courts should a matter be litigated, which leaves the matter quite uncertain and unpredictable in everyday situations. However, what does appear evident is that, consistent with the approach that was adopted with the previous wording contained of indirect discrimination, that of 'requirement or condition', PCP will be afforded a broad interpretation,[63] with each individual term being alternatives rather than cumulative.[64] By approaching PCPs in this manner it enables and encourages tribunals to offer a wide range of protection.

The finding of a PCP is a question of fact for the tribunal, and as such it is extremely difficult to provide any definitive guidance on what will or will not be deemed to be a PCP. There are the obvious examples that will be deemed to be PCPs, such as contractual terms in relation to working hours, holiday entitlements or work benefits amongst others, which all will fall within this concept. In addition to the obvious, previously held PCPs will

---

[63] Although there is reference to criterion, the terms of 'provision' and 'practice' are considered to be much wider in application: this is supported by the approach adopted by the CJEU, where indirect discrimination is approached in a much broader and less technical manner: *Enderby v. Frenchay HA* [1993] ECR I-5535 ECJ (Case C-127/92).

[64] *British Airways plc v. Starmer* EAT/0306/05/SM;[2005] IRLR 862.

offer useful indications too. Below is a short list of matters that have been considered to be a PCP previously before the courts; however, it must be noted that there will never be a finite and closed list, but submissions on PCPs will be open in any given situation:

- *British Airways plc v. Starmer*[65]: A discretionary management decision that only applied to the claimant, and not to the workforce as a whole.

- *R v Secretary of State for Employment, ex parte Equal Opportunities Commission*[66]; *Allonby v. Accrington and Rossendale College*[67]: A requirement to work full-time hours.

- *Price v. Civil Service Commission*[68]: a requirement to be under the upper age limit of 35 when applying for a particular civil service job.

- *Panesar v. Nestle & Co Ltd*[69]: a rule prohibiting employees from wearing beards or having long hair.

- *London Underground Ltd v. Edwards (No 2)*[70]: A requirement to work a flexible shift pattern.

- *Copsey v. WWB Devon Clays Ltd*[71]: an obligation to work on a particular day of the week, in this case the day being a Sunday. The same applies to a particular time of a day.

A PCP is explained by the EHRC with a need to be "construed widely", and would include matters such as "any formal or informal policies, rules, practices, arrangements, criteria, conditions, prerequisites, qualifications or provisions". A PCP is also explained to "potentially include decisions to do something in the future – such as a policy or criterion that has not yet been applied – as well as a 'one-off' or discretionary decision".[72]

The importance of establishing and evidencing the PCP is shown in *Bethnal Green and Shoreditch Education Trust v Dippenaar*[73], where it was held by the EAT that a failure to provide evidence of the existence of a PCP led to a

---

[65] *British Airways plc v. Starmer* EAT/0306/05/SM;[2005] IRLR 862

[66] *R v. Secretary of State for Employment, ex parte Equal Opportunities Commission* [1994] IRLR 176.

[67] *Allonby v. Accrington and Rossendale College* [2001] EWCA Civ 529.

[68] *Price v. Civil Service Commission* [1978] ICR 27.

[69] *Panesar v. Nestle & Co Ltd* [1980] IRLR 64.

[70] *London Underground Ltd v. Edwards (No 2)* [1998] IRLR 364.

[71] *Copsey v. WWB Devon Clays Ltd* [2005] IRLR 811.

[72] EHRC Code of Practice on Employment, para. 4.5.

[73] *Bethnal Green and Shoreditch Education Trust v Dippenaar* [2015] UKEAT 0064/15/JOJ.

finding that the purden of proof could not be shifted in an indirect discrimination claim.

Once it has been established that a PCP exists the next question for the tribunal is whether that PCP has placed the complainant group at a particular disadvantage.

4.4.2.Putting at a Particular Disadvantage

Once one has established that there is a PCP being applied, the next step that one must consider is the impact that the PCP has on one group when compared to a comparator group, that are in materially the same circumstances but without the protected characteristic that forms the focus of the complaint.[74] From here it is often down to statistics[75], as statistical data still plays a useful role in helping a complainant or group of complainants convince a court that there ought to be a presumption of discrimination, bringing with it a reversal of the burden of proof.[76] The importance of statistics is due to PCPs often looking neutral on their face and applied to all persons irrespective of the protected characteristics: consequently, indirect discrimination focusses not on the application of the PCP, but on their impact. Using statistics can identify those PCPs that are having a disproportionately unfavourably impact upon a group of persons when compared to others in a similar situation.

This approach is explicitly spelled out by the ECtHR in *Hoogendijk v The Netherlands*[77]:

> [T]he Court considers that where an applicant is able to show, on the basis of undisputed official statistics, the existence of a prima facie indication that a specific rule – although formulated in a neutral manner – in fact affects a clearly higher percentage of women than men, it is for the respondent Government to show that this is the result of objective factors unrelated to any discrimination on grounds of sex.

---

[74] This follows closely the approach adopted under direct discrimination: it is similarly important in claims for indirect discrimination to isolate the protected characteristic from other differences that may explain the difference in treatment; otherwise it is not possible to establish that the treatment was because of the protected characteristic as opposed to any other material reason that is not linked to a protected characteristic.

[75] Although not always.

[76] The reversed burden of proof is discussed at **Chapter 8.1**.

[77] *Hoogendijk v The Netherlands* Application no. 58641/00, Admissibility Decision of 6 January 2005.

It is clear that statistical data will continue to be of importance in a number of cases where indirect discrimination is a point in issue; however, it is not the sole way of establishing disadvantage.

Before considering the concept of 'particular disadvantage' it is worth noting that one thing that has remained constant throughout the development of indirect discrimination protection is that the complainant must be careful to select an appropriate group with which to make a comparison. The two cases of *Pearse v. Bradford Metropolitan District Council*[78] and *Jones v. University of Manchester*[79] are indicative of this. In the *Pearse* case the comparative group selected was too wide, and should have been limited to those individuals who had the necessary qualifications required to apply for the particular post, whereas the *Jones v. University of Manchester* case is an example where too narrow a comparative group was selected. In both cases the claims failed due to selecting the incorrect comparative groups.

Once the appropriate comparative group has been identified the next stage is to consider whether the complainant group has been 'put at a particular disadvantage' when compared to this group. Just to highlight a couple of court decisions that demonstrate how unclear this is: The case of *Fulton v. Strathclyde Regional Council* [1986] held that where 90% of women could comply with the requirement of full-time working, this was not considerably smaller than the statistics of 100% of men being able to comply. So in this case a 10% difference was not deemed considerably smaller. However, in *R v. Secretary of State for Employment ex parte Seymour Smith and Perez*[80], the CA decided that a difference of less than 10% was considerably smaller. And in the case of *London Underground Ltd v. Edwards (No.2)*[81] a difference of 5% in the ability to comply was held to be enough to satisfy 'considerably smaller'. However, the CA in this case, something which is supported by the ECJ in *Seymour Smith*[82] when this was appealed all the way to the ECJ, suggested that the difference in proportions was only one thing which should be considered. The courts must also take into account the length of time the persistent and constant disparity has been

---

[78] *Pearse v. Bradford Metropolitan District Council* [1988] IRLR 379.

[79] *Jones v. University of Manchester* [1993] ICR 474.

[80] *R v. Secretary of State for Employment ex parte Seymour Smith and Perez* [1995] IRLR 464 (CA)

[81] *London Underground Ltd v. Edwards (No 2)* [1998] IRLR 364

[82] *R (Seymour-Smith) v Secretary of State for Employment* [2000] UKHL 12 and (1999) (Case C-167/97)

evidenced over. The longer the period of time the smaller the differences in proportions can be. However, when considering such case law it must be noted that such decisions were reached in an era where statistical evidence was key, with a need to establish 'considerably smaller' ciompliance or that a higher proportion could not comply. The current approach, that of establishing 'a particular disadvantage' appears to place less emphasis on statistical evidence and enables courts and tribunals to adopt a more common-sense approach to the matter. Of particular importance in this respect are the words of Baroness Hale in Homer:

> The new formulation was...intended to do away with the need for statistical comparisons where no statistics might exist. It was intended to do away with the complexities involved in identifying those who could comply and those who could not and how great the disparity had to be. Now all that is needed is a particular disadvantage when compared with other people who do not share the characteristic in question.[83]

Although statisitical evidence will continue to play a role, as this gives clear evidence from which indirect discrimination can be identified, a lack of such evidence will not automatically bring an end to the claim, with the courts and tribunals able to consider the reality of the situation: a clear step forward in terms of the protection in this area, especially to cover situations where statistical evidence is either costly to produce or just difficult to produce or maintain.

The Commission for Racial Equality, as it then was, suggested that for certainty purposes we should adopt a similar rule as that applied in the US. That is that where the proportion of the complainant's group who can comply is 80% or less then there is discrimination.

In addition to establishing that a group to which the complainant belongs[84] is being put at a particular disadvantage the claimant must also establish

---

[83] *Chief Constable of West Yorkshire Police v. Homer* [2012] UKSC 15.

[84] Interestingly the requirement for the complainant to share the characteristic of the disadvantaged group may be inconsistent with the EU approach to indirect discrimination, following the CJEU's decision in *CHEZ Razpredelenie Bulgaria AD v Komisia za zashtita ot diskriminatsias* [2015], ECJ (Grand Chamber), 16 July, C-83/14: it was decided that indirect discrimination protection extends to persons who, although not themselves a member of a group with the protected characteristic concerned, nevertheless suffers a particular disadvantage. Although this decision was made in the particular context of the supply of goods and services under the Race Directive, by anology it is likely to be extended to indirect discrimination across all protected characteristics in employment. In essence this is an extension of the protection to cover associative indirect discrimination.

the reasons behind the disadvantage[85] as well as individual disadvantage.[86] Importantly, the CA in *Home Office (UK Border Agency)* did not use the requirement of individual disadvantage to introduce an additional evidential burden, through noting that in principle the complainant can rely on the same statistics that establishes group disadvantage to support the submission that they were personally disadvantaged by the PCP. This would be sufficient to prove facts which, in the absence of any alternative explanation, the tribunal could conclude that discrimination is proved, thereby shifting the burden of proof.[87]

4.4.3.Proportionate Means of Achieving a Legitimate Aim

It is possible to raise a justification in relation to indirect discrimination and this is where the employer can show that the measure adopted is a proportionate means of achieving a legitimiate aim.[88] Unlike direct discrimination where the justification is limited to only instances of direct age discrimination, the justification with respect indirect discrimination is available across all the protected characteristics.

Justification means that unequal treatment that would otherwise be unlawful discrimination is made lawful through an acceptable explanation behind the treatment. The justification has long been in place, and various guises of it can be seen in the various legislative instruments that were in existence prior to the Equality Act coming into force; however, the express wording of the justification did differ depending on which legislation one was considering. Despite differences in language the justification did operate in a similar way. The justification follows that which was decided by the ECJ in relation to unequal pay justification in the case of *Bilka Kaufhaus*[89], where it was held that the provision is justified if it:

(a) corresponds to a real need on the part of the employer;

(b) is appropriate to that end; and

(c) is necessary to achieve that objective.

---

[85] Sir Colin Rimer in the CA in *Home Office (UK Border Agency) v Essop & Ors* [2015] EWCA Civ 609 stated that 'it is conceptually impossible to prove a group disadvantage for the purpose of section 19(2)(b) without also showing *why* the claimed disadvantage is said to arise' [para. 59].

[86] Sir Colin Rimer in the CA in *Home Office (UK Border Agency) v Essop & Ors* [2015] EWCA Civ 609, para.61.

[87] Sir Colin Rimer at para.65.

[88] EqA s.19(2)(d).

[89] *Bilka-Kaufhaus GmbH v. Weber von Hartz* [1986] IRLR 317 ECJ (Case C-170/84)

This approach by the ECJ was accepted and adopted by the CA in *Hampson v. Department of Education and Science*[90].

When considering this justification it is simple to identify that the the first two parts of the test are relatively straightforward for an employer to establish. The need on the part of the employer is clearly subjective in nature and not one that the tribunal will interfere with; it is often left for the employing business to identify what their undertaking's real needs are as it is impossible for a tribunal to reach any conclusion on that matter. The need for the the measure to be appropriate to that need is simply requiring that the mesure in some way achieves that aim, or it can be shown to be capable of doing so. It is with respect necessity where the test becomes more complex, as this introduces the idea of proportionality. This third aspect will require an employer to assess the various options available to them that would achieve the same aim, which corresponds to their subjective need, and select the measure that cuases the least discriminatory effect. If the complainant can establish that there were other options available to the employer that would have satisfied their identified need and these would have had less discriminatory impact then the measure being considered would not be considered necessary, and the justification would fail. This places a great responsibility on the employer to evaluate any options that may be available to achieve the end result in mind.

4.5.   Harassment

4.5.1. Early protection against harassment

The initial approach to harassment under the equality legislation prior to the Equality Act was to try and fit it under one of the accepted forms of discrimination, namely as a special form of direct discrimination. This approach was primarily as a consequence of harassment not being explicitly protected against within the relevant legislation. However, adopting such an approach had the undesirable consequence of requiring a comparison, since direct discrimination had and was developing as a protection on the basis of comparing situations between a complainant and a comparable worker in materially the same circumstances. With much of the case law being on sexual harassment, this need for a comparator often led to employers being able to raise the defence that male workers would equally be disgusted or uncomfortable with the action being complained of, and as such sexual harassment was being found not to have taken in place in circumstances where it appeared to be so. For example, a claim for sexual harassment would not succeed where a female worker made a claim

---

[90] *Hampson v Department of Education and Science* [1989] ICR 179 (CA)

following being offended by pornographic pictures being displayed in the work place if male colleagues were similarly offended, despite the conduct of putting up such photos clearly being of a sexual nature and having the effect of creating an uncomfortable environment for the female complainant.[91] Despite a number of cases trying to circumvent this defence through identifying particular acts as 'gender-specific', the need for a comparator was reaffirmed, with the idea of gender-specific acts as a means of establishing harassment being rejected, by the House of Lords in *Pearce v Governing Body of Mayfield School*.[92] The consequence of this decision was that harassment pre-Equality Act, although existing as a protection, had clear limitations.

4.5.2. Harassment protection under the Equality Act

Harassment as a separate claim and a recognised form of discrimination in its own right came through amendments made to UK legislation as required by European developments, in particular through Framework Directive 2000/78/EC and the Equal Treatment Amendment Directive 2002/73/EC. This development of protection from harassment is currently contained in the Equality Act at s.26, and is defined as covering situations where:

(1) A person (A) harasses another (B) if—
    (a) A engages in unwanted conduct related to a relevant protected characteristic, and
    (b) the conduct has the purpose or effect of—
        (i) violating B's dignity, or
        (ii) creating an intimidating, hostile, degrading, humiliating or offensive for B.

(2) A also harasses B if—
    (a) A engages in unwanted conduct of a sexual nature, and
    (b) the conduct has the purpose or effect referred to in subsection (1)(b).

(3) A also harasses B if—
    (a) A or another person engages in unwanted conduct of a sexual nature or that is related to gender reassignment or sex,
    (b) the conduct has the purpose or effect referred to in subsection (1)(b), and
    (c) because of B's rejection of or submission to the conduct, A treats B less favourably than A would treat B if B had not rejected or submitted to the conduct.

---

[91] *Stewert v. Cleveland Guest (Engineering) Ltd* (1994) IRLR 440.

[92] *Pearce v Governing Body of Mayfield School* [2003] IRLR 517.

(4) In deciding whether conduct has the effect referred to in subsection (1)(b), each of the following must be taken into account—

(a) the perception of B;

(b) the other circumstances of the case;

(c) whether it is reasonable for the conduct to have that effect.

(5) The relevant protected characteristics are—

age;

disability;

gender reassignment;

race;

religion or belief;

sex;

sexual orientation.

The approach to harassment under its current provision does not differ much in practice to the approach that was adopted when it considered as part of of direct discrimination, and can be seen in the *Reed and Bull v. Stedman*[93] case. This case concerned a manager who bullied a secretary, and the act of bullying was sexual in nature. The EAT stated that for harassment the question that needed to be asked was whether the applicant had been the subject of a detriment and whether the detriment was on the grounds of sex. The EAT held that:

> The essential characteristic of sexual harassment is that it is words or conduct which are unwelcome to the recipient and it is for the recipient to decide for themselves what is acceptable to them and what they regard as offensive. A characteristic of sexual harassment is that it undermines the victim's dignity at work. It creates an 'offensive' or 'hostile' environment for the victim and an arbitrary barrier to sexual equality in the workplace.

In essence this is the approach that we still adopt when faced with considering whether harassment has taken place, although the current legislative provision is not limited to the protectedcharacteristic of sex. However, in order for ease of consideration, as was done with both direct and indirect discrimination, it is worth breaking up the statutory provision relating to harassment in to its constituent parts.

4.5.3.'unwanted conduct'

In determining whether harassment has taken place it is generally the case that the act or action must occur more than once, as providing evidence of discontent at an act provides strong evidence that a second act was clearly unwanted. This continues with the approach that was adopted pre-

---

[93] *Reed and Bull v. Stedman* [1999] IRLR 299

Equality Act, and is what comes from the cases of *Porcelli v. Stathclyde Regional Council*[94] and *Reed and Bull v. Stedman*. In *Porcelli* sexual harassment was defined as unwelcome acts involving physical acts of a sexual nature and conduct falling short of such acts. There was also a Code of Practice issued by the EC, as it then was defining sexual harassment as 'unwanted conduct of a sexual nature, or other conduct based on sex affecting the dignity of men and women at work. This can include unwelcome physical, verbal or non-verbal conduct'.

However, it has also been held that a single act of harassment if sufficiently serious will satisfy the detriment required for a harassment claim, and this is seen in *Bracebridge Engineering v. Darby*.[95] In this case the sufficiently serious conduct was an indecent assault. It would seem absurd that something so serious and something which is clearly unwanted would need to happen again.

It is obviously going to be a difficult task, in some cases, to draw a line between those acts that do not become unwanted until the perpetrator is made aware that it is and the incident happens again, and those acts that are inherently unwanted. A common sense approach will prevail in these cases.

The only other minor point worth highlighting is that the conduct being complained of must be detrimental to the claimant; the test for this is the same as that for direct discrimination, and will only be considered a detriment if the treatment or conduct is of such a kind that a reasonable worker may take the view that in all of the circumstances, it was to his or her detriment.[96]

4.5.4. Comparator

The statutory definition of harassment in effect reverses the House of Lords decision of *Pearce*, and removes the need to identify a suitable comparator for the purpose establishing conduct that can be deemed harassment. This removal of a comparator is through introducing the need to show 'unwanted' conduct, rather than the former approach of 'less favourable' treatment, which is contained within the definition of direct discrimination. The focus is now on the conduct itself, rather than looking for a comparator against which the treatment can be deemed less favourable.

---

[94] *Porcelli v. Stathclyde Regional Council* [1986] ICR 564.

[95] *Bracebridge Engineering v. Darby* [1990] IRLR 3.

[96] This approach was confirmed as applying equally in the context of harassment by the CA in *Grant v. HM Land Registry* [2011] EWCA Civ 769.

4.5.5. 'related to a relevant protected characteristic'

It should be noted that this does not introduce the need to establish a causative link between the conduct and the relevant protected characteristic. The original provision in the Equality Act required a causative link through the use of the phrase 'on the grounds of'. However, this was amended to only requiring the conduct to be 'related to' following a number of decalarations made by Burton J following a challenge by the Equal Opportunities Commission in *EOC v Secretary of State for Trade and Industry*.[97] Removing the causative link from the provision brought the UK's approach to harassment in line with that present in the relevant European Directives.

4.5.6. 'purpose or effect'

In line with that already discussed under direct discrimination it is clear that including the idea that that conduct has the 'purpose or effect' means that there is not a need to establish motive and intention in all cases where harassment is being considered. The provision is much wider than that, and has the potential also to cover those situations where there was no intention to cause harassment, but the effect is to do so. However, this does not mean that the intention is wholly irrelevant, it just does not act as a 'defence' in all cases. It is worth noting in this respect that the approach evident in s.26 mirrors the test that was established in *Richmond Pharmacology*,[98] in which the EAT stated that the presence or absence of intent would be a factor that would be taken into consideration when deciding whether it was reasonable to consider the conduct to be a detriment.

There is another interesting extension brought into the harassment provision through this phrase, and that is that the conduct in question does not need to be aimed at the complainant. It is easily conceivable that conduct aimed at another, or even conduct aimed at nobody in particular, can still have the effect of creating a particular type of environment in which harassment can be said to occur. This greatly extends the scope of harassment.

4.5.7. Subjective/objective approach

Under the previous approach to harassment it was unclear, due to conflicting decisions, whether the test as to whether conduct could be deemed unwanted was objective or subjective. Case law such as *De Souza v.*

---

[97] *EOC v Secretary of State for Trade and Industry* [2007] EWHC 483.

[98] *Richmond Pharmacology v Dhaliwal* UKEAT/0458/08; [2009] IRLR 336 .

Automobile Association,[99] which saw the Court of Appeal express that it must be conduct such that "a reasonable worker would or might take the view that he had been thereby disadvanted in the circumstances in which he had thereafter to work" contrasted with decisions including *Reed and Bull v. Stedman*,[100] where the EAT held that the test was a subjective one, and that it was "for the recipient to decide for themselves what is acceptable to them and what they regard as offensive". Fortunately, this has now been cleared up through express statutory language, with the Equality Act adopting a similar approach to harassment as that already considered under direct discrimination in relation to the finding of less favourable treatment. The approach is a mix between the subjective and objective. It takes account of the perception of the complainant, which will be accepted as being the case, unless it was an unreasonable view to hold in the circumstances of the case. Clearly, the views of the complainant will be of paramount importance. In essence this ensures that the impact on the complainant will be central to the considerations of the tribunal, which makes sense given that harassment is very personal to the complainant, but this is balanced against the need for such views to be reasonable, and as such will ensure that circumstances where an individual is hyper-sensitive in circumstances where it would appear absurd to consider harassment to have taken place will not fall within the provision.

4.5.8.Protection from Harassment Act 1997

Individuals may wish to make use of the Protection from Harassment Act 1997 ('PHA') as a means of protecting against harassing acts rather than relying on s.26 of the Equality Act. This may be the preferred option in some situations, due to the certain advantages that the PHA has over the Equality Act:

- there is a six year limitation period under the PHA, as opposed to three months under the Equality Act;
- damages can be awarded for anxiety under the PHA;
- the employer has the opportunity to raise a defence of taking all reasonably practicable steps to rebut a submission that they are vicariously liable for acts of harassment under the Equality Act, whereas no such defence exists under the PHA;
- unlike the position under the Equality Act, which, as identified above, has a quite specific definition of harassment, the PHA has no definition restricting the concept of harassment; and

---

[99] *De Souza v. Automobile Association* [1986] IRLR 103.

[100] *Reed and Bull v. Stedman* [1999] IRLR 299.

- harassment under PHA can be argued on any grounds, and is not restricted to a finite range of protected characteristics.

Although Parliament's intention was probably not to introduce such a wide-ranging piece of legislation that filled the same space as that of harassment as protected under the Equality Act, Parliament has made no attempt to take a step back from the wide application attached to the PHA by the House of Lords in *Majrowski v. Guy's and St Thomas's NHS Trust*.[101] Accordingly, the PHA remains a valid means of protecting against harassment in the workplace.

4.6. Victimisation

Victimisation occurs when a person is subjected to a detriment because he or she has brought proceedings, considering bringing proceedings, assisting somebody else bring proceedings, or where the employer considers any of these to be the case, under the Equality Act, unless the allegations were false and made in bad faith.

In determining whether victimisation takes place it is not the protected characteristic of the individual that is of concern, it is just the fact that they have been subjected to a detriment for one of the reasons expressed above. In *St Helens MBC v. Derbyshire and others*[102] the House of Lords adopted a broad purposive approach to victimisation, with a focus on the conduct, and whether this had the intention or effect of frustrating the non-victimisation protection.

The correct approach to victimisation was considered by the House of Lords in *Chief Constable of Yorkshire v. Khan*.[103] Mr Khan was refused a reference because he was pursuing a race discrimination claim and the employer wished to preserve his position. The House of Lords considered that if the 'but for' test did apply, that is 'but for' the discrimination claim, then the references would have been provided. However, the reason references were withheld in this case was for the employer to preserve its position. Consequent to this consideration, the House of Lords decided that the correct approach to victimisation was to ask whether the detriment was 'by reason that' the applicant had carried out the protected act. If it was, then victimisation is established. What the *Khan* case appears to suggest is

---

[101] *Majrowski v. Guy's and St Thomas's NHS Trust* [2005] IRLR 340.

[102] *St Helens MBC v. Derbyshire and others* [2007] UKHL 16.

[103] *Chief Constable of West Yorkshire Police v. Khan* [2001] UKHL 48; [2001] ICR 1065

that, unlike other areas of discrimination, the motivation of the discriminator remains relevant for the purposes of victimisation.

Victimisation protection appears to extend beyond the actions of the employer, with the House of Lords in *Waters v Commissioner of Police of the Metropolis*[104] accepting that victimisation may also arise where an employer fails to prevent acts of employees against a fellow employee, where those acts cause a detriment and are as a result of having carried out a protected act.

4.7.   Vicarious Liability of Employers

Importantly an act of discrimination by a fellow employee can also result in action being taken against the employer, with employers being vicariously liable for the acts of their workforce in certain circumstances. The principle of vicarious liability is provided for at section 109 of the Equalty Act:

> (1) Anything done by a person (A) in the course of A's employment must be treated as also done by the employer...

In other words, whenever an act of discrimination takes place in the course of employment, then the employer will be vicariously liable for all of those acts of discrimination, whether or not it was done with the employer's knowledge or approval. The idea of 'in the course of employment' was subject to debate before the courts as employers attempted to restrict the use of vicarious liability. However, an important case in providing an expansive approach to this concept is best seen by the Court of Appeal in the case of *Jones v. Tower Boot Co. Ltd,*[105] where it was held that the words 'in the course of employment' should have their everyday meaning, which is presumably to say that if the harassment is carried out at work, during work time, by employees undergoing their work duties then the employer will be liable under this provision. An even wider approach to these words can be seen by the EAT in the case of *Chief Constable of the Lincolnshire Police v. Stubbs*[106] where it was held to extend to after work hours, if the social situation could be regarded as an extension of work. In this case an after work leaving party had a sufficiently close nexus with the employment to fall under these words.

However, the principle of vicarious liability is subject to a defence:

> (4) In proceedings against A's employer (B) in respect of anything alleged to have been done by A in the course of A's employment it is a

---

[104] *Waters v Commissioner of Police of the Metropolis* [2000] IRLR 720

[105] *Jones v. Tower Boot Co. Ltd* [1997] IRLR 168

[106] *Chief Constable of the Lincolnshire Police v. Stubbs* [1999] IRLR 81

> defence for B to show that B took all reasonable steps to prevent A—
> (a)from doing that thing, or
> (b)from doing anything of that description.

An employer is able to raise a defence that they should not be held liable for the discriminatory acts as they have taken such steps as were reasonably practicable to prevent the employee from doing that act, or doing in the course of his employment acts of that description. Things that appear to satisfy this defence include implementing a system of proper supervision and publishing an equal opportunities policy. According to the case of *Canniffe v, East Riding of Yorkshire Council*[107] the employment tribunal must consider whether the employer took all reasonable steps to prevent an employee from committing a discriminatory act, and then consider what further steps could have been taken which were reasonably practicable.

A case that highlights at least an example of an approach by an employer that satisfied the defence is that of *Martins v. Marks & Spencer Plc,*[108] where the Court of Appeal held that:

> There can be no doubt that Marks & Spencer made out the defence on the findings of fact about the effective arrangements made for the 'special interview' to ensure that the members of the panel had no knowledge of the reason of the interview; their equal opportunities policy; their compliance with the Code of Practice issued by the Commission of Racial Equality in relation to selection procedures, criteria and interviewing; and their selection of the interview panel to include Mr Walters as a person with an interest in recruiting from ethnic minorities.

All these actions amounted to a sufficient defence.

One thing that is clear and important to note is that the defence will not be established where the approach by the employer is merely a paper exercise with a view to precluding such vicarious liability; there is a clear need to show that any attempt to prevent discrimination or to educate the workforce against discriminatory action must also be evidenced to be taking place in practice. A simple paper trail without any suggestion of implementation will not suffice.

---

[107] *Canniffe v, East Riding of Yorkshire Council* [2000] IRLR 555

[108] *Martins v. Marks & Spencer Plc* [1998] ICR 1005.

4.8. Instructions to Discriminate and aiding a contravention

The Equality Act covers instructions to discriminate through s.111 making it unlawful to instruct, cause or induce another person[109] to act in a manner against a third person that contravenes Part 5 (Work) or s.108 (relationships that have ended) or s.112 (a basic contravention) of the Act. It will be held to be unlawful discrimination where such takes place.[110] Section 111(5) provides a broad range of actors who may bring proceedings in a case involving such a case, giving standing to the person who is instructed,[111] the third person in which the conduct is instructed against,[112] and the EHRC. Including the EHRC enables the Commission to investigate without the need for a complainant or in circumstances where a detriment may be difficult to establish.

Closely linked to the prohibition on instructions to discriminate is the prohibition on aiding a contravention of the Equality Act protections. This is dealt with at s.112 of the Equality Act, where it is stated that a person must not knowingly help another to do anything which contravenes Part 5 (Work) or s.108(1) or (2) or s.111 (a basic contravention). There is an exception built within s.112 where an individual who is asked to help relies on a statement which does not contravene the Act in circumstances where it was reasonable to do so.

4.9. Discriminatory Advertisements

Section 39 of the Equality Act through covering provisions 'for deciding to whom to offer employment' precludes discriminatory advertisements. Any terminology within adverts, such as 'older person', 'young and attractive' or 'British looking' would fall foul of this protection. Arguably if an advert contains a sexual connotation, such as postman or barman or waitress, this will also be taken to indicate a discriminatory intention, unless it is rebutted elsewhere in the advert.

---

[109] EqA s.111(8) clarified that a reference in this section to causing or inducing a person to do something includes a reference to attempting to cause or induce the person to do it.

[110] In *Weathersfield Ltd v Sargent* [1999] IRLR 94 for example, Mrs Sargeant was held to have been discriminated against on the grounds of race when she was constructively dismissed for refusing to operate a racially discriminatory policy.

[111] There is a need to establish that they have been subjected to a detriment as a result of the instruction.

[112] Likewise there is a need to establish a detriment.

In order to establish a claim based on a discriminatory advert the complainant will need to establish that they have suffered some detriment. In other words, they will need to evidence that 'but for' the wording of the advert then they would have made an application but were deterred from doing so. Where there is no genuine intention to accept a post should they be offered it, then the complainant will fail in evidencing that a detriment has been suffered and the claim will fail.[113]

4.10. Disability Discrimination Protections

Discrimination on the grounds that an individual has a disability is further protected against through additional approaches that go beyond the traditional model of anti-discrimination protection. The additional protections are:

1. discrimination arising from disability; and
2. the duty to make reasonable adjustments.

The protection against discrimination arising from disability ensures that persons with a disability are offered wider-ranging protection. It is often not the disability that leads to the discriminatory treatment (which would be caught by direct discrimination principles) but it is the consequences of that disability. This ensures that individuals are not denied protection through an employer submitting that the treatment that the person with a disability received was not directly caused by their disability but was because of something else, and futher that other individuals without that disability acting in the same manner would have been treated in the same negative way. This expands the protections horizontally to ensure a wider level of protection is afforded.

The extended protection for individuals can be further seen when one considers the duty placed on employers to make reasonable adjustments for workers who have a disability. This extension is clearly a substantive equality measure, given that it does not require equal treatment, but in fact requires preferential treatment to be given to individuals in certain circumstances. When one considers that individuals with a disability can potentially face prohibitive barriers to employment, which can include physical barriers which can be altered at a reasonable cost, it is easy to accept the justification behind this approach. This is explained in the EHRC's Statutory Code of Practice on Employment where it is stated that the duty to make reasonable adjustments is

---

[113] *Keane v. Investigo*, UKEAT/0389/09/SM, 11 December 2009.

a cornerstone of the Act which requires employers to take positive steps to ensure that disabled people can access and progress in employment. This goes beyond simply avoiding treating disabled workers, job applicants and potential job applicants unfavourably and means taking additional steps to which non-disabled workers and applicants are not entitled.

The scope of each of these two additional protections will be discussed in turn below.

4.10.1. Discrimination arising from disability

Discrimination arising from disability replaces the previous protection of s.3A(1)[114] that was contained in the DDA. Section 15 provides that:

1) A person (A) discriminates against a disabled person (B) if—
   a) A treats B unfavourably because of something arising in consequence of B's disability, and
   b) A cannot show that the treatment is a proportionate means of achieving a legitimate aim.
2) Subsection (1) does not apply if A shows that A did not know, and could not reasonably have been expected to know, that B had the disability

The first part of section 15 is in direct response to the House of Lords decision in *London Borough of Lewisham v. Malcolm*.[115] The House of Lords held that as s.3A required the treatment of a person with a disability to be 'less favourable' then there was a need for a suitable comparator, which would be satisfied through comparing the treatment afforded to a disabled person with that afforded to a person in materially the same circumstances but non-disabled. This made such claims very difficult to succeed.[116] For example, if a person with no disability was not allowed to enter a restaurant with a dog, then it was not discrimination under DDA s.3A to refuse entry to a person who is blind based on them wishing to bring their guide dog with them as each would be treated the same and thus no less favourable treatment present. Section 15(1) of the Equality Act departed from the need to establish 'less favourable treatment' to only requiring evidence of unfavourable treatment, thus focussing solely on whether the

---

[114] DDA s.3A indicated that it was discrimination if a disabled person was treated less favourably for a reason which related to the disabled person's disability.

[115] *London Borough of Lewisham v. Malcolm* [2008] UKHL 43.

[116] See Horton, R. (2008), 'The end of disability related discrimination in employment?' *Industrial Law Journal*, 376-383; Orme, E. (2008), 'Malcolm v Lewisham LBC: nasty surprise or logical conclusion?' *Journal of Housing Law*, 103-107.

person with a disability has been subjected to a detriment,[117] and removing the need for a comparator.[118]

Knowledge of a person's disability is clearly an important aspect that needs to be addressed, given that the employer will not be held to have unlawfully discriminated against an individual under s.15 if the employer did not know or could not have reasonably have been expected to know of the disability.[119] The need for knowledge on behalf of the employer both here and in other aspects of disability discrimination protection begs the question of whether the Government ought to reconsider the current statutory embargo that applies to the section 60 pre-employment health and disability questionnaires. This is certainly a useful tool in establishing knowledge, or at the very least providing constructive knowledge of a disability. The EHRC's Code of Practice of Employment provides some guidance on the matter of knowledge, and places the obligation on the employer to "do all they can be reasonably expected to do to find out if the worker has a disability". It will be no defence to simply submit that as an employer they buried their head in the sand and ultimately did not know of a disability that a person has. There is a clear obligation placed on the employer to take positive steps.[120]

Even where there has been treatment that is unfavourable because of something arising in consequence of an individual's disability this will not be deemed to be unlawful discrimination where the treatment is a proportionate means of achieving a legitimate aim. Given that this justification mirrors that which has already been discussed in relation to

---

[117] On the matter of whether there is a detriment see the discussion at **Chapter 4.3.1**.

[118] This is confirmed in the EHRC's Code of Pracice on Employment, where it is stated at para 5.6 that for the protecton afforded EqA s.15 '…there is no need to compare a disabled person's treatment with that of another person… it is only necessary to demonstrate that the unfavourable treatment is because of something arising in consequence of the disability.' Interestingly, it is suggested by Cabrelli (2014), at p.476, that the inclusion of the phrase 'because of' in s.15(1) may enable the courts to introduce a comparator requirement through the back door given that it reflects that which is used in s.13 in relation to direct discrimination. Cabrelli further suggests that the use of the term 'unfavourably' has the connotation of requiring disadvantageous treatment, which in itself would require some comparison (either covert or subconsciously) in order for the disadvantageous treatment to be established. However, as this has yet been considered in the judicial forum this is certain a question that remains unanswered at present.

[119] See EqA s.15(2).

[120] At least part of this obligation arguably could be satisfied through pre-employment health and disability checks should the statutory embargo be repealed.

indirect discrimination consideration of what is required in order to establish whether the treatment is a proportionate means of achieving a legitimate aim.

This provision will affect a number of different circumstances where the unfavourable treatment is due to an action or non-action that is a consequence of a disability; this protection focusses not on treatment based on the disability itself, but on treatment based on a consequence of a disability, before then considering whether the treatment could be justified. For example, in circumstances where an employee can not wear particular personal protective equipment, such as safety boots, due to a disability, dismissing that employee may be justified if there are is no alternative employment with the employer available.[121] Although the detriment, or the dismissal, arises from not being able to wear such clothing as direct consequence of a disability, the treatment is justified, with on the basis of health and safety as a legitimate aim. Obviously if alternative work where such personal protective equipment was not required then dismissal may not have been considered a proportionate response.

The EHRC in the Code of Practice for Employment also provides a useful example at paragraph 5.3:

> An employer dismisses a worker because she has had three months' sick leave. The employer is aware that the worker has multiple sclerosis and most of her sick leave is disability-related. The employer's decision to dismiss is not because of the worker's disability itself. However, the worker has been treated unfavourably because of something arising in consequence of her disability (namely, the need to take a period of disability-related sick leave).

It is clear that the focus in this protection is once removed from the disability itself. In circumstances where an individual is complaining of unfavourable treatment and trying to make a causative link with a disability one can almost ask the question: but for the disability would the circumstance that caused the unfavourable treatment have been present? If the answer is "no" then the causative link between unfavourable treatment and a matter arising out of disability will be established.

---

[121] *Farmiloe v. Lane Group Plc* [2004] PIQR P22.

4.10.2. Duty to make reasonable adjustments

The duty to make reasonable ajustments has been described as " ...central to most, if not all [disability discrimination] claims",[122] and is often described as a cornerstone of the Equality Act. This duty goes beyond simply treating those with a disability the same to non-disabled workers or applicants. Although the duty applies to all businesses, irrespective of size, one must bear in mind that it is a duty that is limited by reasonableness, and thus the extent of the duty will vary depending on the circumstances of the employer. It must also be noted that the duty applies throughout the employment life, from recruitment, through the operation of the engagement, and during dismissal.

There are three aspects to the duty to make reasonable adjustments, which are set out in s.20(3)-(5) of the Equality Act, of which failure to comply with is a failure to comply with the duty to make reasonable adjustments under s.21(1) of the Equality Act, and is thus discrimination:

> (3) The first requirement is a requirement, where a provision, criterion or practice of A's puts a disabled person at a substantial disadvantage in relation to a relevant matter in comparison with persons who are not disabled, to take such steps as it is reasonable to have to take to avoid the disadvantage.
>
> (4) The second requirement is a requirement, where a physical feature puts a disabled person at a substantial disadvantage in relation to a relevant matter in comparison with persons who are not disabled, to take such steps as it is reasonable to have to take to avoid the disadvantage.
>
> (5) The third requirement is a requirement, where a disabled person would, but for the provision of an auxiliary aid, be put at a substantial disadvantage in relation to a relevant matter in comparison with persons who are not disabled, to take such steps as it is reasonable to have to take to provide the auxiliary aid.

The duty follows closely the previous incarnation of the duty to make reasonable adjustments contained at DDA s.4A, and in practice will follow a similar approach. Consequently, case law decided under s.4A DDA will be instructive as to how the s.20 duty will operate. There is one difference worth noting between the current approach to the duty to make reasonable adjustments under the Equality Act when compared to the initial approach under the DDA and that is that the Equality Act retains the 2004

---

[122] Hughes P. (2004), 'Disability Discrimination and the Duty to Make Reasonable Adjustments: Recent Developments', *Industrial Law Journal*, 358, 363.

amendment that removed justification from this protection and as such the duty will not be subject to justification.[123]

Broadly speaking, the first of these requirements covers the practice of working, the second is concerned with the physical makeup of the workplace, including building access, wheres the third is concerned with auxiliary aids, and will cover matters such as specialist computer software.

It is important to note that the duty to make reasonable adjustments in the work context is not limited to the current workforce, and similar to the other protections is also extended to cover job applicants.[124] However, unlike the extension afforded to direct discrimination under the Equality Act also to include associative discrimination, the duty to make reasonable adjustments does not extend to individuals who are associated with a disabled person.[125]

The duty to make reasonable adjustments is entirely personal and individual to the worker with a disability. It is in this regard that it can be contrasted with indirect discrimination. The s.20 duty focusses on an individual and requires a claimant to establish that there is a PCP, physical feature of the work premises or lack of auxiliary aid that is placing them at a substantial disadvantage when compared to persons who are not disabled, whereas indirect discrimination focusses on disabled persons as a group.

Before considering the operation of the duty there are two other matters contained within s.20 of the Equality Act which needs to be highlighted:

s.20(6)—that where the first or third requirements relate to the provision of information, the steps which it is reasonable to take include steps for ensuring that in the circumstances concerned the information is provided in an accessible format, and

---

[123] It made sense removing this justification given that in practical terms it made no difference to the scope of the protection given that the concept of reasonableness, on which the duty is predicated, covered matters that would be used to justify the decision not to make an adjustment.

[124] This is extended through the concept of 'interested disabled person', which is introduced at EqA Sch.8.

[125] This was what was decided by the CA, following the EAT decision, in *Hainsworth v. Ministry of Defence* [2014] EWCA Civ 763, when Mr Hainsworth argued a failure in this duty when he did not have his place of work moved in order to enable his disabled daughter to undergo training. The CA held that the duty was placed on an employer and was owed only to their workforce.

> s.20(7)—that a person who is subject to a duty to make reasonable adjustments is not (subject to express provision to the contrary) entitled to require a disabled person to pay to any extent the costs of complying with the duty.

Both of these two provisions are self explanatory. But it is important to note that the financial burden on making reasonable adjustments rests with the employer.

The EAT in *Environment Agency v. Rowan*,[126] provided much needed guidance on the apporach that tribunals should adopt when considering whether there is a breach of the duty to make reasonable adjustments,[127] expressing that the tribunal must identify:

> (*a*) the provision, criterion or practice applied by or on behalf of an employer, or;
> (*b*) the physical feature of premises occupied by the employer;
> (*c*) the identity of non-disabled comparators (where appropriate); and
> (*d*) the nature and extent of the substantial disadvantage suffered by the claimant.

The EAT made it clear that it would not be possible to determine whether there has been a breach of the duty without questioning each of these factors first, as it is these matters that will assist the tribunal in deciding whether an such adjustment was reasonable or not.

Knowledge

Similar to the position under the s.15 protection against discrimination arising from discrimination there is an express need for knowledge of a person's disability on behalf of the employer for the duty to arise; in other words, where the employer does not know of the disability or could not reasonably have been expected to know of the disability, then no duty to consider reasonable adjustments arises. This requirement is contained at paragraph 30 of Schedule 8 to the Equality Act:

> (1) A is not subject to a duty to make reasonable adjustments if A does not know, and could not reasonably be expected to know—
> > (a) in the case of an applicant or potential applicant, that an interested disabled person is or may be an applicant for the work in question;
> > (b) [in any case referred to in Part 2 of this Schedule], that an interested disabled person has a disability and is likely to be

---

[126] *Environment Agency v. Rowan* [2008] IRLR 20.

[127] Although this guidance was laid down in relation to the duty under the DDA, it still appears equally applicable to the duty under the Equality Act.

placed at the disadvantage referred to in the first, second or third requirement.

This acts to ensure that in circumstances where the employer had no knowledge, or it was unreasonable to suggest that they should know that no liability for a failure to make reasonable adjustments will exist.

Due to the wording in paragraph 30 of Schedule 8 mirroring the former approach that was contained in s.4A(3) DDA, case law decided under that provision is likely still to be relevant to the application of the current approach. This means that the guidance provided by the EAT in *Secretary of State for the Department of Work and Pensions v Alam*,[128] is still of importance. In considering the aspect of knowledge the EAT held that two questions need to be considered:

(1) Did the employer know both that the employee was disabled and that his disability was liable to affect him in the manner set out in section 4A(1)?

If the answer to that question is: "no" then there is a second question, namely,

(2) Ought the employer to have known both that the employee was disabled and that his disability was liable to affect him in the manner set out in [the relevant provision]?

If the answer to that question was also "no", then there was no duty to make reasonable adjustments.

In normal circumstances where the employer is explicitly told of a disability, or where there is an occupational health report that identifies a disability, then the question of knowledge is pretty straightforward. However, it becomes more complex when there is no actual knowledge and the tribunal needs to consider whether the employer reasonably ought to have known. By including constructive knowledge this imposes a positive obligation on to the employer to investigate matters that give cause for concern. The EHRC provides an example in the DDA Code of Practice: Employment and Occupation. At paragraph 5.12 an example of an individual who is suffering from depression and was found often to be crying whilst at work was given. It was suggested that such behaviour may have required the employer to investigate further and consider any suitable reasonable adjustments, as a failure to do so could result in a finding that the employer could reasonably have been expected to know of the worker's circumstances. Determining whether an employer could reasonably be

---

[128] *Secretary of State for the Department of Work and Pensions v Alam* [2010] IRLR 283

expected to have known of a worker's disability is a question of fact, and one that will be weighed up by the tribunal.[129]

PCP

There is no statutory definition of a PCP, although it is a term that many are familiar with due to its use in discrimination legislation over the years. It is clearly a concept that has been applied in a broad manner within tribunals and the courts in order to ensure that the legislation achieves its purpose. As such the term PCP has been held to cover a wide array of matters from selection criteria for vacant posts, through to work rules that maintain the working relationship,[130] all the way through to issues concerning dismissal.[131] The broad interpretation applied to PCP can be derived from the EHRC's Code of Practice on Employment, where it is expressed to include " ...any formal or informal policies, rules, practices, arrangements or qualifications including one-off decisions and actions..." The Code makes reference to one-off decisions and actions which ensures that the duty is not restricted solely to discriminatory processes that last a period of time, which may have been implied through the reference to practice in PCP.

Physical feature

Unlike PCP, the Equality Act does provide a definition of physical feature for the purposes of the s.20 duty to make reasonable adjustments:

> Physical feature is defined to include any of the following, whether they are permanent or temporary:
> - any feature arising from the design or construction of a building on the premises;
> - any feature on the premises of any approach to, exit from or access to such a building;
> - any fixtures, fittings, furnishings, furniture, equipment or material in or on the premises; and
> - any other physical element or quality of any land comprised in the premises.[132]

For example, the Court of Appeal in *Royal Bank of Scotland Group v David Allen*,[133] upholding the decision of the EAT, held that installing a platform

---

[129] *Jennings v Barts and The London NHS Trust* [2013] EqLR 326.

[130] *O'Hanlon v Commissioners for HM Revenue and Customs* [2007] IRLR 404, CA.

[131] Including in *Fareham College v. Walters* [2009] IRLR 991 where it was decided that avoiding a dismissal was a failure of the duty to make reasonable adjustment.

[132] EqA s.20(10)

lift to enable access into a bank would have been a reasonable adjustment. Although this case predates the Equality Act this is an example of the type of adjustment that this may require.

Auxiliary aids

The EHRC Code indicates that an auxiliary aid "is something which provides support or assistance to a disabled person [and] can include provision of a specialist piece of equipment such as an adapted keyboard or text to speech software".[134]

Supplementing this definition are the specific examples that are contained within the explanatory notes:

> An employer provides specially-adapted furniture for a new employee with restricted movement in his upper limbs. This is likely to be a reasonable adjustment for the employer to make.

> A large employer is recruiting for posts which routinely attract a high number of applications. He arranges for large print application forms to be available for any visually-impaired people applying for a job. This is likely to be a reasonable adjustment for the employer to make.

Substantial disadvantage

The duty to make reasonable adjustments only arises where the PCP, physical feature or lack of auxiliary aid places the disabled worker at a 'substantial disadvantage'. Consequently, a claimant has the burden of establishing a causal link between the PCP, physical feature or lack of auxiliary aid and the disadvantage being complained of, with the disadvantage being something more than minor or trivial.[135] If there is no causal link then the duty will not arise.

Comparator[136]

The need to establish a substantial disadvantage raises the need of a comparator, as it is only through a comparison that one can establish that a substantial disadvantage has been experienced by a disabled worker.

---

[133] *Royal Bank of Scotland Group v David Allen* EWCA Civ 1213.

[134] EHRC Code of Practice on Employment, para 6.13.

[135] Substantial is defined as being more than minor or trivial at EqA s.212.

[136] In *Foster v Cardiff University* [2013] EqLR 718 it was found that adopting a comparator approach to the duty to make reasonable adjustments would not be incompatible with Framework Directive 2000/78/EC, which expressed the duty in terms of providing disabled persons with 'reasonable accommodation'.

Interestingly, with regards the duty to make reasonable adjustments s.23 of the Equality Act does not apply, and thus this raises the question of who will be a suitable comparator for these purposes? It is expressed in the EHRC Code of Practice on Employment that " ...there is no requirement to identify a comparator or comparator group whose circumstances are the same or nearly the same as the disabled person's".[137] In other words, the courts and tribunals have not been bound by the need for a like-for-like comparison, and have been able to develop the concept of comparator in this specific area to ensure that the protections achieve their ultimate purpose, which has resulted in broad and inclusive developments.

In considering the position of comparators in the context of disability Cox J in *Fareham College Corporation v Walters*,[138] stated that "in many cases the facts will speak for themselves and the identity of the non-disabled comparators will be clearly discernible from the provision, criterion or practice found to be in play". In other words a common sense approach must be taken in this respect, with a greater focus on the impact caused by a PCP rather than individual circumstances of a potential comparator or comparable group. A similar broad approach can be derived from the Langstaff J's judgment in *Royal Bank of Scotland v Ashton*,[139] where he held that "an Employment Tribunal—in order to uphold a claim that there has been a breach of the duty to make reasonable adjustments and, thus, discrimination—must be satisfied that there is a provision, criterion or practice which has placed the disabled person concerned not simply at some disadvantage viewed generally, but at a disadvantage which is substantial and which is not to be viewed generally but to be viewed in comparison with persons who are not disabled." Although a comparison is still required, the approach is much broader, and not as restrictive as that contained within s.23 of the Equality Act.

When is an adjustment a reasonable one?

Where it has been found that there is a PCP, a physical feature or lack of auxiliary aid which places a disabled person at a substantial disadvantage when compared to persons who are not disabled, then the employer is required to take such steps as it is reasonable to have to take to avoid the disadvantage or to provide the auxiliary aids.

---

[137] Paragraph 6.16 of the EHRC's Code.

[138] *Fareham College Corporation v Walters* [2009] IRLR 991.

[139] *Royal Bank of Scotland v Ashton* [2011] ICR 632.

This duty is preferential treatment with a view to recognising the needs that a person with a disability has and trying to accommodate those needs in a manner that removes obstacles to working; this is a prime example of the Equality Act introducing a means of achieving some form of substantive equality. In doing so it ensures that an individual who is clearly capable and able to perform work duties is not isolated and precluded from entering the labour market.

The duty to make reasonable adjustments is not limited to the current workforce, and applies equally to job applicants as it does to workers. In other words, the employer may be required to make adjustments to accommodate disabilities in relation to attending and participating in interviews or other selection processes.

Although not replicated in the Equality Act, a non-exhaustive list contained in DDA s.18B(1) provided guidance of matters that would be relevant in deciding whether something was a reasonable adjustment or not:

18B Reasonable adjustments: supplementary
(1) In determining whether it is reasonable for a person to have to take a particular step in order to comply with a duty to make reasonable adjustments, regard shall be had, in particular, to—
   (a) the extent to which taking the step would prevent the effect in relation to which the duty is imposed;
   (b) the extent to which it is practicable for him to take the step;
   (c) the financial and other costs which would be incurred by him in taking the step and the extent to which taking it would disrupt any of his activities;
   (d) the extent of his financial and other resources;
   (e) the availability to him of financial or other assistance with respect to taking the step;
   (f) the nature of his activities and the size of his undertaking;
   (g) where the step would be taken in relation to a private household, the extent to which taking it would—
      (i) disrupt that household, or
      (ii) disturb any person residing there.

(2) The following are examples of steps which a person may need to take in relation to a disabled person in order to comply with a duty to make reasonable adjustments—
   (a) making adjustments to premises;
   (b) allocating some of the disabled person's duties to another person;
   (c) transferring him to fill an existing vacancy;
   (d) altering his hours of working or training;
   (e) assigning him to a different place of work or training;

(f) allowing him to be absent during working or training hours for rehabilitation, assessment or treatment;

(g) giving, or arranging for, training or mentoring (whether for the disabled person or any other person);

(h) acquiring or modifying equipment;

(i) modifying instructions or reference manuals;

(j) modifying procedures for testing or assessment;

(k) providing a reader or interpreter;

(l) providing supervision or other support.

Given the close connection between the current approach to reasonable adjustments under s.20 of the Equality Act and that which was previously contained within DDA s.4A, and that the matters contained with the list are largely replicated at para 6.32 of the EHRC's Statutory Code of Practice on Employment then these lists will still be of some practical use.[140] They provide examples of the type of adjustments that may need to be considered in relation to the disabled workforce. Equally important is to note that even under the DDA this was a non-exhaustive list, and could be added to through judicial development. For example, even though not expressed in the list it has been held that creating a new job for a disabled employee, if it was a reasonable adjustment in the circumstances of a case, may be required.[141]

Clearly an important aspect in determining the reasonableness of an adjustment is evaluating the extent to which the adjustment removes or alleviates the disadvantage.[142] The evaluation of this involves an objective consideration.[143] If an adjustment is assessed as having no potential discernible positive impact on a barrier to the participation of a person with a disability then undertaking such an adjustment would not be achieving what the duty aims to achieve, and would thus not be required. This leads to the logical conclusion that if there is nothing in the employer's power that can be done that will enable a worker to return to work or enter the workforce, then it would not be unreasonable to implement no adjustments.[144]

---

[140] HHJ Richardson in *Carranza v General Dynamics Information Technology Ltd* [2015] IRLR 43, stated that he as "… no doubt that the same approach applies to the Equality Act 2010".

[141] *Chief Constable of South Yorkshire Police v. Jelic* [2010] IRLR 744, which applied the principle developed by the House of Lords in *Archibald v. Fife Council* [2004] IRLR 651, UKHL 32.

[142] This follows the approach that was explicit in the DDA at s.18B(1)(a).

[143] *Royal Bank of Scotland v Ashton* [2011] ICR 632.

[144] *HM Prison Service v Johnson* [2007] IRLR 951.

There is a distinction drawn between adjustments that are work related and adjustments that are personal, with the duty only extending to adjustments that are to job-related arangements; the duty does not extend to a duty to provide a worker with a personal carer who would assist with personal needs of a disabled worker.[145] This is going beyond the scope of the duty.

Where it is submitted by a complainant that an employer has failed in their duty to make reasonable adjustments then the burden rests with the employer to satisfy the tribunal that they have satisfied their duty. The employer cannot rely on the complainant's inability to suggest potential adjustments that would assist their participation in the workforce as a defence to such a complaint, but there is a burden placed on the employer to provide evidence of their their own considerations and assessments of those considerations.[146]

The duty to make reasonable adjustments has, in reality, been one of the most important aspects of the Equality Act in relation to protecting workers with a disability. The provision has been litigated frequently over the years, with the trend being that the tribunals and courts will adopt a wide and purposive approach when considering reasonable adjustments. Although the list above, as replicated from the DDA in the EHRC Code of Practice, provides a useful starting point when considering what a reasonable adjustment will entail, judicial decisions have highlighted how the duty extends beyond these, and as such there is an obligation placed on employers to give considerable thought as to what adjustments may be needed on a case by case basis. It is easy to envisage some of the more obvious adjustments that a disability may require such as wider doors, automatic doors, larger toilets or frequent and regular rest breaks. The EHRC Code of Practice on Employment also provides some useful examples throughout,[147] including modifying the format of instructions and manuals, relocating of minor or subsidiary duties to another worker, flexible working hours with additional breaks, moving workstation to a more accessible building and additional time off work for rehabilitation purposes. A further source of useful examples is case law, which, in some cases, provides examples that go beyond what may be considered the obvious:

---

[145] *Kenny v. Hampshire Constabulary* [1999] IRLR 76.

[146] *Cosgrove v. Ceasar and Howie* [2001] IRLR 653.

[147] Paras. 6.32-6.35.

- In *Archibald v. Fife Council*[148] the House of Lords adopted a highly purposive approach to the duty and went as far as finding that the duty would include, on these facts, the transferring of the worker into an existing vacancy, even in preference to a better-qualified candidate.

- In *Southampton City College v. Randall*[149] the EAT, again particular to its facts, held that the duty could extend to require an employer to create a job for the worker.

- *Garrett v. Lidl Ltd*[150] saw the EAT find that moving an employee to another place of work within the company group may be a reasonable adjustment if it achieves the desired aim of alleviating a burden caused by a disability.

- In *Chief Constable of South Yorkshire Police v. Jelic*[151] it was held by the EAT that swapping the role of an employee with a disability with another colleague may be a reasonable adjustment in certain circumstances.

Although the courts will try to adopt a liberal and purposive approach to the duty to make reasonable adjustments, it must always be remembered that the duty only extends to that which is reasonable: placing an unreasonable burden on the employer does not fall within this provision. When considering the duty factors such as the impact on the rest of the workforce,[152] the operational needs of the employer, the size of the undertaking, the extent that the discriminatory effects will be alleviated, and the financial costs[153] will all have to be taken into account.

Two areas that have received great consideration and which, despite initial cases suggesting that they did form part of the duty, have witnessed a change of approach before the courts are: consultation with disabled workers, and whether contractual terms can be reasonably adjusted. In both areas, the courts have re-evaluated their previous approach to hold that they both go beyond the limits of the duty: in respect of consultation this can be seen in Elias P's judgment in *Tarbuck v. Sainsbury's Supermarkets*

---

[148] *Archibald v. Fife Council* [2004] IRLR 651, UKHL 32.

[149] *Southampton City College v. Randall* [2006] IRLR 18.

[150] *Garrett v. Lidl Ltd* [2009] UKEAT 0541_09_1612.

[151] *Chief Constable of South Yorkshire Police v. Jelic* [2010] IRLR 744.

[152] *Chief Constable of Lincolnshire Police v. Weaver* [2008] UKEAT/0622/07.

[153] *O'Hanlon v Commissioners for HM Revenue and Customs* [2007] IRLR 404, CA.

EQUALITY AND ANTI-DISCRIMINATION LAW

Ltd;[154] in respect of contractual terms this can be read across both *Royal Liverpool Children's NHS Trust v. Dunsby*[155] and *O'Hanlon v. HMRC.*[156]

The potential of the duty to make reasonable adjustments is clear to see, and this approach is certainly one to applaud. Unlike much of the Equality Act, this duty imposes a proactive aspect to securing equality. It does not rely on a breach of the Equality Act before action will need to be taken and as such is not negative in nature, but the duty is a positive one. By focussing on the removal of workplace barriers it has the potential to improve practices in the labour market such that it can have a positive impact on a wider proportion of workers with disabilities; this contrasts with the individualistic impact present under many of the other equality areas of the UK,[157] both within and outside the Equality Act.

---

[154] *Tarbuck v. Sainsbury's Supermarkets Ltd* [2006] IRLR 664.

[155] *Royal Liverpool Children's NHS Trust v. Dunsby* [2006] IRLR 751.

[156] *O'Hanlon v Commissioners for HM Revenue and Customs* [2007] IRLR 404, CA.

[157] Although this must be read alongside the remedial action of recommendation, which is open to the tribunal to make on the finding of unlawful discrimination.

5. Defences

There are a number of general defences that apply across the Equality Act that need to be understood. Unlike the position of objective justification which renders unequal treatment lawful, a defence is considered and thus applies after there is a finding of unlawful discrimination. In other words, this will ordinarily be the final aspect that will be considered in relation to any discrimination complaints under the Equality Act.

As these general defences are defences against a fundamental freedom that is enjoyed by all citizens the courts tend to apply them fairly narrowly. Courts appear to be retaining a tight rein on these defences and are thus not easy to invoke, except in fairly particular and narrow circumstances.

One of the most important defences to what would otherwise be unlawful justification is that of positive action, which has been expanded under the Equality Act. This is a concept that is often confused with the idea of positive discrimination, which is regularly cited as a means to rebalancing the workforce with regards persons with particular characteristics, most notably as a means of addressing the gender inequality of the UK workforce. However, there is no such practice allowed in the UK or in any EU Member State: if anything the phrase is something of an oxymoron. Discrimination is discrimination, and should not be viewed as positive, irrespective of the context.

Before turning to consider the operation of positive action in the UK this chapter will first consider the well rehearsed defence of 'Genuine Occupational Requirements'. This chapter will then conclude by briefly considering the areas of statutory defence, illegality and national security.

5.1. Genuine Occupational Requirements

It is often in the access to employment where most discrimination takes place, with various barriers and requirements put in place by an employer which restricts certain individuals from applying for an advertised position, or at least makes it more difficult for a successful application to be achieved. However, in recognition that there is, in certain contexts, a need for certain characteristics that are inherently important for a role, Part 1 of Schedule 9 to the Equality Act introduces[1] the concept of a 'genuine occupational requirement' (hereinafter 'GOR').

---

[1] Technically speaking this is maintaining the former position that was contained in the suite of anti-dicrimination legislation to some extent, although the use of genuine occupational requirement as opposed to genuine occupational qualification arguably widens the scope of

A GOR is effectively a statutory exemption from the provisions of the Equality Act; in other words, if the less favourable treatment is due to a GOR for the job then any less favourable treatment caused by the GOR will not be unlawful discrimination.

A GOR can be applied only where it can be established that there is an occupational requirement and the application of that requirement is a proportionate means of achieving a legitimate aim.[2] The Equality Act has not maintained the position that was previously evident in both the SDA and the RRA where specific examples were provided. In some sense this can be seen to widen the scope of this defence; however, what is more likely is that this simply enables new inherent job requirements to be easily incorporated into the defence. It is still likely to be the case that the courts will adopt a stringent and restrictive approach to GORs, which will act to ensure that the protections of the Equality Act are not evaded easily. To invoke the derogation an employer will need to establish that there is a requirement to have a person with a particular protected characteristic such that it goes to the root of the whole role. It is often used, for example, in the casting of actors. The role of James Bond is male and, as such, seeking male actors would be considered an inherent requirement of the role and so not giving equal access to female actors will not result in direct discrimination.

The key in respect of this derogation from the non-discrimination protection is to identify a legitimate aim and to ensure that the requirements being placed on the role do not go beyond what is truly necessary to achieve the aim intended. Any attempt that goes beyond the minimum that is required to achieve the legitimate aim will not fall within this derogation.

5.2. Positive Action

The idea of positive action is that which is often confused with positive discrimination. However, it is worth understanding from the outset that neither domestic nor European law allows for positive discrimination to take place. Instead, we have the concept of positive action, which is a restricted approach to giving some form of priority to a protected characteristic in limited circumstances. Positive action is very much a

---

the exemption. It is argued by Smith and Baker in *Smith & Woods Employment Law* (ed. 10), p. 308 that the defence as it currently stands appears wider than that contained within the Race Directive (2000/43) and may in fact as a consequence be in breach of European obligations, although it may be saved through the introduction of the proportionality requirement.

[2] EqA Sch. 9, Para. 1

substantive equality tool, in that it appreciates historic barriers that have impeded the progress of persons with particular protected characteristics and enables action to be taken that is with a view to overcoming those barriers. It is argued[3] that positive action is a desirable tool given that the individualistic adversarial approach to equality protection in the UK is incapable of dealing with deep rooted systemic discrimination. As with much of equality law, positive action is a useful means of highlighting that individuals are capable of performing roles irrespective of their characteristics, but this time through practice. Positive action can lead to individuals being put on a role which they would not previously have been given, and could, in theory at least, show to others within that sector that such a person is capable and as such breakdown a discriminatory barrier. This has the consequence of giving employers a wider and more diverse talent pool from which they will be comfortable and capable of selecting from, which brings with it much needed benefits to the economy.[4]

Positive action concerns either the maintenance or adoption of specific measures that have the aim of either preventing disadvantages or compensating for previous disadvantages that a particular group has suffered.

Positive action received early consideration in a series of cases discussed under the Equal Treatment Directive ('ETD'); namely *Kalanke*[5], *Marschall*[6] and *Abrahamsson*[7]. Together these cases defined the limits on how far positive action could be taken in order to compensate for the previous disadvantages suffered by, in these particular cases, female workers over the years. Each of these cases will be considered in detail to highlight how the ECJ considered that the principle of positive action should operate.

This is an area of equality law which has been greatly influenced by case law from the ECJ. As such positive action will be considered in two parts:
(i) the approach adopted by the ECJ, before; and
(ii) the position as it currently appears in the Equality Act 2010.

---

[3] See Cabrelli (2014), p.426.

[4] Fredman, S. (1997), Reversing Discrimination, *Law Quarterly Review* 575.

[5] *Kalanke v. Freie Hansestadt Bremen* [1995] ECR I-3051 (Case C-450/93).

[6] *Marschall v. Land Nordrhein-Westfalen* [1997] ECR I-6363 (Case C-409/95).

[7] *Abrahamsson and Leif Anderson v. Elisabet Fogelqvist* [2000] ECR I-5539 (Case C-407/98).

5.2.1. A guiding Light in the ECJ case law: Kalanke, Marschall and Abrahamsson

The earliest of these cases, *Kalanke*, adopted quite a strict narrow-minded view as to what the concept of positive action could include. This case concerned a law in Bremen Germany,[8] which provided for automatic priority to be given to female workers for appointment and promotion where the candidates had the same qualifications but females were deemed to be under-represented in that particular sector; under-representation being expressed to occur if female workers did not make up at least half of the staff in the post in question.

The issue in this case arose when the shortlisting process left only two equally qualified candidates, Mr Kalanke and Ms Glissmann, of which Ms Glissman was given priority. Mr Kalanke appealed the decision up to the First Chamber of the German Federal Labour Court on a point of law, which accepted that resolution of the dispute was dependant essentially on the validity of the local law. The First Chamber accepted that had the board been wrong in applying the law then its decision would consequently be unlawful as it gave an advantage, solely on the grounds of sex, to an equally qualified female candidate. The Court sought a preliminary ruling from the ECJ essentially asking whether the derogations found in Article 2(4) or the principle of proportionality governing Article 2(1) of the ETD would preclude national rules which gave automatic priority to under-represented groups.

The ECJ offered the rationale behind Article 2(4) as being designed to allow measures which "although discriminatory in appearance, are in fact intended to eliminate or reduce actual instances of inequality which may exist in the reality of social life."[9] In addition, the ECJ considered the third recital in the preamble to Recommendation 84/635/EEC of 13 December 1984 on the promotion of positive action for women,[10] which stated that:

> existing legal provisions on equal treatment, which are designed to afford rights to individuals, are inadequate for the elimination of all existing inequalities unless parallel action is taken by governments, both sides of industry and other bodies concerned, to counteract the prejudicial effects

---

[8] Law on Equal Treatment for Men and Women in the Public Service of the Land of Bremen of 20 November 1990.

[9] *Kalanke* at para. 18.

[10] OJ 1984 L 331, at p.34.

on women in employment which arise from social attitudes, behaviour and structures.[11]

The ECJ in effect highlighted that there are inequalities still present in the workplace that required intervention in order to be eliminated. It was further appreciated at paragraph 19 that Article 2(4) does in fact permit national measures that give women a specific advantage in the workplace, including promotion, so long as it was introduced with the view of bringing an improvement in their ability to compete in the labour market free of such discrimination.

However, despite the acceptance that in certain circumstances such national measures would be accepted as valid under Article 2(4), and citing *Johnston v. Chief Constable of the Royal Ulster Constabulary*,[12] the ECJ stated that any derogation from an individual right must be interpreted strictly. As a result of the Court's desire to protect the individual, it was held that "[n]ational rules which guarantee women absolute and unconditional priority for appointment or promotion go beyond promoting equal opportunities and overstep the limits of the exception in Article 2(4) of the Directive"[13]. The ECJ was clearly placing strict limits on the application of positive action to ensure that it was not available as a means of appointing individuals of a particular sex regardless.

Positive action was not considered again by the ECJ until 1997 in the *Marschall* case. This case once more saw the German courts seeking advice on the interpretation of Article 2(1) and Article 2(4) of the ETD. This case concerned the *Law on Civil Servants of the Lander of 1 May 1981*, which provided:

> Where, in the sector of the authority responsible for promotion, there are fewer women than men in the particular higher grade post in the career bracket, women are to be given priority for promotion in the event of equal suitability, competence and professional performance, unless reasons specific to an individual male candidate tilt the balance in his favour.

The problem in this case arose when Mr Marschall applied for a promotion. However, he was rejected as it was the intention to appoint a female candidate to that particular position. Mr Marschall objections were rejected being told that there was an equally qualified female candidate who

---

[11] *Kalanke* at para. 20.

[12] *Johnston v. Chief Constable of the Royal Ulster Constabulary* [1986] ECR 1651, para 36 (Case 222/84)

[13] *Kalanke* at para. 22.

applied for the post, and as females were under-represented in the particular career bracket she had to be promoted.

Mr Marschall brought an action before the Administrative Court, who on finding that Mr Marschall and the female candidate were equally qualified for the post, decided that the outcome of the proceedings was again dependent upon the compatibility of the provision in question with Article 2(1) and 2(4) of the ETD. The Court sought guidance from the ECJ.

This case saw a difference of opinion between the parties who made submissions to the ECJ as to whether such a national rule fell within Article 2(4). The majority of Governments, including the Spanish, Austrian, Finnish, Swedish and Norwegian Governments as well as the Lander in question and the European Commission considered that such a rule was in fact a provision that constituted a measure for promoting equality of opportunity between the sexes, and thus fell within the scope of Article 2(4). Furthermore, it was considered that the provision in question, as it was not absolute and unconditional priority, fell within the limits highlighted in the *Kalanke* case. However, the French and the UK Governments held a different opinion, claiming that the national rule was still giving a particular group priority, which, as in the *Kalanke* case, went further than what was intended by Article 2(4). It was argued that the saving clause[14] only applied in exceptional circumstances and would have little application in practice, and as such female candidates were, in the majority of cases, receiving preference.

The ECJ in this case focussed on whether the clause concerning reasons specific to an individual male candidate tilting the balance would save the clause and bring it within Article 2(4)[15]. On this occasion the ECJ held that the national rule did fall within the Article 2(4) derogation. The Court distinguished this case from the *Kalanke* case on the basis of the saving clause, stating that:

> Unlike the rules at issue in *Kalanke*, a national rule which, as in the case in point in the main proceedings, contains a saving clause does not exceed those limits if, in each individual case, it provides for male candidates who are equally as qualified as the female candidates a guarantee that the candidatures will be the subject of an objective assessment which will take account of all criteria specific to the individual candidates and will

---

[14] "... unless reasons specific to an individual male candidate tilt the balance in his favour..."

[15] The focus on the clause was based on this being the only real difference between the national rule in the *Kalanke* case and the national rule being discussed in the *Marschall* case.

EQUALITY AND ANTI-DISCRIMINATION LAW

override the priority accorded to female candidates where one or more of those criteria tilts the balance in favour of the male candidate...[16]

The final case which assists in explaining the scope of the rules surrounding positive action is the *Abrahamsson* case. This case concerned the validity of a number of Swedish equality laws, including the Swedish Law on Equality of 1991, the Swedish Regulations on Universities of 1993 and the Swedish Regulation concerning certain professors' and research assistants' posts created with a view to promoting equality of 1995, each of which allowed for positive action where the aim was to promote equality in the workplace. Both the 1993 and the 1995 Regulations had a *Marschall*-esque saving clause indicating that "[p]ositive discrimination must, however, not be applied where the difference between the candidates' qualifications is so great that such applications would give rise to a breach of the requirement of objectivity in the making of appointments."[17]

In accordance with the 1995 Regulations the University of Goteburg announced that they had created a professorial position, and that this post would be part of an agenda aimed at promoting equality of the sexes in professional life, and as such positive discrimination might be applied. Ms Abrahamsson, Ms Destouni and Ms Fogelqvist, and Mr Anderson were among eight candidates who applied for the post.

The experts' reports on the selection process clearly showed Ms Destouni to be the favoured candidate, with Mr Anderson coming second and Ms Fogelqvist third; however, following this decision Ms Destouni opted to withdraw her application. Despite a majority of the appointments committee members considering there to be significant differences between Mr Anderson and Ms Fogelqvist with regards suitability for the post, the Rector of the University decided to appoint Ms Fogelqvist to the professorial chair. The Rector reasoned that the decision was in keeping with 1995 Regulations and to the University's plan for equality between men and women, he further stated that the "difference between the respective merits of Mr Anderson and Ms Fogelqvist was not so considerable that positive discrimination in favour of the latter constituted a breach of the requirement of objectivity in making the appointments"[18].

Two of the unsuccessful candidates, Mr Anderson and Ms Abrahamsson, appealed the decision to appoint Ms Fogelqvist due to the differences in

---

[16] *Marschall* at para. 33.

[17] Article 3 of the Swedish Regulation concerning certain professors' and research assistants' posts created with a view to promoting equality of 1995.

[18] *Abrahamsson* at para. 20.

qualifications between the two candidates, and further that the positive action simply went too far. A central issue that needed to be answered in order to determine the success of the appeals was whether the application of the 1995 Regulations fell within the Article 2(4) derogation and as such a preliminary ruling was sought from the ECJ. In essence the Swedish Government was seeking advice as to whether Article 2(1) and 2(4) of the ETD precluded national legislation which provided for positive discrimination in favour of candidates of an under-represented gender. In asking these questions the Swedish Government was essentially questioning the legality of their widespread gender mainstreaming policies.[19]

In answering the questions posed, the ECJ highlighted that the national legislation in question enabled preference to be given to a candidate of an under-represented gender who did not possess qualifications that were equal to the candidate of the opposite sex, so long as they were sufficiently qualified to fill the post.[20] The ECJ continued and indicated that under that particular Swedish legislation a candidate belonging to the "under-represented sex and possessing sufficient qualifications for that post had to be chosen in preference to a candidate of the opposite sex who would otherwise have been appointed, where that measure is necessary for a candidate belonging to the under-represented sex to be appointed".[21] This in turn suggested that the legislation in question acted in a manner that automatically granted preference to candidates of the under-represented sex, so long as they had adequate qualifications for the post, subject to the qualification that objectivity of appointment was not breached due to a great difference between the merits of the candidates of each sex. Consequently, the ECJ ruled that Article 2(1) and 2(4) would in fact preclude such national legislation.

On the question of whether Article 2(1) and 2(4) precluded national legislation which offered preferential treatment to the under-represented sex over a candidate of the opposite sex where both candidates hold either

---

[19] Gender mainstreaming is the process of adapting initiatives so as be more inclusive of individuals regardless of gender. Sweden is one of three states that are credited with introducing mainstreaming language into policy initiatives of the EU. An interesting account of the continuing development of gender mainstreaming at EU level can be seen in Beveridge, F. (2007), Building Against the Past: the impact of mainstreaming on EU gender law and policy, *European Law Review*, pp.193-212.

[20] This was unlike the national legislation considered under previous case law: *Kalanke* and *Marschall*.

[21] *Abrahamsson* at para. 51.

equal or substantially equal merits, the ECJ reaffirmed the decision of *Marschall*, stating that such a rule would be compatible with Community law so long as the position of the candidates was established through objective assessment, so long as the assessment took into account the specific personal situations of all the candidates. The ECJ also made it clear that Community law is in no way determined by the level of appointment made, and thus will have comparable application whatever the post to be filled.

As these cases have highlighted the ECJ has generally been cautious in its approach to allowing positive action to override the principle of fairness. Only in limited circumstances, where the positive action is not unconditional and absolute, will the ECJ allow national rules to fall within the derogation of Article 2(4). There was much fear attached to the *Marschall* case that a member state would simply have to attach a proviso, regardless of its application in practice, in order to ensure that the national law rule fell within the derogation. However, this avenue appears to have been tightened up somewhat by the *Abrahamsson* case, a practice that is likely to be continued in the application of the positive action principle.

This raises the question as to whether adverts that actively encourage applicants with certain protected characteristics to apply will be deemed unlawful as, on the face of the advert, there is an implicit suggestion that such candidates will be given priority. According to the ECJ in *Badek v Hessischer*[22] this practice is not precluded, so long as unconditional priority is not given in the selection process. So long as the approach is merely targeting with a view to encouraging applications then this will be fine within this context.

5.2.2. Positive Action in the Equality Act 2010

Positive Action is contained within the Equality Act at sections 158 and 159, and was expanded to include promotion when it was replicated within the Act. The current position is as follows:

Section 158, Positive action: general
(1) This section applies if a person (P) reasonably thinks that—
  (a) persons who share a protected characteristic suffer a disadvantage connected to the characteristic,
  (b) persons who share a protected characteristic have needs that are different from the needs of persons who do not share it, or
  (c) participation in an activity by persons who share a protected characteristic is disproportionately low.

---

[22] *Badek v Hessischer* (2001) CMLR 79.

(2) This Act does not prohibit P from taking any action which is a proportionate means of achieving the aim of—

    (a) enabling or encouraging persons who share the protected characteristic to overcome or minimise that disadvantage,

    (b) meeting those needs, or

    (c) enabling or encouraging persons who share the protected characteristic to participate in that activity...

There are two elements that need to be understood when considering the general position on positive action:

1. the employer needs to establish that they reasonably think that a person suffers a disadvantage, either because of a protected characteristic itself, or because of different needs that a characteristic introduces, or where it is thought that persons with a particular characteristic has had a disproportionately low participation rate in the activity in question; and

2. the general provision on positive action can only be used by an employer where it considers that the measure being considered is a proportionate mean of achieving a legitimate aim. Unlike other provisions within the Equality Act which make use of this phrase there is a closed list of legitimate aims found at s.158(2), of which at least one must be the aim of the measure in question.

There is reference to a need for an employer to establish that they 'reasonably think' a particular situation is in existence when considering positive action under s.158, and this raises the question of what does this mean? According to the EHRC's Code of Practice on Employment the threshold is relatively low:

> In order to take positive action, an employer must reasonably think that one of the above conditions applies; that is, disadvantage, different needs or disproportionately low participation. This means that some indication or evidence will be required to show that one of these statutory conditions applies. It does not, however, need to be sophisticated statistical data or research. It may simply involve an employer looking at the profiles of their workforce and/or making enquiries of other comparable employers in the area or sector. Additionally, it could involve looking at national data such as labour force surveys for a national or local picture of the work situation for particular groups who share a protected characteristic. A decision could be based on qualitative evidence, such as consultation with workers and trade unions.[23]

---

[23] Para 12.14.

As one can appreciate, to reasonably think something does require some research and analysis to take place, but as is evident in the EHRC guidance, this is not an onerous task and the employer can make use of simple analytical tools.

Section 159, Positive action: recruitment and promotion

(1) This section applies if a person (P) reasonably thinks that—
    (a) persons who share a protected characteristic suffer a disadvantage connected to the characteristic, or
    (b) participation in an activity by persons who share a protected characteristic is disproportionately low.

(2) Part 5 (work) does not prohibit P from taking action within subsection (3) with the aim of enabling or encouraging persons who share the protected characteristic to—
    (a) overcome or minimise that disadvantage, or
    (b) participate in that activity.

(3) That action is treating a person (A) more favourably in connection with recruitment or promotion than another person (B) because A has the protected characteristic but B does not.

(4) But subsection (2) applies only if—
    (a) A is as qualified as B to be recruited or promoted,
    (b) P does not have a policy of treating persons who share the protected characteristic more favourably in connection with recruitment or promotion than persons who do not share it, and
    (c) taking the action in question is a proportionate means of achieving the aim referred to in subsection (2).

(5) "Recruitment" means a process for deciding whether to—
    (a) offer employment to a person,
    (b) make contract work available to a contract worker,
    (c) offer a person a position as a partner in a firm or proposed firm,
    (d) offer a person a position as a member of an LLP or proposed LLP,
    (e) offer a person a pupillage or tenancy in barristers' chambers,
    (f) take a person as an advocate's devil or offer a person membership of an advocate's stable,
    (g) offer a person an appointment to a personal office,
    (h) offer a person an appointment to a public office, recommend a person for such an appointment or approve a person's appointment to a public office, or
    (i) offer a person a service for finding employment.

The operation of positive action in s.159 differs from the general approach to positive action in that its focus is on the actual decision-making by the employer when considering whether to offer a position to an individual or whether to offer promotion. However, this does not enable an individual to be given automatic priority simply due to their protected characteristic, as to do so would be in breach of the European position, as expressed earlier on in this chapter. The European position is effectively built into s.159(4), which only enables the protected characteristic of an individual that the employer reasonably thinks has suffered a disadvantage connected to a protected characteristic, or where there is disproportionately low participation rates of persons with that protected characteristic, in circumstances where there is more than one candidate who is equally qualified for the post, and using the protected characteristic the as the tie breaker is a proportionate means of overcoming or minimising the disadvantage suffered, or where it enables such a person to participate in the activity.

The positive action provisions do not preclude introducing measures and means of encouraging participation or applications, or introducing measures that remove practical barriers to participation, so long as these approaches are being introduced due to objective criteria which show that such a group has been disadvanted; however, it does preclude measures that go beyond this, and are seen as targeting a group specifically such that a decision has already been made to favour this group over any other. Positive action does not remove meritocracy and cannot be used to select a lesser qualified individual solely on the basis of a protected characteristic. It is a last resort principle to some extent.

The principle of positive action is a useful principle to have incorporated into the Equality Act. It has the potential to overcome some deep-seated barriers to participation, which are often rooted in discriminatory theory. Being capable of attacking such systemic issues is both a positive approach, and a balanced one, such that its operation does not in effect discriminate against other groups in order to give priority. That, in itself, could be damaging due to resentment it could cause in a workplace, and it could also give rise to feelings of being a token appointment. By adopting such a balanced approach equality is being protected and progressed. The key advantage of such a principle is that it can act to encourage persons to apply for a position who would not have applied previously. Moreover, when a person with a characteristic who would not previously have been considered for an activity is in post then they can break down barriers further simply by being there and doing the job. This can either be through colleagues seeing that the characteristic in question is an arbitrary reason for exclusion, but also by providing others with that same characteristic a role model in a position to which they can aspire, which could further encourage participation of those with characteristics that are under-represented.

5.3. Statutory Defence

There are certain specific statutory provisions that are outside of the scope of the Equality Act, which are contained within Schedule 22 to the Act, and have been made effective through s.191.

5.4. Illegal contracts

The impact of whether the Equality Act protection applies in circumstances where an individual is employed on a contract that is tainted with illegality will wholly depend on the nature of the claim. If the status of the contract has nothing to do with that which is being complained of, then the provisions of the Equality Act will operate as in any other circumstance, such as if the complaint concerns a simple direct discrimination issue.[24] However, if the claim and subsequent remedy involves relying on the contract then the protections would not operable, on the simple basis that an illegal contract would be unenforceable and therefore it could not be relied upon to give effect any such claim.

5.5. National Security

According to s.192 of the Equality Act "[a] person does not contravene this Act only by doing, for the purpose of safeguarding national security, anything it is proportionate to do for that purpose". Furthermore, there is a restriction placed on the remedy of Recommendation where it is being made in a national security case, with it being restricted to recommendations that affect the complainant only.[25]

---

[24] *Hall v Walston Leisure Centre* [2000] IRLR 578

[25] EqA s.125.

6. Scope of the Equality Act 2010

The Equality Act is an inclusive act in terms of its scope, and offers protection across the spectrum of the working relationship and to other 'workers' that would not be traditionally viewed as employees. As such it brings a wide range of workers within its broad reach. This ought to be commended as a welcome approach.

6.1. Working Arrangments

The Equality Act provides protection across the entirety of the working relationship, covering periods before employment to offer protection to applicants, during employment so as to offer protection to the current workforce, and finally to post-employment such as to protect ex-workers. This broad spectrum aproach ensures that a worker is offered some level of protection in all of the key aspects of a labour relationship. In particular the extension to provide protection post-employment is most welcome, especially when one considers that power of a reference. This approach can be seen at s.39 of the Equality Act, with s.39(1) focussing on prospective workers or applicants, and s.39(2) focussing on the current workforce:

(1) An employer (A) must not discriminate against a person (B)—
   (a) in the arrangements A makes for deciding to to offer employment;
   (b) as to the terms on which A offers B employment;
   (c) by not offering B employment.

(2) An employer (A) must not discriminate against an employee of A's (B)—
   (a) as to B's terms of employment;
   (b) in the way A affords B access, or by not affording B access, to opportunities for promotion, transfer or training or for receiving any other benefit, facility or service;
   (c) by dismissing B;
   (d) by subjecting B to any other detriment.

Both job applicants and employees are further protected against discrimination through s.39 (3) and (4).

(3) An employer (A) must not victimise a person (B)—
   (a) in the arrangements A makes for deciding to whom to offer employment;
   (b) as to the terms on which A offers B employment;
   (c) by not offering B employment.

(4) An employer (A) must not victimise an employee of A's (B)—
   (a) as to B's terms of employment;

    (b) in the way A affords B access, or by not affording B access, to opportunities for promotion, transfer or training or for any other benefit, facility or service;

    (c) by dismissing B;

    (d) by subjecting B to any other detriment.

Reference to subjecting a person to a detriment remains the same in this context as it does throughout the Equality Act and refers to putting a person at a disadvantage. This can cover, as was seen in relation to direct discrimination through *Burton v. De Vere Hotels,*[1] not only the causing of the detriment but where an employer allows an employee to be subjected to a detriment in circumstances where he can control that treatment.

Initially, under the pre-Equality Act legislation, there was judicial conflict as to whether the reference to dismissing in the scope of the protections also included constructive dismissals. This was ultimately concluded in the affirmative by the CA in *Nottinghamshire County Council v Meikle;*[2] this has now been codified at s.39(7) of the Equality Act.

6.1.1. Employees, Applicants and Contract Workers

The Equality Act 2010 protects both employees and applicants (applying to become employees) from unlawful discrimination by virtue of s.39 as seen above, with the term 'employment' being defined widely in s.83 of the Equality Act as including:

- employment under a contract of employment, a contract of apprenticeship or a contract to personally to do work;
- Crown employment;
- employment as a relevant member of House of Commons staff; AND
- employment as a relevant member of House of Lords Staff.

Additionally, the Act explicitly applies to services in the armed forces in the same way as it does to those in private employment (s.83(3)).

It is clear from s.83(2) of the Equality Act that the protections, similar to the previous anti-discrimination regime, apply to individuals who are employed under a contract of employment, but also goes far beyond this. Reference to a contract of employment suggests that case law decided under ERA s.230 is important; however, it must also be be noted that by including reference to those working under "a contract personally to do work" means that the protections are afforded beyond the employer/employee relationship. The Court of Appeal considered this

---

[1] *Burton v. De Vere Hotels* [1996] IRLR 596.

[2] *Nottinghamshire County Council v Meikle* [2004] IRLR 703.

wording in *Gunning v. Mirror Group Newspapers*.[3] It was held that the correct approach was to focus on the dominant purpose of the contract, and consider whether this was to place an obligation to undertake work personally. Applying this approach to the facts in this case led to a finding that a contract between a proprietor of a business that established a commercial relationship with a newspaper to collect and distribute newspapers to newsagents was not a contract to undertake work personally. Although there were some aspects of the contract that required some work to be done personally, the dominant purpose of the contract when taken as a whole was a commercial contract for the distribution of newspapers.

There are plenty of examples where an expansive definition has been applied to scope of the non-discrimination protections. In particular, in *Quinnen v. Hovells*[4] it was held that this would even cover the self-employed provided that they were providing a personal service.

Despite the expansive approach to s.83 of the Equality Act, it is still unlikely to cover agency workers who are placed with an end-user in most circumstances. In order for a contract to be implied between the agency worker and the end-user it will need to be established that implication is necessary, with implication not being necessary if the agency arrangement is deemed to be a genuine agency arrangement.[5] In other words, so long as the contractual position between the three parties are not sham contracts merely to avoid employment protections then there will be no contract between the agency worker and the end-user, and thus nothing which can fall within s.83 of the Equality Act. Despite this there may be some level of protection for agency workers through the Agency Worker Regulations 2010, which are predicated on non-discrimination principles, so long as they fall within the scope of these regulations.

Contract workers or contractors[6] are afforded protection against discrimination from a principal by virtue of s.41 of the Equality Act. It could be argued that agency workers could be afforded protection as a contract worker, although this may be limited due to the reference to a

---

[3] *Gunning v. Mirror Group Newspapers* [1986] IRLR 27.

[4] *Quinnen v. Hovells* [1984] IRLR 227.

[5] See LJ Mummery in *James v. Greenwich LBC* [2008] IRLR 302.

[6] This is defined as a person who is employed by one person but is supplied to another person (the "principal") to provide services under a contract to which the principal is a party (see EqA s.41 (5)-(7)).

need for the individual to be employed;[7] case law in the area of agency workers suggests that unless there are particular specific circumstances that sees the agency retaining substantial control over the agency worker[8] then it is unlikely that there will be a finding of an employer/employee relationship between the agency and worker.[9] This lack of being employed by the agency is likely to preclude such an engagement with an end-user falling under the concept of contract worker.

6.1.2.Police Officers

It is well established that police officers do not work under a contract of employment or any other contract to undertake personal service but instead are 'in office'.[10] The protections are extended to police officers under s.42 (3)-(6) of the Equality Act.[11]

6.1.3.Partnerships and Limited Liability Partnerships

Partnerships and LLPs are dealt with under ss.44 and 45 of the Equality Act, which prohibit:

- discriminating against or victimising a person in the arrangements they make for deciding to whom to offer a position as a partner; on the terms which they offer a position as a partner; or by not offering a person a position as a partner;[12]
- discriminating against or victimising a partner as to the terms of the partnership; in the way access is afforded to opportunities for promotion, transfer, or training or for receiving any other benefit, facility, or service; by expulsion; or by subjecting a partner to any other detriment;[13]
- harassing partners or applicants for partnership;[14]
- failing to make reasonable adjustments.[15]

---

[7] EqA s.41(5).

[8] Such as that witnessed in *McMeechan v Secretary of State for Employment* [1996] EWCA Civ 1166.

[9] See generally *Montgomery v Johnson Underwood Ltd* [2001] EWCA Civ 318 and *Dacas v Brook Street Bureau (UK) Ltd* [2004] EWCA Civ 217.

[10] *Sheikh v. Chief Constable of Greater Manchester* [1990] 1 QB 637.

[11] Police cadets are equally protected by virtue of s.42(2).

[12] See EqA ss.44 (1), 44(5), 45(1) and 45(5).

[13] See EqA ss.44(2), 44(6), 45(2) and 45(6).

[14] See EqA ss.44(3), 44(4), 45(3) and 45(4).

[15] See EqA ss. 44(7) and 45(7)

6.1.4. Barristers and Advocates

Barristers and advocates are prohibited from:

- Discriminating, victimising or harassing applicants for pupillage or tenancy and/or pupils and tenants themselves;[16] and
- Failing to make reasonable adjustments.[17]

6.1.5. Office Holders

Office holders are brought within the scope of the Equality Act through sections 49-52. The Act draws a distinction between personal offices and public offices.

Personal offices are covered through s.49, with a personal office being hold to include offices:

(a) to which a person is appointed to discharge a function personally under the direction of another person, and

(b) in respect of which an appointed person is entitled to remuneration.[18]

Public office is defined at s.50, and covers:

(a) an office or post, appointment to which is made by a member of the executive;

(b) an office or post, appointment to which is made on the recommendation of, or subject to the approval of, a member of the executive; or

(c) an office or post, appointment to which is made on the recommendation of, or subject to the approval of, the House of Commons, the House of Lords, the National Assembly for Wales or the Scottish Parliament.

Although there is a list of offices which fall outside of the ss.49 and 50; this list is contained within Schedule 6 to the Equality Act. The "relevant person", on whom is imposed the obligation not to discriminate and to make reasonable adjustments is defined in s.52.

6.1.6. Other Bodies

Other bodies that fall within the scope of the Equality Act include qualification bodies,[19] trade organisations[20] and employment service

---

[16] See EqA ss.47 (1)-(6) and 48 (1)-(6)

[17] See EqA ss.47(7) and 48(7)

[18] EqA s.49 (2)

[19] EqA s.53

[20] EqA s.57

providers, which includes providers of vocational training and employment agencies.[21] Each of these bodies is prohibited from discriminating, harassing, victimising or failing to to make reasonable adjustments.

---

[21] EqA ss.55-56

7.   Protected Grounds

There are a total of nine protected characteristics contained within the Equality Act. Less favourable treatment because of any of these characteristics will be deemed unlawful discrimination. It is important from the outset to understand that the Equality Act is quite rigid in this respect and does not protect against discrimination per se. The protections are limited in terms of what characteristics are protected. There is scope for these protections to be expanded in due course; however, for the time being it is only those characteristics that are named that are provided with protection. This is unlike the position contained within the ECHR or the EU's Charter of Fundamental Rights, which provides for an open-ended protection non-discrimination and equality right.

Each of the respective characteristics contained within the Equality Act are discussed below, with a view to identifying the breadth of each of them. Of particular note is the difference in approach adopted by the UK and the EU in relation to the concept of disability; it is expected that that UK's former medical approach will continue to converge and align with the EU's social approach to this concept, and as such this is certainly a concept that will need to be monitored in future case law.

7.1.   Age

The protected ground of age was first introduced by the Employment Equality (Age) Regulations 2006, and was in response to the part of the Framework Directive 2000/78/EC which required age discrimination in employment to be prohibited.

Age is currently defined at s.5 of the of the Equality Act, and covers:

> (a) a reference to a person who has a particular protected characteristic is a reference to a person of a particular age group;
> (b) a reference to persons who share a protected characteristic is a reference to persons of the same age group.

Furthermore, it is expressed that a "reference to an age group is a reference to a group of persons defined by reference to , whether by reference to a particular age or to a range of ages".

The EHRC's Code of Practice in Employment at paragraph 2.4 offers some indication as to the type of matters that this will cover, including:

> (1) defining through the use of a particular age;
> (2) defining through the use of a wide age group, such as "people under 50";

(3) defining through the use of a narrow age group, such as "people born in the 1940s"; and

(4) relative age groups, such as "older than me".

Before the protected characteristic of age was introduced in the 2006 Regulations there was no protection in the UK against age discrimination. This was clearly expressed by the House of Lords in *Rutherford v Secretary of State for Trade and Industry*[1] when Mr Rutherford's claim for age discrimination due to the (then) statutory maximum age of 65 for bringing an unfair dismissal or redundancy claim was rejected as the UK at the time was not subject to any age discrimination laws.

Awareness of issues of age discrimination was initially increased through a non-legislative code of practice (June 1999) which highlighted best practice in six key areas of the employment relationship, including recruitment, promotion, training opportunities and the ending of the relationship. However, as this was simply informational, with none of its contents legally enforceable.

7.2. Disability

Protection against discrimination on the ground of disability in employment and other areas was provided for by the Disability Discrimination Act 1995 ('DDA'). In order to comply with the disability discrimination provisions of Framework Directive 2000/78/EC, the DDA was amended by the Disability Discrimination Act 1995 (Amendment) Regulations 2003 (SI 2003/1673), which came into force on 1 October 2004. Further amendments were introduced to DDA through the Disability Discrimination Act 2005 ('DDA 2005').

The burden is placed on the complainant to show that on the balance of probabilities they satisfy the Equality Act's concept of being a person with a disability. Disability is currently defined at s.6 of the of the Equality Act, defining a person to have a disability if that person (P):

(a) has a physical or mental impairment, and

(b) the impairment has a substantial and long-term adverse effect on P's ability to carry out normal day-to-day activities.

It is important to note that not everybody who would colloquially be considered to have a disability would necessarily have one within the context of the Equality Act, as this Act sets out a test with specific requirements that need to be satisfied. This definition substantially mirrors the old definition that was contained at section 1 of the DDA, and so is

---

[1] *Rutherford v Secretary of State for Trade and Industry* [2006] IRLR 551.

likely to follow a similar approach to that that was adopted under this provision. To help clarify the meaning of this definition, alongside case law developments, further explanation of the component parts can be found in Schedule 1 of the of the Equality Act.

It is in *Goodwin v. Patent Office*[2] where the EAT first provided guidance[3] as to the correct approach to determining whether an individual satisfied the legal definition of disability. In essence there are four questions that need to be considered:

1. Does a mental or physical impairment exist?
2. Does this impairment have an adverse effect on the claimant's ability to carry out normal day-to-day activities?
3. Is this adverse effect substantial?
4. Is the substantial adverse effect long term?

If the answer to each of these questions is "yes" then the claimant will be considered to have a disability in accordance with the of the Equality Act. Each of these component parts will be considered in turn below. It was accepted by the EAT in *Goodwin* that these component parts will not always be mutually exclusive issues, with there being overlap of them. Such overlap was particularly noted in relation to the requirement of substantial and long-term, as it will not always be easy to view either of these in isolation. In such circumstances the EAT indicated that a tribunal ought to consider the whole picture and not get too bogged down with deconstructing the parts.[4]

The timing of evaluation of whether a person has a disability ought to be immediately before they are subjected to treatment which they are complaining as being unlawful disability discrimination.[5]

The question of whether an individual has a disability is generally dealt with as a preliminary issue in a pre-hearing review, leaving the tribunal hearing to focus on the merits of the case.

7.2.1. Impairment

Mental or physical impairment is not defined within the Equality Act; however, it is well accepted that they should be given their ordinary

---

[2] *Goodwin v. Patent Office* [1999] IRLR 4.

[3] The *Goodwin* guidance has now been codified in the Equality Act definition of disability.

[4] Paragraph 30.

[5] *Cosgrove v. Ceasar and Howie* [2001] IRLR 653, para.4; *Cruickshank v VAW Motorcase Ltd.* [2002] IRLR. 24.

meaning. It is important that a broad definition is attached as too restrictive an approach will have the effect of frustrating the purpose of the protections.

It is clear that the focus should be on the impairment itself, and not on the cause of the impairment.[6] This is confirmed as being the case in the Equality and Human Rights Commission's Code of Practice, where it is stated that

> **It is not necessary to consider how an impairment is caused, even if the cause is a consequence of a condition which is excluded**. For example, liver disease as a result of alcohol dependency would count as an impairment, although an addiction to alcohol itself is expressly excluded from the scope of the definition of disability in the Act. What it is important to consider is the effect of an impairment, not its cause – provided that it is not an excluded condition.[7]

The term 'impairment' is exceptionally wide, and at least in terms of a physical impairment, is usually quite easy to identify. Examples would include:

- sensory impairments, such as where sight or hearing are affected;
- impairments of organs, such as asthma, cardiovascular diseases, strokes or heart disease;
- progressive impairments, such as motor neuron disease; and
- multo-skeletal impairments, such as back pain or or restricted movement in the joints.

Mental impariments are more difficult to identify, mainly due to the way in which they manifest themselves, making them less obvious than visible impairment; however, the previous restrictive approach of requiring a mental impairment to be clinically well-recognised has been removed.[8]

Examples will include:

---

[6] See the Court of Appeal in *College of Ripon and York St John v. Hobbs* [2002] EWCA Civ 1074, where it was held that there was no requirement to identify the underlying fault or defect that caused a physical impairment to exist. Similarly, in *Walker v Sita* [2013] UKEAT 0097_12_0802, the EAT found that the ET's focus on the cause of the impairment was an incorrect approach, rather it there should merely have been focus on the actual impairment and the effects thereof.

[7] See para A7, Disability: Equality Act 2010 - Guidance on matters to be taken into account in determining questions relating to the definition of disability.

[8] In *Dunham v. Ashford Windows* [2005] ICR 1584, the EAT held that an individual could still suffer from a mental impairment even where it did not amount to a mental illness. Subsequent to this case all reference to a need for a mental impairment to be clinically recognised was removed from equality legislation.

- developmental impairments such as autistic spectrum disorders, dyslexia and dyspraxia;
- learning disabilities;
- mental health conditions, including anxiety, low mood, panic attacks, phobias, eating disorders, bipolar affective disorders, post traumatic stress disorder; and
- mental illnesses, such as depression and schizophrenia.

The specific conditions of cancer, HIV infection and multiple sclerosis are all deemed to be disabilities under the Equality Act, being protected from the point of diagnosis.[9] In addition, persons that are certified as blind, suffer from sever sight imparment, or are deemed partially sighted by a consultant ophthalmologist will all be deemed to be disabled without having to satisfy the other aspects of the definition.[10]

A useful guiding consideration on the concept of impairment was provided by Commisisoner Howell QC in the EAT in *Rugamer v Sony Music Entertainment UK Ltd*[11] where he stated that:

> "Impairment", for this purpose and in this context, has in our judgment to mean some damage, defect, disorder or disease compared with a person having a full set of physical and mental equipment in normal condition. The phrase "physical or mental impairment" refers to a person having (in everyday language) something wrong with them physically, or something wrong with them mentally.

With the focus of impairment being on whether there is something 'wrong' with the individual, whether that is physical or mental, it places great importance on evidence, of which medical evidence is often crucial.[12]

7.2.2. Adverse impact on day-to-day activities
The DDA offered guidance on what areas ought to be considered when measuring whether an impairment had an adverse impact on day-to-day activities:

---

[9] EqA Sch. 1, para.6

[10] EqA Sch. 1, para.7

[11] *Rugamer v Sony Music Entertainment UK Ltd* [2001] IRLR 644, para.34.

[12] The importance of medical evidence being obtained by both paries on the matter of impairment was spelled out clearly by Mummery LJ in the CA case of *McNicol v Balfour Beatty Rail Maintenance Ltd* [2002] IRLR 711: "This appeal highlights the crucial importance (a) of applicants making clear the nature of the impairment on which the claim of discrimination is advanced and (b) of both parties obtaining relevant medical evidence on the issue of impairment." (para 16).

An impairment is to be taken to affect the ability of the person concerned to carry out normal day-to-day activities only if it affects one of the following—
(a) mobility;
(b) manual dexterity;
(c) physical co-ordination;
(d) continence;
(e) ability to lift, carry or otherwise move everyday objects;
(f) speech, hearing or eyesight;
(g) memory or ability to concentrate, learn or understand; or
(h) perception of the risk of physical danger.

This list enabled the complainant to focus their evidence on self-contained issues. Although this list has not been replicated in the Equality Act, a similar approach is adopted in practice, with reference to similar broad issues being raised in submissions concerning whether a person satisfies the concept of disability; however, through removing the list it enables a thorough evaluation of all the circumstances of a person's situation, including matters that were not considered at the time of drafting of the DDA. It is important to note that the approach to day-to-day activity has never been to look at activities in isolation as the effect of a disability may have a cumulative effect which impairs a number of different things.[13]

When questioning the adverse impact on day-to-day activities the tribunal ought to consider all of the circumstances surrounding the case. The focus is not to simply be on those activities that an individual cannot do, but must also look at matters that matters which an individual can do but with difficulty or those which the individual avoids.[14] It is often the case that a disabled person will alter their approaches to an activity in order to cover up their difficulties.

Case law is often a useful place from which to identify broadly the type of activities that will be considered to be normal day-to-day activities. One thing that is clear is that it is not restricted solely to activities at home, but may include those in the workplace. In the *Goodwin* case the Employment Tribunal found that an employee who suffered from paranoid schizophrenia, which in itself caused bizarre behaviour at work was not disabled. They held that the condition obviously had no substantial effect on his ability to carry out day-to-day activities since he had no problems looking after himself at home. The EAT disagreed, and held that all the

---

[13] *Goodwin v. Patent Office* [1999] IRLR 4, paras 34-35.

[14] *Goodwin v. Patent Office* [1999] IRLR 4.

circumstances were relevant, including the way he acted at work. Taking into account all the relevant circumstances would have led to the conclusion that he was in fact disabled.

The tribunals or courts have not made an attempt to provide an exhaustive list or all encompassing definition of what is meant by normal day-to-day activities due to the complexity of such a task; however, the Court of Appeal did provide a useful view in *Goodwin*:

> What is a day-to-day activity is best left unspecified: easily recognised, but defined with difficulty. What can be said is that the enquiry is not focussed on a particular or special set of circumstances. Thus it is not directed to the person's own particular circumstances either at work or at home.[15]

What this does tell us is that a day-to-day activity is not something that is considered a day-to-day activity from the perspective of that particular person; there is clearly an objective element to this exercise such that it is what is normal in the everyday sense that is important for the legal definition of disability.

There are examples in case law that have been held to be normal day-to-day activities that may be useful, which include:

- DIY and car maintenance (*Cruickshank v VAW Motorcase Ltd*[16])
- "It is clear that an ability to prepare vegetables, cut up meat and carry a meal on a tray would all be regarded as examples of normal day-to-day activities." (*Vicary v British Telecommunications Plc*[17])
- "It seems to us obvious that making beds, doing housework (polishing furniture), sewing and cutting with scissors would be regarded as normal day-to-day activities as would minor DIY tasks, filing nails, curling hair and ironing."(*Vicary v British Telecommunications Plc*[18])
- "It seems to us obvious that it would be a substantial impairment on a normal day-to-day activity if the Applicant could not use a hand-held bag or carry washing, other than in small quantities, or unload her shopping trolley other than in small quantities" (*Vicary v British Telecommunications Plc*[19])

---

[15] As per Morison J in *Goodwin*.

[16] *Cruickshank v VAW Motorcase Ltd* [2002] IRLR 24.

[17] *Vicary v British Telecommunications Plc* [1999] IRLR 680, para.12.

[18] At para.13.

[19] At para.14.

In addition to case law the ECHR Code of Practice is also useful, as this gives a number of examples that would be considered normal day-to-day activities. In particular it is expressed that:

> Day-to-day activities thus include – but are not limited to –activities such as walking, driving, using public transport, cooking, eating, lifting and carrying everyday objects, typing, writing (and taking exams), going to the toilet, talking, listening to conversations or music, reading, taking part in normal social interaction or forming social relationships, nourishing and caring for one's self. Normal day-to-day activities also encompass the activities which are relevant to working life.[20]

Unlike the approach to finding an impairment the question of what is a normal day-to-day activity is not one which a medical expert should express an opinion on. This is a matter that is for the tribunal to determine based on the submissions presented to it.[21] The tribunal ought to be focussing on whether the activity in question is a normal day-to-day activity for the employee in question.

7.2.3.Substantial impact

This requirement to be a substantial impact merely reflects society's perception of a disability, with it being reserved for matters that are not minor or trivial[22] and which go beyond a simple difference in a person's ability to do something.

It is difficult to separate substantial impact from the requirement to consider normal day-to-day activities since it is only when viewing activities affected that one can determine whether the impact is indeed substantial.

In *Leonard v. Southern Derbyshire Chamber of Commerce*[23] it was held that in determining whether the effect of an impairment is substantial, a tribunal should not simply balance out what a person can and cannot do. The correct approach is only to consider what the applicant can do with difficulty alongside what he in fact cannot do. In determining whether the impact is substantial a comparison may be considered between a person with an impairment against a person without it in relation to:

---

[20] ECHR Equality Act 2010 Employment Code of Practice, Appendix 1: the meaning of disability, para. 15.

[21] *Vicary* at para.16.

[22] The exclusion of minor and trivial impacts are expressly excluded at EqA s.212(1).

[23] *Leonard v. Southern Derbyshire Chamber of Commerce* [2001] IRLR 19.

- how long it takes to carry out an activity;
- the manner in which the activity is carried out;
- the range of activities impacted upon by the impairment; and
- the effects on behaviour.

Cruikshank v. VAW Motorcast Ltd[24] concerned an employee who was suffering from occupational asthma. The effects of his asthma were worsened and aggravated by the fumes which he had to encounter at work. On these facts, the EAT held that it was possible to take into account such aggravating factors.

These three cases show us that we must look at the effect both outside work and at work, we do not balance the tasks which the applicant can do with the tasks he can not do, and that any factors present at work that aggravate the problem will be relevant in determining whether the adverse effect is substantial.

According to paragraph 5 of Schedule 1 to the Equality Act, the effect of any measures taken to treat or correct an impairment, such as medication, must be discounted. In other words, consideration of whether the impairment would likely satisfy the definition of disability 'but for' the treatment or correction must be considered. So for example medical treatment, the use of prosthesis or other aid ought to be discounted in the evaluation.[25] An obvious example would be to evaluate an individual who is hard of hearing when they are not wearing their hearing aid. However, this discounting does not apply to sight impairments where that impairment is capable of being corrected through an aid such as glasses or contact lenses.[26] In such cases the evaluation of the impact of the sight impairment would be done whilst the glasses or contact lenses were in use.

7.2.4. Long term effect

This point is really straightforward, and is dealt with in Schedule 1 to the Equality Act. Schedule 1 defines a long-term effect as an impairment that is capable of lasting one year or more or for the rest of a person's life in the case of a terminal illness. Where the impairment ceases but is likely to recur then it will be treated as having a long-term effect. The relevant time in deciding whether an impairment would last a year should be the time of the action being brought.

---

[24] *Cruikshank v. VAW Motorcast Ltd* [2002] IRLR 24.

[25] EqA Sch.1 para 5(2).

[26] EqA Sch.1 para. 5(3).

Schedule 1 paragraph 2(2) deals with the issue of conditions that are likely to recur. If a condition has had substantial adverse effect on a person's ability to carry out normal day-to-day activities, has subsequently ceased to have such an effect, but are likely to recur, then they are to be treated as continuing to have that effect for the purposes of the Act.

Furthermore on this issue of a long-term effect, we have an issue with regards progressive conditions. Paragraph 6 of Schedule 1 states that where an employee suffers from a progressive condition he will also be treated as disabled within the Act at the point where the condition has an *effect* on their ability to carry out normal day-to-day activities. Notice there I used an 'effect', rather than a 'substantial effect'. This is aimed at protecting an employee from pre-emptive action, for example dismissal, where an employee has a condition that will eventually bring him within the Act. The requirement here for a progressive condition to receive protection is that some effect has materialised. On this matter an instructive case is *Mowat-Brown v University of Surrey*,[27] which provides an example of a claimant falling within the protection of the Act due to the expectation that a condition will become substantial in the future, despite it having not already reached this threshold. Including progressive conditions within the Act offers protection to those who suffer from conditions such as cancer and HIV where it affects a persons ability to carry out day-to-day activities.

It is important to note that individuals that have had a past disability, where the impairment no longer satisfies the test of disability under the Act are still protected.[28]

7.2.5. Progressive conditions

Progressive conditions, which are deemed to be conditions which worsen over time and are likely to have a substantial impact at some future date, are given special treatment under the Equality Act.[29] Protection is provided in these circumstances at the moment in time where it can be shown that the impairment, which is as a consequence of that condition, has an adverse effect on their ability to carry out normal day-to-day activities. This in effect removes the need to show a substantial impact in order to attract protection. This prevents employers from effectively dismissing or treating less favourably individuals who are suffering from a condition but who have yet to reach the threshold of 'substantial impact'.

---

[27] *Mowat-Brown v University of Surrey* [2002] IRLR 235.

[28] See EqA s.6(4) and Sch.1 para.9.

[29] EqA Sch.1 para.8.

EQUALITY AND ANTI-DISCRIMINATION LAW

A useful example is provided by the EHRC in relation to progressive conditions:

> A woman has been diagnosed with systemic lupus erythematosis (SLE) following complaints to her GP that she is experiencing mild aches and pains in her joints. She has also been feeling generally unwell, with some flu-like symptoms. The initial symptoms do not have a substantial adverse effect on her ability to carry out normal day-to-day activities. However, SLE is a progressive condition, with fluctuating effects. She has been advised that the condition may come and go over many years, and in the future the effects may become substantial, including severe joint pain, inflammation, stiffness, and skin rashes. Providing it can be shown that the effects are likely to become substantial, she will be covered by the special provisions relating to progressive conditions. She will also need to meet the 'long-term' condition of the definition in order to be protected by the Act. [PARA B20]

Common progressive conditions would include cancer and HIV. This effectively provides protection from the moment of diagnosis rather than waiting for the progressive condition to reach a particular threshold level.

An obvious point is that where a progressive condition has been treated successfully, and the adverse effects no longer exist then the special protection afforded will no longer apply.

7.2.6. Past Disabilities

A further expansion to the protection is the inclusion of past disabilities into the scope of the definition of a person with a disability, and this extension can be found at s.6(4) of the Equality Act. This means that anything related to the impairment that was previously deemed to be a disability cannot be used in a manner that subjects an individual to a detriment. This will mean, for example, that if an individual has periods of absence or periods of unemployment that were caused by a previous disability, then this information should not be used when making decisions in relation to that person.

7.2.7. Excluded conditions

There are a number of conditions that are expressly excluded from being a disability under the Equality Act, these being contained in The Equality Act 2010 (Disability) Regulations 2010:[30]

- addiction to, or dependency on, alcohol, nicotine, or any other substance (other than in consequence of the substance being medically prescribed);

---

[30] S.I. 2010/2128.

- the condition known as seasonal allergic rhinitis (e.g. hayfever), except where it aggravates the effect of another condition;
- tendency to set fires;
- tendency to steal;
- tendency to physical or sexual abuse of other persons;
- exhibitionism;
- voyeurism.

Applying the exclusion is fact sensitive, and in most cases should not cause any problems. Where an impairment is found to fall within this list of categories, then clearly it cannot be deemed to be a disability. However, greater difficulties lie where the one of these tendencies are as a result of some other impairment. This then requires careful analysis to determine the true basis for any alleged discrimination: if it is the resultant excluded tendency, then the exclusion applies; whereas, if it is related to the underlying cause of the tendency then the exclusion will not apply. The EHRC provides the following illustrative example:

> A young man has Attention Deficit Hyperactivity Disorder (ADHD) which manifests itself in a number of ways, including exhibitionism and an inability to concentrate. The disorder, as an impairment which has a substantial and long-term adverse effect on the young person's ability to carry out normal day-to-day activities, would be a disability for the purposes of the Act.

> The young man is not entitled to the protection of the Act in relation to any discrimination he experiences as a consequence of his exhibitionism, because that is an excluded condition under the Act.

> However, he would be protected in relation to any discrimination that he experiences in relation to the non-excluded effects of his condition, such as inability to concentrate. For example, he would be entitled to any reasonable adjustments that are required as a consequence of those effects. [PARAGRAPH A13]

This example shows the importance of understanding and investigating what it is that is causing the conduct of such a worker rather than merely applying an exclusion in a blanket fashion, as this may result in other discrimination not being dealt with appropriately, and could lead to claims being instigated.

7.3. Gender Reassignment

Protection against discrimination on the grounds of gender reassignment was first introduced in to the UK through the Sex Discrimination (Gender

Reassignment) Regulations 1999,[31] which amended the Sex Discrimination Act 1975 by inserting s.2A, which expressly prohibited discrimination on the grounds of a person intending to undergo, having undergone or is undergoing gender reassignment. The need for amendment[32] was consequent to the ECJ's decision in *P v. S*,[33] which adopted a broad test in relation to the protected ground of sex such as to cover transsexuality. Not only did this case highlight that discrimination on the grounds of sex is a fundamental right which must be observed, but it also highlighted that sex discrimination protection could not be limited to the fact that a person belonged to one sex or the other, but that gender reassignment discrimination is based essentially, if not exclusively, on the sex of that person.

The definition of gender reassignment is currently found at s.7 of the Equality Act, which states that:

(1) A person has the protected characteristic of gender reassignment if the person is to undergo, is undergoing or has undergone a process (or part of a process) for the purpose of reassigning the person's sex by changing physiological or other attributes of sex.

(2) A reference to a transsexual person is a reference to a person who has the protected characteristic of gender reassignment.

The Equality Act does remove one of the threshold requirements in relation to transgender, removing the need for the individual to be under medical supervision for reassignment purposes in order to attract the protection. This expands the protection slightly. It should also be noted that once a person has undergone gender reassignment and obtained formal recognition under the Gender Recognition Act 2004, that person is entitled to be treated in all respects as a person of the acquired gender, which includes applying for a new birth certificate.

7.4. Marriage and Civil Partnership

Marriage discrimination was previously a protected ground through s.3 of SDA. However, this did not act to cover those that were not married, an

---

[31] SI 1999/1102.

[32] Arguably amendment of the SDA was not strictly necessary following the purposive interpretation adopted by the EAT in *Chessington World of Adventures Ltd v. Reed* [1997] IRLR 556, which interpreted the national legislation in line with that provided by the ECJ in *P v S*.

[33] *P v. S* [1996] ECR I-2143 (Case C-13/94)

approach that has been maintained under the Equality Act (this is discussed below).

Civil partnership was included in the protection of s.3 following amendement through the Civil Partnership Act 2004, s.251.

Marriage and civil partnership is currently defined at s.8 of the Equality Act which states that:

> (1) A person has the protected characteristic of marriage and civil partnership if the person is married or is a civil partner.
>
> (2) In relation to the protected characteristic of marriage and civil partnership—
>   (a) a reference to a person who has a particular protected characteristic is a reference to a person who is married or is a civil partner;
>   (b) a reference to persons who share a protected characteristic is a reference to persons who are married or are civil partners.

What is clear is that s.8 of the Equality Act does not offer protection to an individual who is single. This has been subject to litigation under the Sex Discriminaiton Act 1975. The initial position and quite a strict approach can be witnessed in the case of *Bick v. School for the Deaf*.[34] In this case an employee was dismissed before her wedding day due to the employing school maintaining a policy of not employing married staff, and this was held not to fall within the scope of the act, since the act was not concerned with protecting single people. However, this appears to be no longer the case following the tribunal decision of *Turner v. Stephen Turner*.[35] In this case the complainant was sacked when she announced that she was going to marry her employer's son. The tribunal found that there was discrimination on the grounds of marital status, and that to find differently would have been to defeat the purpose of that particular provision. However, it must be noted that this only applies to direct discrimination claims, as the amended definition of indirect discrimination, only applies specifically to married persons.

7.5. Race

Race discrimination was prohibited through the Race Relations Act 1976 ('RRA'), which built upon and replaced the protections that had previously been contained within the Race Relations Acts 1965 and 1968. This was a

---

[34] *Bick v. School for the Deaf* [1976] IRLR 326.

[35] *Turner v. Stephen Turner* [2005] 138 EOR 31.

wholly national approach until the EU utilised its competences under what was then Article 13 of the TEU.[36] Although there was a difference in the scope of the protections afforded at national level and European level, which led to a distinction in the way protections were applied depending on the form of race discrimination being complained of, this no longer exists.[37]

Section 9 of the Equality Act offers the current definition of Race for the purposes of non-discrimination protection, and states:

(1) Race includes:
    (a)   colour;
    (b)   nationality;
    (c)   ethnic or national origins.

(2) In relation to the protected characteristic of race:
    (a)   a reference to a person who has a particular protected characteristic is a reference to a person of a particular racial group;
    (b)   a reference to persons who share a protected characteristic is a reference to persons of the same racial group.

(3) A racial group is a group of persons defined by reference to race; and a reference to a person's racial group is a reference to a racial group into which the person falls.

(4) The fact that a racial group comprises two or more distinct racial groups does not prevent it from constituting a particular racial group.

(5) A Minister of the Crown may by order:
    (a)   amend this section so as to provide for caste to be an aspect of race;
    (b)   amend this Act so as to provide for an exception to a provision of this Act to apply, or not to apply, to caste or to apply, or not to apply, to caste in specified circumstances.

(6) The power under section 207(4)(b), in its application to subsection (5), includes power to amend this Act.

---

[36] This was a legal base providing the EU with the competence to introduce action against discrimination on a number of different grounds, which included on the ground of race; this legal base is currently found at Article 19 of the Treaty on the Functioning of the Europena Union, following renumbering under the Treaty Lisbon.

[37] This is now condemned to the history books, but there was a distinction in how the race discrimination protections applied depending on whether the discriminatory treatment was being brought on race, ethnic origin or national origin as opposed to colour or nationality.

The term that has received greatest consideration before the courts is the term ethnic origins, which is considred to be much wider than the term 'race'. On this issue the House of Lords in *Mandla v. Dowell Lee*[38] laid down guidance as to what was covered under this concept. The House of Lords indicated that an ethnic group must regard itself as a distinct community by virtue of certain characteristics. These characteristics were to include:

- a long shared history, of which the group is conscious as distinguishing it from other groups, the memory of which keeps it alive; and
- a cultural tradition, including social customs and manner.

In addition to these, the House of Lords said that other factors may be of relevance, such as:

- a common geographical origin or descent from common ancestors;
- a common language (but not necessarily peculiar to the group);
- a common literature;
- a common religion different from that of neighbouring groups; and
- being a minority or being an oppressed or a dominant group within a community.

This led to the finding in this case that a Sikh was held to have an ethnic origin, likewise Jews in *Seide v. Gillette Industries Ltd*[39] were found to be a distinct ethnic origin capable of being protected under the Act. However, according to the Court of Appeal in *Dawkins v. Department of the Environment*[40] Rastafarians do not satisfy these requirements as their history only went back some 60 years, and there was nothing to distinguish them from others of Jamaican or Afro-Caribbean descent.

Although there is an intrinsic link between language and nationality/national origin, the concept of race has not been expanded such as to cover less favourable treatment based on language alone, although it will be covered if language is coupled with a nationality/national origin requirement. For example, the Claimant's in *Gwynned CC v Jones and Doyle*[41] saw their claim claim for indirect race discrimination based on a re *Mandla v. Dowell Lee* fusal of a residential home to employ non-Welsh speaking

---

[38] *Mandla v. Dowell Lee* [1983] UKHL 7.

[39] *Seide v. Gillette Industries Ltd* [1980] IRLR 427.

[40] *Dawkins v. Department of the Environment* [1993] IRLR 284.

[41] *Mandla v. Dowell Lee* [1986] ICR 833.

Welsh persons due to many of their clients being Welsh speaking fail. The race discrimination provisions did not cover such matters.[42]

7.6.   Religion or Belief

As with Race, religion or belief was one of the new competences contained within the old Article 13 TEU, and which formed part of the protections introduced through the Framework Directive 2000/78EC.

Initially the required prohibition of discrimination on the grounds of religion or belief was introduced through the Employment Equality (Religion or Belief) Regulations 2003 (SI 2003/1660), which came into force on 2 December 2003.[43]

Religion or belief is defined in s.10 of the Equality Act, and covers:

(1)   Religion means any religion and a reference to religion includes a reference to a lack of religion.

(2)   Belief means any religious or philosophical belief and a reference to belief includes a reference to a lack of belief.

(3)   In relation to the protected characteristic of religion or belief:
 (a)   a reference to a person who has a particular protected characteristic is a reference to a person of a particular religion or belief;
 (b)   a reference to persons who share a protected characteristic is a reference to persons who are of the same religion or belief.

7.7.   Sex

Prohibition of discrimination on the grounds of sex was provided for through the Sex Discrimination Act 1975 (SDA), which was introduced as a result of the Equal Treatment Directive.

Sex is currently defined at s.11 of the Equality Act which defines sex as including:

(a)   a reference to a person who has a particular protected characteristic is a reference to a man or to a woman;

---

[42] One could envisage a claim from a person of a different nationality having more success from the point of view of their linguistic limits were inherently linked to their nationality. However, this would have then been subject to questions of whether the refusal was a proportionate means of achieving a legitimate aim, which may have been possible given the locality and needs of the residential home's clients.

[43] These Regulations did not extend to the jurisdiction of Northern Ireland (s.1(2)), which instead introduced its own legislation in this area.

(b) a reference to persons who share a protected characteristic is a reference to persons of the same sex.

7.8.   Sexual Orientation

Sexual orientation as a protected characteristic was introduced through the Framework Directive 2000/78/EC and introduced into UK law through the Employment Equality (Sexual Orientation) Regulations 2003 (SI 2003/1661), as amended by the Employment Equality (Sexual Orientation) (Amendment) Regulations 2003 (SI 2003/2827), which came into force on 1 December 2003.

Sexual orientation is defined at s.12 of the Equality Act, which states:

(1)   Sexual orientation means a person's sexual orientation towards:
    (a)   persons of the same sex,
    (b)   persons of the opposite sex, or
    (c)   persons of either sex.

(2)   In relation to the protected characteristic of sexual orientation:
    (a)   a reference to a person who has a particular protected characteristic is a reference to a person who is of a particular sexual orientation;
    (b)   a reference to persons who share a protected characteristic is a reference to persons who are of the same sexual orientation.

7.9.   Pregnant Workers and Maternity

Discrimination pertaining to pregnancy and maternity leave were previously dealt with under a form of sex discrimination, but received explicit recognition as a protected ground in its own right following the Employment Equality (Sex Discrimination) Regulations 2005. The 2005 regulations had the effect of inserting s.3A into the SDA dealing with ground. This was effective from 1 October 2005.

Pregnancy and maternity are maintained as a ground for protection in their own right under the Equality Act at s.4. However, unlike the other protected characteristics there no is statutory definition as to what is covered.

The approach to this protected characteristic will thus still be dependent on jurisprudential developments which took place before the Equality Act was brought into force.

Although the UK initially struggled to deal with the issue of pregnancy discrimination in a suitable manner,[44] the ECJ made great strides in enhancing the protection in a number of seminal decisions in the early 1990s. Of particular note was the removal of the need to establish a comparator in pregnancy discrimination cases.[45] Interestingly it took the courts until 1990 to realise that pregnancy was a unique case since a man could not get pregnant!

---

[44] Much of these difficulties centred on the need for a comparable worker, even leading the EAT making comparisons with a temporary illness, which was likely to last around 9 months: *Hayes v Malleable Working Men's Club and Institute* [1985] IRLR. 367.

[45] *Dekker v Stichting Vormingscentrum voor Jong Volwassenen (VJV- Centrum) Plus* [1991] IRLR 27 (Case C-177/88).

8. Evidencing Unlawful Discrimination

8.1. Burden of Proof

The enactment of the Sex Discrimination (Indirect Discrimination and Burden of Proof) Regulations 2001 and the Race Relations Act 1976 (Amendment) Regulations 2003 brought in to efect the Burden of Proof Directive (97/80/EC) across the protected characteristics, and is now replicated at section 136(2) of the Equality Act:

> If there are facts from which the court could decide, in the absence of any other explanation, that a person (A) contravened the provision concerned, the court must hold that the contravention occurred.

What this means is that the burden is on the complainant initially to establish facts from which the tribunal may presume that there has been direct or indirect discrimination, and thereafter the burden shifts to the respondent who will then have to prove that there has been no such discrimination; the complainant must establish a *prima facie* case of discrimination, and then the burden will shift to the employer to try to give an adequate explanation. Where the burden shifts and there is no adequate alternative explanation then the tribunals will be free to find that discrimination has taken place. This is, in effect, a much easier hurdle to satisfy than the standard burden of proof in civil cases, as it places much of the burden on the respondent.

There have been a number of cases on the issue of burden of proof, and in particular what is required on the part of the complainant: these cases include *University of Huddersfield v. Wolff*[1] and *Webster v. Brunel University.*[2]

In *Wolff* the EAT held that the burden shifts once the tribunal has concluded that a *prima facie* case of less favourable treatment on the grounds of race or sex has been made out and has set out the relevant facts on which it has made its findings, so that the employer knows what it has to justify. Whereas it is clear from *Webster* that the evidence required to shift the burden is not that onerous. The facts of *Webster* are fairly illustrative of the low hurdle that needs to be satisfied: the complainant was employed as a help desk officer, from which she provided IT support to administrative staff across the university. On one such occasion, whilst giving advice over the phone to a member of staff, she heard laughter in the background and heard the use of the word 'Paki'. Deeply upset at this

---

[1] *University of Huddersfield v. Wolff* [2004] IRLR 534.

[2] *Webster v. Brunel University* [2005] ICR 931.

Mrs Webster brought a complaint. Initially at the tribunal, her claim was rejected. Her claim was rejected as the office of the administrative staff concerned was a public place, and there it was open to the possibility that someone other than a member of staff could have been the person using the offensive word. The EAT disagreed with this approach and reversed the decision of the employment tribunal. What the EAT said was that once the employer had established the facts, it had to ask itself if the employer could have been responsible. It did not ask whether they were sure that the employer was responsible. That is crucial to the approach adopted to the burden of proof. Once it has shown that it *could* have been the fault of the employer, the burden shifts to the employer to prove that it was not them at fault. This case highlights how low the threshold is that needs to be satisfied, and surely can only be considered a good thing, especially when one thinks of the evidential burden that would be placed on the complainant otherwise.

A useful tool in satisfying the burden was provided for by s.138 of the Equality Act, which allowed a person who considered that they may have been unlawfully discriminated against or victimised to request information from their employer through a prescribed statutory questionnaire procedure. The importance of this was twofold: firstly, it enabled the worker to request such information, but secondly, where the employer failed to answer the questions, or answered equivocally or evasively the tribunal was able to draw adverse inferences. However, the s.138 statutory questionnaire procedure was abolished on 6 April 2014 through s.66 of the Enterprise and Regulatory Reform Act 2013 ('ERRA'), which was brought into effect by the Enterprise and Regulatory Reform Act 2013 (Commencement No. 6, Transitional Provisions and Savings) Order 2014. Despite this useful tool having been abolished, the Explanatory Notes to ERRA explains that a complainant may still ask such questions and the tribunal may still draw adverse inferences where the Respondent refuses to respond or answer evasively. This is further explained in ACAS guidance[3], which although explaining that an employer will not be legally obliged to answer such questions, the manner of answer may be a factor considered by the tribunal when reaching its overall decision as to whether discrimination has taken place.

8.2. Presentation of a Complaint

In order to bring a claim of discrimination, the standard position is that the complaint must be brought before the tribunal within three months of the

---

[3] ACAS (2014), 'Asking and responding to questions of discrimination in the workplace'

act of discrimination, or where there is a continuing discrimination, the complaint must be brought within three months of the last act of discrimination.[4] A useful example on this is *Calder v. James Finlay Corporation*,[5] where the employers had an unwritten rule that excluded women from a subsidised mortgage scheme, which is clearly an act of discrimination. The employee concerned lodged a complaint some five months after being refused a subsidised mortgage, but within three months of leaving employment. It was held on these facts that the refusal of the mortgage was a continuing act which continued during her employment, and only ceased when she left her employment. As such she was not timed out from bringing a claim. Similarly, in the case of *Cast v. Croydon College*,[6] it was held to be a continuing act of discrimination when an employer refused on three separate occasions to allow an employee to job share after returning from maternity leave, so that the three-month time limit started to run from the date of her resignation, prompted by the refusal.

There is the possibility of the three months' time limit being extended where the tribunal considers that it is 'just and equitable' to do so.[7] This discretion is limited to only exceptional circumstances.[8] The determinative factor in deciding whether to extend the time limit is the balance of prejudice.[9]

---

[4] EqA s.123; more particularly s.123(3).

[5] *Calder v. James Finlay Corporation* [1989] IRLR 55.

[6] *Cast v. Croydon College* [1998] IRLR 318.

[7] EqA s.123(1)(b).

[8] *Robertson v Bexley Community Centre* [2003] EWCA Civ 567.

[9] *Harden v. Wootlif & Anor* [2015] UKEAT/0448/14/1504.

EQUALITY AND ANTI-DISCRIMINATION LAW

9. Remedies for Direct and Indirect Discrimination, Harassment and Victimisation Claims

Although compensation is the primary remedy available to the tribunal where a finding of unlawful discrimination is made, it is not the only one. The employment tribunal is also empowered to make an appropriate recommendation or a declaration. This enables the tribunal to make an award that not only compensates for the damage caused to an individual by discriminatory actions, but it also provides useful powers that have the potential to deal with the root cause of the problem. The Equality Act is not merely concerned with remedying a situation after the event, but also seeks to alter practices to prevent similar discriminatory events from occurring in the future.

9.1. Compensation for direct discrimination, harassment and victimisation claims

Under section 124(2)(b) of the Equality Act the tribunal may "order the respondent to pay compensation to the complainant". There is no statutory limit to the amount of compensation that can be awarded following a finding of unlawful discrimination.[1] Not having an upper limit on compensatory awards introduces a disincentive and deterence to employers, as they may be subject to huge liabilities should they not comply with the Equality Act. This enables full reparation of damages to be recoverable.

Tortious principles are applied when determining the amount of compensation to be awarded,[2] which means that the purpose of a compensatory award is not to provide a just and equitable remedy,[3] but to place the injured party, as far as possible, into the position they would have been in had the act of discrimination not taken place.[4] This also means that

---

[1] The statutory limit that was initially applied was found to be unlawful under EU law and thus removed following the ECJ decision in, *Marshall v. Southampton and South West Hampshire Area Health Authority (No 2)* [1993] ECR 1-4367 (Case C-271/91).

[2] EqA s.124(6) states that compensation in the employmwent tribunal corresponds to the amount which could be awarded by a county court or the sheriff under section 119. EqA s.119(2) and (3) refers to tortious remedies that could be granted by the High Court.

[3] As is the case under unfair dismissal law.

[4] *Ministry of Defence v. Wheeler* [1998] IRLR 23 and *Chagger v Abbey National plc* [2010] IRLR 47.

the general tortious principles relating to causation and remoteness apply to discrimination cases.

Although the general causation rule – that compensation will only be recoverable for injury that is reasonable foreseeable – applies to most discrimination claims, it is disapplied where a claim involves harassment.[5]

Although most cases appear to name a company/employer as the respondent,[6] awards can also be made against the individual who carried out the unlawful discrimination. It is often considered a safer approach to bring an action against the individual at fault alongside the employer, against whom vicarious liability will be argued as this can be viewed as a safety net such that a claim will not simply fail on the basis of the reasonable practicable steps defence that is considered when determining vicarious liability, which would be the case should the employer be named as the sole respondent.[7] In such circumstances the Employment Tribunal has jurisdiction to make an award on a joint and several basis,[8] rather than apportioning liability between the parties in accordance with Civil Liability (Contribution) Act 1978 s.2(1).[9]

The compensatory award can include pecuniary and non-pecuniary losses.

9.1.1. Financial Losses

The types of losses that can be recovered for unlawful discrimination is quite broad, covering almost anything that has a financial value attached to it. As such it will cover the obvious financial losses such as pay and bonuses, but will also cover the fringe benefits associated with the employment, such as loss of use of a company car, medical insurance and

---

[5] This was the decision of the Court of Appeal following *Essa v. Laing Ltd* [2004] ICR 746. It is arguable that this limitation on compensation is removed from all awards of compensation for discrimination, as although the case concerned the specific context of racial harassment, the majority's reasoning was predicated on the intentional nature of the unlawful act.

[6] This is due to the employer being vicariously liable for acts of discrimination in the course of employment, unless they have taken reasonably practicable steps to prevent such discrimination, and they being in the stronger financial position (or insured position) to satisfy any such awards.

[7] Vicarious liability is considered fully in **Chapter 4.7.**

[8] *Munchkins Restaurant Ltd v. Karmazyn* UKEAT/0359/09.

[9] Apportionment is discussed in *Way v. Crouch* [2005] IRLR 603.

loss of pension rights. Compensation may also be awarded for loss of the opportunity to be promoted.[10]

These losses are assessed net rather than gross.

Calculating the financial losses

The calculation for financial losses is made up of two parts:

1. Losses suffered up to the date of the hearing
2. Future losses

Each of these will be calculated and accumulated to give an initial figure, against which deductions may be made. Credit needs to be given for any payments received. This includes deducting any State benefits that the claimant has received from the compensation award.[11] Credit must also be given for any ex gratia payments that the complainant has received from their employer.[12]

The ordinary rules relating to mitigation also apply to discrimination claims, and as such the claimant is under a duty to mitigate each and every head of loss that they are claiming. A claimant will not be able to claim compensation for any loss which could have been avoided by taking reasonable steps.[13] The burden of establishing a failure to mitigate rests with the respondent.

Future handicap in the labour market

The tribunal is able to make a 'Smith and Manchester award'[14] following a finding of unlawful discrimination. Such an award is made based on an assessment by the tribunal as to what risk exists the claimant will suffer a handicap on the open labour market as a result of their treatment.

The Court of Appeal in *Moeliker v. Reyrolle & Co. Ltd*[15] suggested a two-step approach to dealing with such an award in circumstnaces where the claimant is still working:

---

[10] *Ministry of Defence v. Cannock* [1994] ICR 918.

[11] *Chan v. Hackney LBC* [1997] ICR 1014.

[12] See *Ministry of Defence v. Hunt* [1996] ICR 544.

[13] *Wilding v. British Telecommunications Plc* [2002] IRLR 524

[14] This is what future handicap in the labour market is often referred to following the case of *Smith v. Manchester Corporation* (1974) 17 KIR 1.

[15] *Moeliker v. Reyrolle & Co. Ltd* [1976] ICR 253.

1. Is there a substantial or real risk that the claimant will lose their job before the estimated end of their working life? If the answer is "yes", then

2. What is the degree of that risk? When is it likely to materialise? What are the claimant's chances of finding an equally well paid job?

It has also been accepted by the Court of Appeal[16] that compensation can be awarded for 'stigma' damages, where it is this stigma that can act as a handicap to the claimant in the open labour market; however, due to the difficulty in quantifying it was accepted that such a figure will more likely than not be a notional sum.

9.1.2. Non-Pecuniary Losses

Unlike a claim for unfair dismissal,[17] compensation for unlawful discrimination can include an award for injury to feelings and is expressly provided for at s.119(4) of the Equality Act. Consequent to compensation being determined on a tortious basis, the award thus may include awards made for injury to health, aggravated damages as well as exemplary damages.

Injury to Feelings

The burden lies with the claimant to establish that an award for injury to feelings should be made,[18] although what appears to be required is a simple statement of such injuries, which then places the onus on the tribunal to consider the extent of any such injuries.[19]

It is often a difficult exercise to translate injury to feelings into an award, given that it involves translation of matters that have no obvious financial value such as upset, anxiety and humiliation into a financial figure. There is certainly no precise method that can be adopted in order to predict the level of such an award. However, some policy considerations on what tribunals should take into account when considering an award for injury to

---

[16] *Chagger v. Abbey National Plc* [2010] IRLR 47.

[17] Dunnachie and Eastwood held that to the 'just and equitable' compensatory principle for unfair dismissal under ERA s.123 only refers to pecuniary losses. *Johnson v Underwood* further limited compensation awards for injury to feeling through the manner of the dismissal by restricting the development of the implied term of trust of confidence so as to not have application during the dismissal process, as otherwise it would undermine the statutory scheme as devised by Parliament.

[18] *Ministry of Defence v. Cannock* [1994] ICR 918.

[19] *Murray v. Powertech (Scotland) Ltd* [1992] IRLR 257.

feelings were provided by Smith J in *Armitage, Marsden and HM Prison Service v. Johnson*:[20]

(1) Awards for injury to feelings are compensatory. They should be just to both parties. They should compensate fully without punishing the tortfeasor. Feelings of indignation should not be allowed to inflate the award.

(2) Awards should not be too low, as that would diminish respect for the policy of the anti-discrimination legislation. Society has condemned discrimination and awards must ensure that it is seen to be wrong. On the other hand, awards should be restrained, as excessive awards could ... be seen as the way to untaxed riches.

(3) Awards should bear some broad general similarity to the range of awards in personal injury cases. We do not think this should be done by reference to any particular type of personal injury award; rather to the whole range of such awards.

(4) In exercising their discretion in assessing a sum, tribunals should remind themselves of the value in everyday life of the sum they have in mind.

(5) Finally, tribunals should bear in mind . . the need for public respect for the level of awards made.

In order to assist with the assessment awards for injury to feelings the Court of Appeal introduced three broad bands of awards based upon the severity of the case.[21] These bands were given consideration, and subsequently updated by the HHJ McMullen in the EAT case of *Da'Bell v. NSPCC*[22], and currently stand at:

- For 'less serious cases' where the unlawful act is isolated or a one-off, a lower band of between £750-£6000

- For 'serious cases which do not merit an award in the highest band', a middle band of between £6,000 and £18,000

- For the 'most serious cases', which involve 'a lengthy campaign of harassment', a bracket of between £18,000 and £30,000, with awards over £25,000 being reserved for exceptional cases.

However, it must be noted that these brackets are not intended to be hard and fast rules, but merely as a means of assisting the tribunal when utilising their discretion in determining a suitable level of compensation.

---

[20] *Armitage, Marsden and HM Prison Service v. Johnson* [1997] ICR 275.

[21] *Vento v. Chief Constable of West Yorkshire Police* [2003] ICR 318.

[22] *Da'Bell v. NSPCC* [2010] IRLR 19.

As this is a discretionary award the Appelate tribunal/courts should only overturn such a finding where it is established that the tribunal has misdirected itself in law or where the award was so excessive that it was to be considered a perverse decision.[23]

An award for injury to feelings is not taxable.

An important point to note is that an award for injury to feelings and injury to health consequent to unlawful discrimination for awards made after 1 April 2013 will attract the 10% uplift[24] which was introduced into personal injury claims by the Court of Appeal's decision in *Simmons v. Castle*.[25]

Injury to Health

There is a close nexus between injury to feelings and injury to health, and drawing a distinction between the two is often difficult. In most cases an award for both headings is generally made under a single award; however, the tribunal is able to make a separate award if it is satisfied that in doing so it is not providing a double recovery for the same loss.[26]

Injury to health caused by a discriminatory act was recognised as a head of loss which attracted compensation by the Court of Appeal in *Sheriff v. Klyne Tugs (Lowestoft) Ltd*.[27] At least in cases of direct and intentional discriminatioin there is no need to establish that the injury was a reasonably foressable consequence of the discriminatory act,[28] but only that the injury was a direct consequence of it. As such medical evidence plays an important role in establishing the causal link, and failing to provide such evidence could result in the tribunal refusing to award such compensation. However, failure to provide evidence establishing such causal link between the discriminatory act and the injury to health will not impact upon the award for injury to feelings.

Although this category is quite broad, it is generally used to compensate for psychiatric injuries. Awards are made in accordance with ordinary personal injury claims using the Judicial College Guidelines for the Assessment of General Damages in Personal Injury Cases.

---

[23] See *Vento* and *Gilbank v. Miles* [2006] IRLR 538.

[24] *Cadogan Hotel Partners Ltd v. Ozog* (UKEAT/0001/14/DM).

[25] *Simmons v. Castle* [2012] EWCA Civ 1039.

[26] *HM Prison Service v. Salmon* [2001] IRLR 425.

[27] *Sheriff v. Klyne Tugs (Lowestoft) Ltd* [1999] ICR 1170.

[28] *Essa v. Laing Ltd* [2004] ICR 746.

Aggravated Damages

Judge Burke in *Singh v. University Hospital NHS Trust*[29] summarised the position with regards aggravated damages in discrimination claims:

(1) Aggravated compensation may be awarded in a discrimination case: *HM Prison Service v Johnson* [1997] ICR 275.

(2) However, they may only be awarded in a case in which it is established that the discriminator has acted in a high-handed, malicious, insulting or oppressive manner: *Alexander v The Home Office* [1998] IRLR 190.

(3) While any discrimination is offensive and regrettable and may be potentially very distressing, the requirements set out in **Alexander** involve some special element in the conduct of the discriminator which takes the case beyond the ordinary run of discrimination cases. The fact that there has been discrimination and that the victim has been upset or distressed or even injured in his health as a result of the discrimination is not of itself enough.

(4) It is a matter for the Tribunal on the facts of each case to decide whether, if the discriminator has acted in a high-handed, malicious, insulting or oppressive manner, the case is one in which aggravated compensation should be awarded.

(5) An award of aggravated compensation may, but need not be, included in the award for injury to feelings. It may be included, it may be separate: *ICTS UK Ltd v Tchoula* [2000] IRLR 643.

(6) Aggravated compensation may be awarded even though the injury to feelings award in the individual case is in what was described in *Tchoula* as the "lower category" and not the "higher category" of the two very broad categories described in that decision.

(7) An award of aggravated compensation should be compensatory, not punitive: *Armitage v Johnson* [1997] IRLR 162

A further useful summary of the purpose of aggravated damages can be seen in the judgment of LCJ Carswell in *McConnell v. Police Authority for Northern Ireland*[30] where it was stated that:

An award of aggravated damages should not be an extra sum over and above the sum which the Tribunal of fact considers appropriate compensation for the injury to the claimants feelings, and that aggravated damages should not be treated as an extra award which reflects a degree of punishment of a respondent for its behaviour. The right course was to arrive at a figure which included whatever sum was

---

[29] *Singh v. University Hospital NHS Trust* [2003] All ER 131.

[30] *McConnell v. Police Authority for Northern Ireland* [1997] IRLR 625.

thought to be appropriate by way of aggravated damages in order to reflect the sum for injury to feelings.

Exemplary Damages

Exemplary damages are only ever awarded in exceptional circumstances, and are unlikely to be widely used in discrimination cases. The House of Lords made it clear in *Kuddus v. Chief Constable of Leicestershire Constabulary*[31] that such damages are only recoverable if the compensation awarded is considered insufficient to punish the wrongdoes, and where the conduct is either:

(a) oppressive, arbitrary, or unconstitutional actions by agents of the government, or

(b) where the respondent's conduct has been calculated to make a profit which may exceed the the compensation payable to the claimant.

Such an award is only available where the claim is brought under domestic legislation, with it being precluded where the claim is being brought under the Equal Treatment Directive.[32] As one can appreciate from that which is expressed in *Kuddus*, such an award is extremely limited, and although one can imagine situations where this will be applicable in extreme cases of unlawful discrimination, it is unlikely to arise often.

9.1.3. Compensation for indirect discrimination

An award for compensation for indirect discrimination can be made under s.124(4) of the Equality Act, but only where the tribunal "is satisfied that the provision, criterion or practice was not applied with the intention of discriminating against the complainant", and only after having first considered making a declaration or recommendation.[33]

To date there are no cases that have yet considered such an award.

9.1.4. Failure to follow the ACAS Code of Practice

The ACAS Code of Practice on discipline and grievance was issued under of the Trade Union and Labour Relations (Consolidation) Act 1992 s.199, and came into effect by order of the Secretary of State on 6 April 2009, replacing the previous Code issued in 2004. There have been some minor revisions to the Code which came into force on 11 March 2015. Although one usually associates the Code of Practice with dismissal and disciplinary matters it has greater application than that, and has relevance in situations

---

[31] *Kuddus v. Chief Constable of Leicestershire Constabulary* [2002] 2 AC 122.

[32] *Ministry of Defence v. Meredith* [1995] IRLR 539.

[33] EqA s.124(5)

whenever an individual has a grievance, including where there is a complaint on discrimatory grounds.

In effect the Code requires an employee to raise a grievance should they have one with a manager who is not the subject of the grievance and where it cannot be dealt with informally, and for the employer to deal with the matter promptly through investigation, meetings and the reaching of a conclusion.

It must be noted that the Code of Practice does not lay down a process that needs to be followed, with there being express appreciation that different employers and different situations will need to operate in different ways. However, there are some key principles that are expressed within the Code. These include:

- holding a meeting with the employee to discuss the grievance (para 33), with an adjournment of the meeting for necessary investigations to take place if necessary (para 34);

- allowing the worker to be accompanied at the meeting by either a fellow worker, trade union representative, or an official employed by a trade union so long as they have made a reasonable request (paras 35-39); and

- providing the employee with an outcome in writing, along with any appropriate action that will be taken, and allowing a right of appeal should the employee be unhappy with the outcome (para 40).

The importance of complying with the spirit of the ACAS Code of Practice is that the Tribunal has the discretion to increase or decrease compensation by up to 25% where there has been an unreasonable failure to follow the Code. In other words if the employee unreasonably fails to follow the code, either through not raising a formal grievance in circumstances where they ought to, or by non co-operation in the process then they may have their compensation decreased by up to 25%, and, where it is the employer that unreasonably fails to comply then the tribunal may use its discretion to increase any compensation awarded by up to 25%.

It is worth bearing in mind that this is wholly based on the tribunal's discretion, who will hear submissions by both sides as to the unreasonableness of the conduct of the other side, as well as on levels of increase/decrease, before reaching its own conclusion. There are no hard and fast rules in this respect.

9.2.   Recommendation

The employment tribunal can "make an appropriate recommendation" on the finding of unlawful discrimination under Equality Act s.124(2)(c). An appropriate recommendation is:

> ...a recommendation that within a specified period the respondent takes specified steps for the purpose of obviating or reducing the adverse effect of any matter to which the proceedings relate—
>
> (a) on the complainant;
>
> (b) on any other person.[34]

This provision provides the tribunal with an exceptionally wide power and will cover an extremely broad range of steps, so long as the step is being recommended for the purpose of obviating or reducing discriminatory impacts of any matter which has been found unlawful by the tribunal. This order is not limited to specific steps that are to the benefit of the claimant, and can include steps that are beneficial to the workforce as a whole. This can cover, for example, providing racial awareness training[35] or requiring changes to the employer's policies and/or staff handbooks that affect the entirety of the workforce. However, there is not a closed list of which a tribunal can refer to and it would not be possible to attempt to provide an exhaustive list of possible actions. This is a highly flexible tool.

There appear to be some limits on what can be recommended, including ordering an employer to increase a claimant's wage,[36] or recommending that a claimant be automatically appointed to the next available vacancy,[37] or ordering that the claimant be promoted.[38] Although these are likely to continue to be considered going beyond the powers available to the tribunal as a recommendation, they may be open to question given that they were decided under legislation that existed prior to the Equality Act 2010, and at a time when there was reference to a need for steps to be practicable; a requirement which has since been removed.

---

[34] EqA s.124(3).

[35] *Southwark London Borough v. Ayton* EAT/0515/03

[36] This has been held to be a matter for compensatory awards. See *Irvine v. Prestcold* [1981] IRLR 281.

[37] Giving an unconditional priority to the claimant would be unfair to other potential candidates. See *Noone v. North West Regional Health Authority (No.2)* [1988] IRLR 530

[38] *Sharma v. British Gas* [1991] IRLR 101.

Although there is no power available to effectively enforce a recommendation, it is made against the backdrop of s.124(7) of the Equality Act, which enables a tribunal to make an award of compensation (where none was made in the case), or to increase a compensatory award in the event of non-compliance.

The wider power of a recommendation is certainly a useful tool from an equality point of view, especially given that it can be used to alter measures and practices of an employer for the greater good of the workforce, rather than being limited to the claimant. This power will enable a tribunal to require changes that has the potential to deal with the unlawful discriminatory treatment at the root cause, and truly get to the foundation of the complaint. This, in particular, can be viewed as a proactive approach to ensuring equality in the workplace, rather than the reactive approach that the award of compensation is so often viewed.

9.3. Declaration

The third of the available remedies available to the tribunal on the finding of unlawful discrimination is that of an order of declaration, which is expressed at s.124(2)(a) of the Equality Act. It enables the tribunal to "make a declaration as to the rights of the complainant and the respondent in relation to the matters to which the proceedings relate".

The declaration is a fairly simple remedy: the tribunal will expressly declare that the claimant has been unlawfully discriminated against by the respondent in the circumstances heard before it. This can often be viewed as a means to an end, with a number of claimants often merely seeking public recognition that they have been wronged rather than expecting compensation.

EQUALITY AND ANTI-DISCRIMINATION LAW

10.   Equal Pay

10.1.   Introduction

The introduction of legislation on equal pay was aimed at removing sex discrimination from pay systems, and tries to redress the imbalance of the so-called 'gender pay-gap' (the difference in pay between men and women despite doing essentially the same work). The relevant UK law in this area was the Equal Pay Act 1970 (EqPA), as amended by Europe. However, this is now dealt with under the Equality Act 2010. Equalisation of pay is based upon European Law, being enshrined in Article 157 of the Treaty on the Functioning of the European Union ('TFEU').[1] Furthermore, there is also the Equal Pay Directive (Directive 75/117/EEC) ('EPD'), concerning the application of Article 157 TFEU, which states that equal pay is to be paid for the same work or work to which equal value has been attached. The supremacy of EU law over UK national law means that the approach under EPD will be relevant in interpreting the EqPA, and therefore will be considered accordingly in relevant parts of this text.

In considering the application of the Equality Act, the employment tribunals must apply its provisions in accordance with the statutory objective of eliminating discrimination in terms and conditions of employment which exist solely because of a person's sex. For historical reasons, most of the claims made under equal pay legislation are made by women, but the law applies equally to men, where appropriate.[2]

Despite such regulatory attempts to deal with the differences in pay based on gender existing for over 45 years there still remains a problem in the UK, although the differences in pay appear to be decreasing.

Despite the equal pay protection now being given pride of place alongside the ordinary non-discrimination protections within the Equality Act, the systems have long been kept separate, and continue to operate independently.

---

[1] Before renumbering under the Treaty of Lisbon the principle of Equal Pay was found within Article 141 of the EC Treaty. It is important to note that Article 157 TFEU has been held to have direct effect (*Defrenne v Sabena*) and as such this European provision and the related case law defining how it operates can be relied upon before the national courts.

[2] For the purposes of avoiding confusion this chapter is written as if the provisions solely protect females; however, the genders selected throughout the chapter can be easily switched given that the protections apply equally to both men and women.

Before considering the protections that come under the umbrella of equal pay protection it is first worth turning to consider the gender pay issue alongside its causes, in order to highlight the mischief that the protection is attempting to deal with. This then provides a backdrop against which the equal pay provisions can be considered with a view towards whether they are capable of achieving equality in this area.

10.2. The Gender Pay Gap

One of the most obvious manifestations of inequality between the sexes is where there is a difference in the pay that a woman receives when compared to that which a man receives for doing essentially the same job. The Office of National Statistics provides information on the gender pay gap annually, and calculates it through considering the median hourly earnings of men and women exclusive of overtime. The latest statistics (2014) highlight that there is a current gender pay gap in the UK for all employees (which includes full-time and part-time employees) of 19.1%, which is a reduction from 19.8% in 2013, and a significant improvement from the 27.5 % gap that existed in 1997.

On a basic level, differences in pay can be attributed to prejudicial treatment of women in the workplace by employers. Some employers still prejudge the ability of a female worker to be lower than that of a male worker and as a result pay significantly less. However, this is does not provide the full picture, with other factors also contributing to the pay gap. Two of the other key factors involve the hours which women work, or are available to work, and the job sectors in which they work.

An obvious factor behind the gender pay gap can be found through comparing the detailed breakdown in pay provided by the ONS labour market statistics. The data highlights that the pay gap between men and women with regards full-time work is at 9.4% whereas, the gender pay difference is 5.5% when it is for part-time work. The difference in pay between those in full-time work and part-time work is much harsher and exacerbates the problem, with statistics in 2013 suggesting that full-time employees on average earned £13.03 per hour, with part-time workers earning £8.29 an hour, which is a 26.4% difference.[3] If one then considers that out of the 7.464 million part-time roles, 5.628 million (or 75.4%)[4] are

---

[3] These figures were produced in a *Guardian* article entitled 'UK median weekly pay is £517 - but who earns that?', which was first published on 12 December 2013.

[4] These statistics are calculated from the figures that are contained within the ONS 2013 publication *'Full report - Women in the labour market'*, released 25 September 2013.

filled by females, then the gender pay issue becomes much more of a problem: more women are employed at a lower pay rate than part-time male counterparts when also working part time, but at a significantly lower rate than full-time pay rates, which are predominantly filled by men: this has a double impact on the gender pay gap. These statistics highlight that hourly pay is intrinsically linked to working time: the fewer working hours one undertakes, the less per hour that person will receive. This, as suggested, causes a problem from an equality perspective given that it is generally accepted that women have a greater role to play within a family, especially with regards childcare responsibilities, leaving less time to undertake paid work, which in itself deflates the pay that is received. Working time itself presents a sex equality pay issue. The Equality Act does go some way to offering protection against such wage deflation through comparison of contractual terms; this protection is enhanced further through more targeted regulation such as the Part-time Workers (Prevention of Less Favourable Treatment) Regulations 2000 and the regulations that form part of the UK's family friendly policies. These protections are considered in **Chapters 11 and 12**.

A further factor that appears to exacerbate the gender pay gap is job segregation. There are particular industries, generally that are low skilled and low paid, where jobs are predominantly filled by females: such industries include catering, cleaning and caring. On the other hand, there are particular professions and roles, generally high paid, where females are under-represented, including the judiciary, board members and bankers. It is debatable whether the Equality Act is capable of addressing such job segregation.

The remainder of this section turns to consider how the equal pay provisions of the Equality Act operate.

The equal pay provisions covers all contractual benefits that an individual is entitled to receive, and is not limited to merely pay, as the title may suggest.

10.3. The Scope of the Equal Pay Protections

The equal pay provisions covers all contractual benefits that an individual is entitled to receive, and is not limited to merely pay, as the title may suggest.

Previously it has been held to cover, amongst other things, Christmas bonuses[5], travel facilities,[6] training course allowances[7] and pension scheme

---

[5] *Leven v Denda* (2000) IRLR 67.

contributions.[8] This is important, as it means that the protections are not limited just to pay. This broad approach has been accounted for in the EHRC's Code of Practice on Equal Pay:

> These equal pay provisions apply to all contractual terms including wages and salaries, non-discretionary bonuses, holiday pay, sick pay, overtime, shift payments, and occupational pension benefits, and to non-monetary terms such as leave entitlements or access to sports and social benefits.[9]

This differs somewhat from the approach under Article 157 TFEU, which is limited to the 'remuneration' that an employee receives from their employer.

It was intimated in the case of *Shields v. E Coomes (Holdings) Limited*[10] that the EqPA and the SDA were supposed to act together to form one homogenous code of domestic legislation, with the EqPA covering only contractual terms, and the SDA covering discrimination outside contractual rights and benefits.[11] The Equality Act has maintained this approach of trying to ensure sex equality across the entire working relationship.

As with the scope of discrimination law, the equal pay provisions have been given a wide scope and apply to those engaged under a contract of employment, a contract of apprenticeship, or a contract to do work personally.[12]

The operation of equal pay protection is contained neatly within ss.64-79 of the Equality Act, with the system currently in place reflecting closely the previous approach contained within the EqPA. However, there have been some developments in the text of the provisions and through case law in this area since the Equality Act was first introduced. One point that remains consistent is that equal pay protection manifests itself through the implication of a sex equality clause into all contracts that fall within the

---

[6] *Garland v British Rail Engineering Ltd* [1983] 2 AC 751.

[7] *Davies v Neath Port Talbot County BC* [1999] IRLR 769.

[8] *Worringham v Lloyds Bank* [1981] IRLR 178.

[9] Paragraph 31.

[10] *Shields v. E Coomes (Holdings) Limited* [1978] IRLR 263.

[11] The focus of the general sex discrimination provisions is expressed at para 32 of the EHRC's Equal Pay Code of Practice. Other sex discrimination provisions apply to non-contractual pay and benefits such as purely discretionary bonuses, promotions, transfers and training and offers of employment or appointments to office.

[12] EqA s. 80(2). This follows closely the approach discussed in **Chapter 6.1.1**.

scope of the Equality Act's provisions, and consequently, understanding this clause is crucial to understanding equal pay protection.

10.4. The Sex Equality Clause

Section 66 of the Equality Act implies an 'equality clause' into every worker's contract. Equal pay is essentially determined through a comparison between the complainant and a selected comparator of the opposite sex.[13] The sex equality clause can only be utilised positively by the complainant where there is a comparator worker of opposite sex, who is employed by the same employer or an associated employer,[14] and where the complainant and comparator are employed on 'like work'; 'work rated as equivalent' or 'work of equal value', at the same establishment, or at an establishment where similar terms and conditions are applied. It is only when each of these aspects are satisfied that a suitable comparator will be found, and the implied sex equality clause will have effect.[15]

The effects of the implied sex equality clause are straightforward: under s.66(2) of the Equality Act any term or condition that is less favourable than that in the contract of the comparator will be equalised to be as favourable; where no such corresponding term exists, one will be deemed to exist. This indicates an exceptionally wide approach to equal pay, covering *all* contractual benefits and terms.

A similar approach is seen under Article 157 at EU level where it is stated that:

> Each Member State shall ensure that the principle of equal pay for male and female workers for equal work or work of equal value is applied.

This is further emphasised in Article 4 of the recast Equal Treatment Directive, which requires that:

---

[13] It is important to always bear in mind that equal pay protection is a form of sex discrimination protection. It is only concerned with differences in pay that can be attributed to the sex of the complainant; it is not concerned with ensuring that all workers are fairly paid.

[14] It is made clear in *Hasley v. Fair Employment Agency* [1989] IRLR 106 that statutory agencies, even where they are controlled by the Government, will not be considered as associate employers for the purposes of equal pay protection; although this is the current state of affairs under the Equality Act it is questionable whether this is compatible with approach adopted at European level, in particular in light of *Scullard v Knowles and Southern Regional Council* [1996] IRLR 344.

[15] Each of these is discussed in greater detail below.

> For the same work or for work to which equal value is attributed, direct and indirect discrimination on grounds of sex with regard to all aspects and conditions of remuneration shall be eliminated.

This identifies that the European and UK approaches to equal pay are fairly similar. Both are concerned with sex discrimination, both are based on a comparator approach, and both require the less favourable aspects of pay to be equalised where there are differences that can be attributed to sex.

One final point to note on the issue of the implied sex equality clause is that equal pay protection requires an equalisation of the individual terms of each respective contract. In *Hayward v. Cammel Laird Shipbuilders Ltd (No.2)*[16] it was questioned whether the contract as a whole should be considered or whether a term-by-term comparison was required. The House of Lords held that the Act required a term-by-term comparison, with each individual less favourable term being equalised: detriments or benefits in one contract are not balanced against the detriments and benefits in the comparator contract.[17] This is best explained through a hypothetical example. Mrs A receives £200 per days' work plus £10 lunch tokens. Mr B receives £250 per days' work and £5 lunch tokens. The contract is not considered in the whole. Instead an individual term approach must be taken. That means comparing the daily rate of pay: Mrs A would complain about being paid £50 less per day with Mr B being able to complain of the £5 difference in lunch voucher value. That is how the equal pay protection works.

This term-by-term approach is further enhanced by the ability of the complainant to select multiple comparators if such an approach is beneficial to their claim. In other words, a complainant can select different comparators for each individual term of their contract if they can identify such differential treatment being applied.[18]

This chapter now turns to consider the concept of suitable comparable worker, and thus will consider the constituent parts of the concept highlighted above:

- in the same employment or associated employer;

---

[16] *Hayward v. Cammel Laird Shipbuilders Ltd (No.2)* [1987] 3 WLR 20.

[17] It was confirmed by the European Court in *Jorgensen v Foreningen AF Speciallaeger Sygeskringens Forhandlingsudvalg* [2000] ECR I–2447 (Case C-226/98), that adopted a rolled up approach and considering the contract as a whole was the incorrect approach to equal pay protection.

[18] Paragraph 59 EHRC Code

- engaged in like work, work rated as equivalent or work of equal value;
- at the same establishment or a different establishment where common terms and conditions apply.

10.5. Choosing a Suitable Comparator

10.5.1. Need for an actual comparator

It is important to always bear in mind that the Equality Act requires a comparison with a member of the opposite sex in order to pursue an equal pay claim.[19] Where no such comparison can be made, no claim exists under the equal pay protections. Finding a comparator has not proved an easy task, especially in those areas where women were the predominant workers, for example in the textile, catering or cleaning industries. This was considered one of the major drawbacks to this statutory system; women in work where low pay and poor terms and conditions were standard were often left without a comparator and thus no available claim.

One approach that was considered a means of easing such difficulties was to enable comparison with a predecessor. Whether this was allowed was considered in *Macarthys Ltd v Smith*.[20] The Court of Appeal refused a stockroom manageress the ability to compare her wages with her predecessor in the post, who happened to be male and paid significantly more. The Court of Appeal believed that as the EqPA was worded in present tense terms no such comparison could be made. However, the European Court of Justice thought otherwise, and decided that under Art 157 TFEU (which was Art 119 EC Treaty at the time) an applicant could compare their position with their predecessor. This approach was extended to the EqPA by the EAT in *Diocese of Hallam Trustee v Connaughton*,[21] which has been maintained under the Equality Act. This does ease some of the difficulties in finding a comparator where none currently exists. However, this may not go far enough. It is still the case (or at least arguable) that an actual comparator is needed, and it has not been extended to a hypothetical comparator as allowed under the general sex discrimination provisions.[22]

---

[19] See EqA s.64

[20] *Macarthys Ltd v Smith* [1980] ICR 672

[21] *Diocese of Hallam Trustee v Connaughton* [1996] IRLR 505.

[22] It was held in *Walton Centre for Neurology NHS Trust v. Bewley*, UKEAT/0564/07 that a successor in a job was not a suitable comparator in an equal pay claim due to the uncertainty that would exist in any exercise that tried to consider what the relative wages would have been had the complainant and successor been employed contemporaneously.

Making use of predecessors is now a settled and accepted approach in relation to equal pay claims. Ultimate acceptance of predecessors as suitable comparators can be seen through its inclusion at s.64(2) of the Equality Act. Furthermore, para 60 of the EHRC's Equal Pay Code of practice makes it clear that the complainant and selected comparator does not need to be working contemporaneously, and as such a predecessor is suitable.

An interesting, and novel approach to furthering protection of equal pay was introduced by the Equality Act s.71,[23] to cover situations where no actual suitable comparator can be found. Given the limitation in relation to successors as a suitable comparator for equal pay claims if no suitable comparator can be found the equal pay claim should, at least in theory, fail.[24] However, under s.71, where a woman has evidence of direct sex discrimination in relation to her contractual pay but there is no actual comparator doing equal work, so that a sex equality clause cannot operate, she can claim sex discrimination based on a hypothetical comparator. In other words, where no suitable comparable worker exists for the purposes of an equal pay claim, the complainant can make use of direct sex discrimination, and take advantage of the fact that the wording of direct discrimination allows for the use of hypothetical comparators.

This begs the question as to who will be a suitable comparator for the purposes of the equal pay provisions. The answer to this lies within s.79 of the Equality Act, which makes it clear that, in addition to the need for being of the opposite sex to the complainant, there is also the requirement that the comparator falls within one of four categories:

- employed by the same employer as the complainant and works at the same establishment; or
- employed by an associate employer of the complainant's employer and works at the same establishment; or
- employed by the same employer as the complainant, however, works at a different establishment but to which common terms apply; or
- employed by an associate employer of the complainant's employer, however, works at a different establishment but to which common terms apply.

---

[23] This is further expressed at para 61 of the EHRC Equal Pay Code of Practice.

[24] This was the case under the EqPA.

Same employer…

There is no need to give any meaningful consideration here to the situation concerning the 'same employer' as this is self-evident. Obviously where the complainant identifies a colleague who has a contract with the same employer, and they have the same place of work then the comparator requirements will be satisfied. This is often viewed as the typical situation which gives rise to an equal pay claim and the one that most people would be able to identify with.

Associated employer…

The Equality Act provides a definition of an associated employer at s.79(9), where it is stated that for the purposes of a comparable worker, employers are associated if:

(a) one is a company of which the other (directly or indirectly) has control, or

(b) both are companies of which a third person (directly or indirectly) has control.

This clearly indicates that determining whether employers are associated will ultimately depend on the relationship between two companies. Where one is capable of having a controlling influence over the other, or where there is a third party company which has the powers to control the two companies which employ the complainant and proposed comparator respectively, then this provision will be satisfied. Determining the relationship between companies will require consideration of the company documents.

Common terms apply…

There is no great need to consider the part relating to being employed at the same establishment as this is pretty straightforward, and one that should not cause any problems. However, there are some interesting cases in relation to the employment at different establishments where common terms and conditions are present which provide some useful guidance as to what the courts will take into account when determining whether a comparator is suitable or not.

British Coal Corporation v Smith[25] concerned a claim by some 1,200 canteen workers and cleaners across a number of different establishments, who were claiming an equalisation of pay with 150 workers who were either surface mineworkers or in clerical posts. On these facts it is clear that the claimants and the selected comparators were not employed at the same

---

[25] *British Coal Corporation v Smith* [1996] ICR 515.

establishment. However, the terms and conditions of the applicants and the selected comparators were governed under a national agreement that covered all of the workers who were party to these proceedings. Despite a number of variations in the terms of conditions, attributable to the different locations of the workers, the House of Lords held that they were suitable comparators and that the terms and conditions need not be identical, but only had to be "on a broad basis, substantially comparable". So the fact that the terms and conditions were subject to this national agreement with only slight differences mainly based on location did not prevent a claim arising. The important point being the common terms and conditions.

The issue of terms and conditions received similar consideration in the case of *Leverton v. Clwyd County Council*[26]. In this case a nursery nurse sought to compare herself with higher-paid clerical workers employed by the county council at a different establishment. The House of Lords reversing the earlier decision of the Court of Appeal in this case held that the clerical workers were valid comparable workers. Lord Bridge giving the leading judgment held that where there was a common collective agreement as in this case, then that would "seem to represent the paradigm, though not necessarily the only example, of the common terms and conditions contemplated by the Act."

An interesting approach to the matter of 'broadly similar terms and conditions' was adopted by the Court of Session in the case of *North v Dumfries and Galloway Council*. The case concerned female staff at a number of schools[27] across the same region, all of which were employed by the same local authority, who sought to have their roles compared with male manual workers who were also employed by the same local authority, although they worked out of depots rather than schools. When considering the matter of comparators the Court of Session indicated that in order to satisfy the need for common terms and conditions to be applied in the different establishments, the Court would have to be satisfied that if the selected comparators were transferred to the claimants' place of work, their terms and conditions would remain unchanged. As the Court was not satisfied that this would be the case the claim failed.

These cases highlight the ability of the equal pay provisions to have application in cross-establishment situations, and in this regard extend the

---

[26] *Leverton v. Clwyd County Council* [1989] IRLR 28.

[27] *North v Dumfries and Galloway Council* [2013] UKSC 45 This included a range of different positions including nursery nurses and classroom teaching assistants amongst others.

ability of the Equality Act to provide equality of pay beyond the boundaries of a singular establishment. Furthermore, the decisions above also highlight that the courts have attached a broad construction to the phrase 'common terms and conditions', which has further extended the ambit of the protection. Through adopting an approach which only requires that the terms and conditions applied in cross-establishment situations to be 'on a broad basis, substantially comparable' has ensured that the purpose of the protections can be achieved; this has avoided minor differences being capable of frustrating the equal pay protections in this context.

Although the approach of the courts can be applauded from the perspective of giving the statutory language as wide a construction as possible, the approach to a comparable worker has still been criticised for being too narrow, through the need for a common employer or associated employer. However, to enable comparisons outside of this framework across a sector would be extremely difficult to manage in practice, and thus may even be counterproductive.[28]

10.5.2. Equal Work

Equal pay protection is predicated on the need for equal pay to be provided for equal work. As with many aspects of this protection equal work has been attributed a fairly broad interpretation and is defined as covering three well-known concepts: like work, work rated as equivalent and work of equal value.[29] Each of these is a mutually exclusive concept which covers three quite different situations. Cumulatively they operate to ensure a broad ambit is given to the equal pay regime.

It is important to understand what is meant by the three distinct notions that make up equal pay, as unless the complainant can show that they undertake 'like work', 'work rated as equivalent' or 'work of equal value'

---

[28] A claim was issued on the premise that EU law enabled the selection of a worker in the same sector but not working for the same employer or associated employer as a suitable comparable worker in *Lawrence v Regent Office Care Ltd* [2002] ECR I- 7325 (Case C-320/00). However, the ECJ did not accept this approach as being covered by Article 141 (now Article 157 TFEU). Ultimately the ECJ held that the equal pay provisions did not cover such a claim as there is a need for a single source from which the pay condition is derived; without such a single source then there is no body to which responsibility for ensuring equal pay can be placed. To have decided otherwise would have been a strange result as this would have effectively bound all employers within a sector to pay that was the market norm, with no room for manoeuvre.

[29] EqA s.65

with that of the identified comparable worker then the equal pay protection will have no effect. Each of these areas is discussed below.

10.5.3. Like Work

The most obvious way of claiming equal pay is by showing that the complainant is engaged on 'like work' with their selected comparator.[30] Like work is defined as being where

> [the complainant's] work and the [comparators'] is of the same or broadly similar nature, and the difference (if any) between the things she does and the things they do are not of practical importance in relation to the terms of their work.[31]

Breaking down the definition of like work it is clear that there are two things that need to be considered:
1. Are the duties that are undertaken the same or broadly the same?
2. Are the differences in duties that are identified of rel practical importance to the role?

An illustrative case that explains the idea of like work and what ought to be the focus is *Capper Pass Ltd v. Lawton*,[32] which suggests that the focus is on the task that is being completed, and that the provision should be interpreted in a broad manner so as not to defeat the purpose of the legislation. In this case, it was held that a female cook who made between 10-20 lunches for directors in their dining room was engaged in like work with two assistant male chefs who had the task of cooking a substantially larger number of meals for the remaining factory workers, they prepared some 350 meals each day. There were other differences in this case that were considered, such as that Mrs Lawton worked 40 hours per week and had no one supervising her, whereas the men worked 45 hours per week and were under the supervision of the head chef. As mentioned the EAT upheld the decision by the ET that she was engaged on like work and was thus entitled to equal pay. What the EAT said was that the work did not have to be identical, it did not have to be exactly the same, it was sufficient if it was broadly similar and the differences were not of practical importance. The EAT considered that to have decided otherwise would have seriously reduced the impact and ability of the legislation to rectify unequal pay. In this case the process and skill required to complete their

---

[30] However, such an approach as a means of achieving equal pay is almost obsolete given the obviousness of such a breach. The majority of the claims brought before the tribunal now rest on the work rated as equivalent or work of equal value approach.

[31] See EqA s.65(2)

[32] *Capper Pass Ltd v. Lawton* [1976] IRLR 366

respective duties was found to be essentially the same. This highlights an extremely broad approach which will be adopted by the tribunals and courts when considering whether work will be deemed like work.

In *Capper Pass* the issue of 'practical importance' was also considered, highlighting the two-pronged aspect to the definition of like work. Where the employer can show that the differences were of practical importance in relation to the terms and conditions of employment then the applicant will not be found to be engaged on like work with her selected comparator. The case law appears to suggest that 'practical importance' can be considered across three broad themes:

1. Where different duties exist
2. Where different hours are worked
3. Where there are different responsibilities

Different Duties

In *Shields v E Coomes (Holdings) Limited*[33] the issue of practical importance was considered from the perspective of different duties. This case concerned the employment of staff in the respondent's betting shop. The applicant was paid 62p per hour, whereas her male counterparts were paid £1.06 per hour. The employer claimed that this was due to the different duties involved, in particular, the men acted as security if trouble were to break out. As the men had never been called upon to perform any security function, the CA held that the jobs were essentially the same. It was expressed that the focus ought to be on the practical reality of the role and not on the bare contractual obligations. The CA was ensuring that employers were not able to avoid equal pay protection through simply inserting sham clauses into a contract, which on paper at least would suggest different roles. The CA provided useful guidance in *Coomes* and stated that there ought to be an examination and assessment of the nature and extent of any differences, and account must be taken of the frequency with which any such differences occur. This is now contained at s.65(3), where in determining 'of practical importance' it is necessary to have regard to—

(a) the frequency with which differences between their work occur in practice, and
(b) the nature and extent of the differences.

---

[33] *Shields v E Coomes (Holdings) Limited* [1978] IRLR 263.

Different Hours

The case of *Dugdale v Kraft Foods Ltd*[34] provides a useful example of the second of the categories that makes up the 'of practical importance' part of like work, that being where males and females are employed to work different hours. In *Dugdale* the male and female parts of the workforce were found to be undertaking broadly similar work for the same employer: in essence they were all quality control workers. However, there was a contractual difference, with male workers required to work a compulsory night shift, with an option to work a Sunday morning shift. The original employment tribunal considered that this was of practical importance, which justified the higher basic rate of pay the men received. However, the EAT, although accepting that being required to work unsocial hours could be 'of practical importance', held that this could only have effect in relation to terms connected to the unsocial hours. Unsocial hours had no impact on terms related to ordinary working hours, such as the basic rate of pay. The consequence was that when the case was remitted back to the employment tribunal a majority of the applicants in the case succeeded in their claim to have their basic rate of pay equalised to that contained within the contract of the male workers.

An important point ought to be noted in relation to different pay based on different working hours: enhanced pay that is provided to workers who do broadly similar work to a suitable comparator but work unsocial hours or in unfavourable conditions should be at a level that reflects the inconvenience of the duties but not used as a means of ensuring more favourable terms based on sex. On this point Phillips J expresses that the equal pay provisions:

> [do] not mean that men, or women, cannot be paid extra for working at night or at weekends, or at other inconvenient times; if the additional remuneration is justified by the inconvenience of the time at which it is done the claim will not succeed. For, while every contract of employment is deemed to include an equality clause, it only has to take effect so that the terms of the woman's contract shall be treated as so modified as not to be less favourable than the man's. Thus the industrial tribunal — without falling into the error of setting itself up as a wage fixing body — may adjust the woman's remuneration upon a claim by her so that it is at the same rate as the man's, discounting for the fact that he works at inconvenient hours, and she does not.[35]

---

[34] *Dugdale v Kraft Foods Ltd* [1976] IRLR 368.

[35] *National Coal Board v. Sherwin* [1978] IRLR 122.

It is important, when considering any differences in pay due to working hours, that a causative link can be identified between the difference in pay and the sex of the worker. A complainant will not succeed in an equal pay claim where the differences in pay, which is based on the working hours involved, is a consequence of the role in question rather than the sex.[36]

Different responsibilities

The issue 'of practical importance' was again considered in *Eaton Ltd v. Nuttall*[37], but this time in the context of different responsibilities. In this case the fact that a male production scheduler handled 1,200 items worth between £5 and £1,000 as opposed to the female production scheduler who handled 2,400 items of a value below £2.50 resulted in them not being engaged on like work. This difference was considered 'of practical importance' since an error on the part of the man would have resulted in greater financial consequence for the employer. The EAT can be seen to be accepting that it is correct for a tribunal to take into account the responsibilities a person has within a job when considering whether like work is being undertaken.

10.5.4. Work rated as equivalent

A second way in which the s.66 equality clause takes effect in a works contract is to show that the work of the complainant and the selected comparator is rated as equivalent. In establishing such a claim the job of the applicant must be rated as equivalent to that of the comparator following a job evaluation study. This route is based on a study undertaken in the workplace. Section 65(4) states:

(4) A's work is rated as equivalent to B's work if a job evaluation study—
    (a) gives an equal value to A's job and B's job in terms of the demands made on a worker, or
    (b) would give an equal value to A's job and B's job in those terms were the evaluation not made on a sex-specific system.
  (5) A system is sex-specific if, for the purposes of one or more of the demands made on a worker, it sets values for men different from those it sets for women.

---

[36] This can be easily identified by considering the positions of male and female workers within the two roles that are being considered for comparison. If there is equal treatment between the sexes within each role respectively, then the chances are that the differential pay treatment between the roles is as a consequence of the role itself rather than being caused by the sex of the complainant: see *Kerr v Lister & Co Ltd* [1977] IRLR 259.

[37] *Eaton Ltd v. J Nuttall* [1977] IRLR 71 EAT.

According to s.80(5) of the Equality Act and para 38 of the EHRC Code, in order to establish a claim through this route the factors of particular importance are the demands being placed on the worker in terms of effort, skill and decision-making.

A job evaluation scheme is a way of systematically assessing the relative value of different jobs, through focussing on objective criteria that is free from sex discrimination; this is a means of rectifying previous approaches by employers which placed greater value on the work undertaken by men when compared to those roles undertaken by women. Work is rated as equivalent if the jobs of both the complainant and the selected comparator have been objectively assessed as scoring the same number of points and/or as falling within the same job evaluation grade.[38] A small difference in the assessment result may or may not reflect a material difference in the value of the jobs, depending on the nature of the job evaluation exercise.

The Equality Act does not lay down any detailed requirements for such a scheme but once it has been carried out there is a presumption that the tribunal will uphold the JES unless there are reasonable grounds for suspecting that it was discriminatory, as was stated in *Green v. Broxtowe DC*.[39]

Some guidance was offered by the EAT in the *Eaton Ltd v. Nuttall*[40] case on the issue of the JES. It was said that the scheme had to be:

> thorough in analysis and capable of impartial application. It should be possible ... to arrive at the position of a particular employee at a particular point in a particular salary grade without taking other matters into account except those unconnected with the nature of the work. It will be in order to take into account such matters as merit or seniority, etc., but any matters concerning the work (e.g. responsibility) one would expect to find taken care of in the evaluation study. One which does not satisfy that test, and requires the management to make a subjective judgment concerning the nature of the work before the employee can be fitted into the appropriate place in the appropriate salary grade, would seem to us not to be a valid study.[41]

---

[38] For an example where a female complainant's role was not evaluated as being equivalent to her male comparator but did fall within the same broad salary grade and as such was entitled to the grade in question *see Springboard Sunderland Trust v Robson* [1992] IRLR 261 (EAT).

[39] *Green v. Broxtowe DC* [1977] IRLR 34.

[40] *Eaton Ltd v. J Nuttall* [1977] IRLR 71 EAT

[41] At page 555.

Similar views are presented by the CA in *Bromley v. H & J Quick*[42]. Dillon LJ stated that:

> Sir Ralph Kilner Brown criticised the use of the word 'analytical' as a gloss on the section. In my judgment, the word is not a gloss, but indicates conveniently the general nature of what is required by the section, viz. that the jobs of each worker covered by the study must have been valued in terms of the demand made on the worker under various headings. The original application of [work rated as equivalent route] necessarily required that the woman's work and the man's should each have been valued in terms of the demand made on the worker under appropriate headings.[43]

What this effectively means is that subjective views on the nature of the work are of no relevance. In order to be considered a suitable and valid job evaluation scheme, the scheme must be analytical and objective, with scores to be attributed to objective headings that provide analysis of the roles in terms of effort, skill and decision making. Subjective schemes will be deemed inappropriate for this purpose, as will slotting a job into a pay grade on a 'whole job' basis,[44] and can lead to the tribunal to rejecting the scheme.

A point well highlighted by Cabrelli[45] is that a job evaluation scheme is not a 'precise science'. There is no formula that can simply be applied to the circumstances of a case in order to provide an answer. Tribunals are thus required to adopt a pragmatic approach when considering such schemes. Elias J (P) touches upon this point in *Bainbridge v Redcar & Cleveland BC (No. 2)*[46], when he considered job evaluation schemes in general:

> In effect there are two elements to a job evaluation study. First, there is the evaluation of the jobs; then there is the fixing of grade boundaries. These may be more or less complex. It is not uncommon for jobs to be fitted into grades where there may be real distinctions in the value of the jobs. It may be simpler for an employer to introduce pay scales which embrace a relatively wide class of jobs even although the value of the jobs at the higher end of a particular grade may be significantly higher than those lower down. That may be a pragmatic and sensible approach

---

[42] *Bromley v. H & J Quick* [1988] 2 CMLR 468.

[43] Page 478.

[44] This was considered in *Bromley*; such an approach negates to evaluate the required headings and impacts upon the transparency of the decision making.

[45] Cabrelli D. (2014), at p.538.

[46] *Bainbridge v. Redcar & Cleveland Borough Council (No.2)* [2007] IRLR 494.

> enabling the employer to select relatively simplified pay scales, even though it does not closely relate pay to value.

Obviously the approach adopted by employers will be wholly specific to their own requirements; however, the more complex an approach to pay grades adopted the more careful the evaluative analysis of roles should be.

As the wording of this statutory route suggests, it is about ensuring equal pay for roles that are deemed equivalent. It enables an assessment between roles that are, on the face of it, completely different. If following the completion of the JES the conclusion is that the two roles in question are deemed not to be equivalent, then any claim under this approach will fail. This is the obvious result where there is a large objective difference in the equivalence of the role, but also where there are small, but significant, differences in the roles.[47]

The wording of the statutory provision concerning work rated as equivalent is the main limitation attached to this approach to equal pay protection: a job evaluation scheme is not mandatory, but is a wholly dependent on the discretion of the employer. It is clear from s.65 of the Equality Act itself that this route is only available 'if' a job evaluation study gives equal value to two compared roles. However, should an employer choose not to undertake a job evaluation scheme then there will be no comparator under this equal pay route in order to maintain an action: the protection through work rated as equivalent is easily frustrated by an employer's decision not to co-operate: work of equal value effectively fills this lacuna, as discussed in more detail below.

10.5.5. Work of equal value

The third way in which the equality clause may be invoked is where the work of the complainant and the selected appropriate comparator can be shown to be doing work that is of equal value. This heading was not introduced until 1983, and resulted from the ruling of the ECJ in *EC Commisson v. United Kingdom*,[48] when it decided that the two bases of comparison (that of like work and work rated as equivalent) did not go far enough to satisfy the requirements of the Equal Pay Directive. The express requirement of the Directive was to provide equal pay for work of equal value. The more restricted approach under the EqPA would only enable an equal value in circumstances where the employer had voluntarily undertaken some form of job evaluation (such as that which forms the basis

---

[47] *Home Office v Bailey* [2005] IRLR 369.

[48] *EC Commisson v. United Kingdom* [1982] ICR 578.

of the work rated as equivalent route). That system was, therefore, extremely limited. Not only did it not provide the required scope of protection but it also arguably, may have enabled the employment of a 'token male' to evade the protections afforded under the Act. As a consequence of the judgment the UK government amended the EqPA through the Equal Pay (Amendment) Regulations 1983,[49] which inserted the new heading of 'work of equal value'.[50]

The current approach to work of equal value, which simply replicates the previous provision in the EqPA, can be seen at s.65(6) of the Equality Act, where it is stated that:

> A's work is of equal value to B's work if it is—
> (a) neither like B's work nor rated as equivalent to B's work, but
> (b) nevertheless equal to B's work in terms of the demands made on A by reference to factors such as effort, skill and decision-making.

Similar to the approach witnessed under 'work rated as equivalent', work of equal value focusses on the demands of the role, with particular reference to the factors of effort, skill and decision making. This means jobs that are completely different in nature can be assessed against one another to see whether they are of equal value; this approach has been used an awful lot in equal pay claims across councils, where manual roles have been compared with administrative positions.

Unlike under the other two headings, the employment tribunal has a greater role in determining the values of the positions in question, at least in some sense. Although not determining the values of the roles itself, the tribunal, when faced with a question of whether work is of equal value the tribunal has two options:

1. it may proceed to determine the question itself; or
2. it may require a member of the independent panel of experts to undertake an evaluation and prepare a report.[51]

If the second of these options is followed then the expert will be asked to produce a report, which will need to consider the skill, effort and tasks undertaken by the complainant and comparator in deciding whether the work is of equal value.

---

[49] SI 1983/1794.

[50] The amendment was introduced across an amended s.1 and the insertion of s.2A into the EqPA.

[51] See EqA s.131.

Interestingly, even after requesting a report to be prepared the tribunal retains the power to withdraw this requirement at any time. However, if a report is requested and not withdrawn then the tribunal will be precluded from reaching a conclusion without first receiving the report.

The report (similar to that under the 'work rated as equivalent' route) is produced as evidence; although not binding on the tribunal it is very rare to reject its conclusions. This presumption of following the report can be rebutted where either there are reasonable grounds to suggest that it was discriminatory on the grounds of sex itself, or that it is otherwise unreliable.[52]

Two cases worth considering on the issue of work of equal value are the cases of *Pickstone and Others v. Freemans plc*[53], and that of *Murphy v. Bord Telecom Eireann*[54].

In the *Pickstone* case Mrs Pickstone was employed as a warehouse operative and wanted to claim her work was of equal value to that of a warehouse checker. It was argued by the respondents that this route was not possible as there was one man doing the same work as Mrs Pickstone, and the route of work of equal value was only available when like work or work rated as equivalent does not apply. The House of Lords rejected this interpretation of the statute; although accepting that section 1(2) of the EqPA (now s.65(6) of the Equality Act) gave mutually exclusive routes to claiming equal pay, it only did so once an appropriate comparator had been selected. This is an important decision as it highlights that the courts will not allow for a token male to be employed to defeat the legislation. This also highlights that it is for the complainant to select their comparator, and it is on selecting an appropriate comparator that the route towards equal pay will also be selected. This in itself suggests that a prudent complainant may evaluate all of their options with regards potential comparators before launching a claim.

The *Murphy* case considered whether a woman would lose her equal pay claim if her work was assessed at a higher value. The courts said no, what they are looking for is that the work is of at least equal value to that of her comparator. This is certainly logical and to have decided otherwise would have devalued the protection. Such a purposive approach was clearly required in the face of such a submission by the respondent.

---

[52] See EqA s.131.

[53] *Pickstone and Others v. Freemans plc* [1989] AC 66.

[54] *Murphy v. Bord Telecom Eireann* [1988] IRLR 267.

Arguably the equal value route to equal pay provides the greatest potential to close the gender pay gap. Unlike the 'like work' route this approach is not limited to finding a comparator that is doing broadly similar work, and unlike the 'work rated as equivalent' route it does not rely on the discretion of the employer to undertake a JES. In contrast, this heading enables cross-comparisons across diverse job roles, which is primarily initiated by the complainant. The potential of the equal value route was discussed by Fredman, when she stated that:

> In one important respect, the [equal pay protection] holds out the promise of radical change. This takes the form of the principle of equal value. By penetrating job labels to examine the characteristics of women's work, the notion of equal value opens up dramatic possibilities for transcending evaluations of women's work which depend on deeply held stereotypes and entrenched inequalities in women's bargaining power. Properly handled, the concept of equal value reveals the extent to which women's work shares characteristics usually attributed only to men's work, such as heavy work and responsibility. It also requires recognition of chronically undervalued elements of women's work, such as manual dexterity and caring. As a result, a cook has been compared to a carpenter; a home help to a refuse collector and learning support assistants to painters, drivers and street cleaners.[55]

However, despite accepting the potential of this route, Fredman[56] does conclude that there are many problems with work of equal value that limits its success:

- the route is often protracted and complex;
- the report is only evidence which can be challenged; and
- the existence of a JES undertaken by the employer introduces limits to any further study that attaches relative weight to a role, unless it can be established that this initial JES itself was discriminatory or out of date.

Despite such limitations, it is still possible to say that the 'work of equal value' heading has some potential to address, at least in part, one of the factors identified that causes the gender pay gap to continue, that being job segregation. However, it must be noted that this heading does not enable complete cross-industry and cross-role comparison, as it is still limited to dealing with situations where the terms and conditions are derived from a single source (as noted above, having the same employer or associated employer, and being employed in the same establishment or different establishment where common terms and conditions apply), as well as

---

[55] Fredman, S. (2008), 'Reforming Equal Pay Laws', *Industrial Law Journal*, at pp.207-208.

[56] Page 208.

having other limitations as identified by Fredman. So although 'work of equal value' does not appear to provide all the answers, and will not be able to deal completely with situations where job segregation deflates wages, amongst other things, it does enable some success for individuals in roles that previously would not have fallen within the scope of the equal pay protections. To that extent s.65 of the Equality Act is a useful provision that acts in some way to try to ensure pay equality.

10.6.   The Genuine Material Factor Justification

Where there are contractual pay differences between what is afforded to a worker of one sex with that of a suitable comparator of the opposite sex, and it is accepted that the two parties either engage in like work, work rated as equivalent or work of equal value, the employer can still justify certain actions by showing that the different treatment was because of a genuine material factor (hereinafter 'GMF'): this justification is contained at s.69 of the Equality Act.

Interestingly, and often overlooked, is that the GMF justification operates in a very similar way to that considered under ordinary non-discrimination principles contained within the Equality Act. As with direct discrimination, direct pay discrimination cannot be justified using this justification. This is made clear by s.69(1)(a) which precludes the treating of one person less favourably because of that person's sex when compared to another person (of the opposite sex) from the scope of the justification. This clears up the uncertainty that previously surrounded the GMF under the EqPA.

The consequence of the approach under the Equality Act, of explicitly identifying a distinction between direct and indirect pay discrimination, enables a consistency of approach to flow across the Equality Act in this respect. As a result of the wording of s.69 only indirect pay discrimination can be justified. Justification of indirect pay discrimination is provided for by the remainder of s.69:

> (1)(b) if the factor is within subsection (2), is a proportionate means of achieving a legitimate aim.

> (2)   A factor is within this subsection if A shows that, as a result of the factor, A and persons of the same sex doing work equal to A's are put at a particular disadvantage when compared with persons of the opposite sex doing work equal to A's.

What this justification thus requires, in order to justify a difference in pay between a complainant and a suitable comparator, is for the employer to show that the difference in contractual entitlement was due to a material difference that was other than sex. Paragraph 76 of the EHRC's Equal Pay Code assists in explaining the operation of the GMF justification. It highlights that the employer must identify the non-sex related factor(s), as well as proving that:

- it is the real reason for the difference in pay and not a sham or pretence;
- it is causative of the difference in pay between the woman and her comparator;
- it is material: that is, significant and relevant; and
- it does not involve direct or indirect sex discrimination.

The Code effectively codifies these requirements as they were developed by the House of Lords in *Glasgow City Council v Marshall.*[57] This provides a useful framework under which the justification can be scrutinised.

Understanding the practical application of the GMF justification is vitally important in the context of equal pay, as it is often central to whether an equal pay claim succeeds or not. Often a case will ultimately be decided by whether a GMF justification can be established for two reasons:

1. Although direct pay discrimination is precluded, these in any event are rare. The majority of actions will be based on indirect pay discrimination, and as a consequence the GMF justification will be operational.

2. The reversed burden of proof under s.136 of the Equality Act has effect in relation to equal pay claims. So the same low threshold applies of merely establishing facts at which point the burden reverses. This makes it much easier for a claimant to initiate a claim and establish that a difference in pay could have been because of their sex, which then, through s.136, effectively passes the burden on to the employer to establish a GMF justification to explain why there are such differences in pay.

It is a combination of these two factors that elevate the GMF justification to being of central importance in equal pay discussions.

One thing that is clear, and albeit an obvious point to make, is that if this justification is successfully established then the equality clause will not bite and equalise the contractual terms that have been argued as less favourable due to sex. A further point worth noting is that the GMF justification is case specific (given that the employer is required to identify factor(s) specific to their own requirements), and as such each case will be determined on its individual merits. However, case law can be used to suggest a number of

---

[57] *Glasgow City Council v Marshall* [2000] IRLR 272.

established accepted practices and principles which may be applicable in future challenges.

One of the seminal cases on the GMF justification is *Rainey v Greater Glasgow Health Board,*[58] which suggests that a justification based on 'market forces' may succeed. Mrs Rainey worked as a prosthetist in the Scottish NHS, and was employed on the Physics and Technicians pay scale. Due to shortages in the workforce the NHS targeted experienced private sector prosthetists for recruitment. Their recruitment drive included an attractive salary package, with the Health Board offering commercial pay rates, which was £2,790 p.a. more than that earned by Mrs Rainey, and led to an appointed male being paid more than her. The House of Lords in these circumstances held that this difference in pay was objectively justified: market forces meant that in order to recruit from the private sector the Health Board had to offer an attractive pay structure, bearing in mind private sector pay. The materiality of the difference was expressed to be present if it was 'significant and relevant'. In reching this conclusion the House of Lords in effect followed the approach formulated in *Bilka-Kaufhaus GmbH v. Weber von Hartz,*[59] which requires the employer to show that:

- there is a real need on the part of the business for the difference;
- the difference was appropriate to achieving that end; and
- the measures are necessary to achieve that end.

If one considers the justification based on market forces carefully it is easy to see how this may have a significant impact upon equal pay protection, if not scrutinised appropriately. The labour market arguably changes on a daily basis, and as such appointments are always made when different market forces exist.[60] The key to ensuring that such a factor does not drive a horse and cart through the protections, is careful scrutiny of the

---

[58] *Rainey v Greater Glasgow Health Board* [1987] IRLR 26.

[59] *Bilka-Kaufhaus GmbH v. Weber von Hartz* [1986] IRLR 317 ECJ (Case C-170/84)

[60] Denning MR made an early attempt to limit the operation of the GMF justification in *Clay Cross (Quarry Services) Ltd v. Fletcher* [1979] ICR 1, stating that the justification ought to be limited to personal factors as to decide otherwise would lead to discrimination that existed within the market simply continuing and being replicated. This approach was overruled in *Rainey,* which expressed that justifications based on economic or administrative grounds would be permissible.

appropriateness and necessity aspect devised in *Bilka Kaufhaus*, or the proportionality aspect contained within s.69 of the Equality Act.[61]

Similarly, at European level, market forces has been accepted as a factor that can justify differences in pay. Of particular note in this regard is the judgment of the ECJ in *Enderby*, where it was expressed that

> [t]he state of the employment market, which may lead to an employer to increase the pay of a particular job in order to attract candidates, may constitute an objectively justified economic ground.

There is an obvious conclusion to make with regards market forces, and that is that it will be driven by supply and demand. This makes it fairly difficult for the equal pay provisions to impact upon gender pay differentials in skilled, highly competitive sectors. In such sectors where supply of workers is low then an employer may find it easier to introduce differences in pay and readily invoke the GMF justification to mask any such discrimination. However, it may not be so easy to utilise in lower paid and lower skilled sectors, or in times of recession, when supply is high as in such circumstances there will be less of a need to offer enhanced pay packages. From this perspective, arguably, the equal pay provisions may well be less successful in higher skilled sectors, which as a consequence have a deflationary impact on the mean average pay of females when compared to males, further perpetuating the gender pay gap.

Other practices that have been found to satisfy the GMF defence include:
- differences in pay for greater length of service (*Capper Pass Ltd v. Lawton*[62]);
- different pay rates based on locality, in particular London (*NAAFI v. Varley*[63]); and
- 'red-circling', which is the practice of relocating a long-serving employee but keeping them on the same pay (*Snoxell and Davies v. Vauxhall Motors Ltd*[64]).

---

[61] Although it is certainly questionable whether a proportionality approach offers a sufficient level of scrutiny as this appears a lower threshold than the need for necessity. Proportionality appears to require a balancing exercise between harm done and cost of alleviating harm further, whereas necessity suggests the need to appreciate all means of achieving the end need of the employer, with the least impactful measure adopted.

[62] *Capper Pass Ltd v. Lawton* [1976] IRLR 366.

[63] *NAAFI v. Varley* [1976] IRLR 408.

[64] *Snoxell and Davies v. Vauxhall Motors Ltd* [1977] IRLR 123.

- The EHRC'c Code of Practice on Equal Pay, at paragraph 77, provides the examples of personal differences such as experiences or qualifications or where the different roles involve unsocial working hours, rotating shifts or night work.

These provide at least some examples of the type of factors that will be considered legitimate aims within the GMF justification framework; however, this is far from an exhaustive list. It is open for an employer to put forward almost any reason as a factor that ought to be considered a legitimate aim, with *Bilka Haus* providing that it ought to be accepted as legitimate if the aim is something which is of real need for the business in question.

There is an interesting introduction into the Equality Act which seeks to deal with transitional arrangements in pay structures, this being found at s.69(3) of the Equality Act, which states that:

> For the purposes of [the GMF justification], the long-term objective of reducing inequality between men's and women's terms of work is always to be regarded as a legitimate aim.

The problem that this is dealing with is that which is highlighted in *Redcar & Cleveland v. Bainbridge.*[65] Where a new structure is being introduced to rectify historic pay inequality that has been discovered, it will be difficult to persuade the male portion of the workforce to accept a new structure which sees their pay decrease. So, the employer often opts to retain the male workforce on their current scheme with transitional pay schemes introduced to narrow the gap with a view to eventually having pay parity.[66]

The problem with s.69(3) is that it enables such an approach to be adopted in some circumstances and actually enables the continuing of pay disparity so long as the gap is being narrowed, with a long-term view, which is undefined,[67] of reducing the inequality. However, there is some saving grace through the phrasing of the provision in that it does not express that such an approach will always be justified, but simply that such an

---

[65] *Redcar & Cleveland v. Bainbridge* [2008] EWCA Civ 885.

[66] Often employers do not introduce a new structure immediately that places all workers on the same pay due to the costs involved, but try to alleviate the financial impact through intermediary steps which spreads the jumps in additional costs out across a period.

[67] Although arguably the views expressed in *Bainbridge* will still be relevant, in particular the acceptance that such a scheme may potentially be justified in limited circumstances, in particular where the intermediary scheme is short-term in nature.

approach will always be regarded as a legitimate aim. In other words, there will still be a requirement for the employer, in such circumstances, to establish that the transitional pay system is a proportionate means of achieving that accepted legitimate aim.[68] This safety net of proportionality acts to limit the impact of s.69(3) and ensures that employers are precluded from merely putting forward a non-determinable long-term aim of reducing inequality in pay to justify pay differentials.

10.7. Bringing a Claim

Knowledge of the pay conditions within an employer's business is often a huge limiting factor that restricts the operation of the equal pay provisions: pay and other remuneration is often viewed as a private matter, and one that very few of the workforces openly discuss. This obviously makes it difficult to know whether a colleague or a comparable worker doing like work, work rated as equivalent or of equal value is paid more. Without such knowledge it is impossible to know whether an equal pay claim exists. Furthermore, some employers even went as far as inserting clauses within their employment contracts which prevented the workforce from discussing their pay, making acquiring such knowledge even more difficult, if not impossible.

In an attempt to address the problem of gathering the requisite knowledge of differences of pay the Equality Act introduced two useful initiatives:
1. the principle of pay transparency, and
2. the right to obtain information.

10.7.1. Pay Transparency

According to the ECJ case of *Handels og Kontorfunktionaerernes Forbund i Danmark v Dansk Arbejdsgiverforening (acting for Danfoss)*,[69] where a pay system lacks transparency then there is a greater risk of it being found to be

---

[68] This in essence follows the approach adopted in *Bainbridge*, where Mummery LJ stated that: "We accept that a large public employer might be able to demonstrate that the constraints on its finances were so pressing that it could not do other than it did and that it was justified in putting the need to cushion the men's pay reduction ahead of the need to bring the women up to parity with the men. But we do not accept that that result should be a foregone conclusion. The employer must be put to proof that what he had done was objectively justified in the individual case. [para 175]".

[69] *Handels og Kontorfunktionaerernes Forbund i Danmark v Dansk Arbejdsgiverforening (acting for Danfoss)* [1989] IRLR 532.

discriminatory.[70] The ECJ in this decision in effect placed a burden on the employer to prove that a pay system is not discriminatory where it is established that the system as a whole lacks transparency when there is evidence that the average pay of women is less than that of men.[71] This rebuttable presumption is very much framed in accordance with the reversed burden of proof: the complainant needs to establish that there is some difference in average pay, and that the reasons for the difference are unclear as the pay scheme lacks transparency, at which point the burden passes to the respondent to explain that there are other reasons not associated to sex that explain the pay differential.

In order to further address the pay transparency, alongside the rebuttable presumption described above, s.77 was introduced into the Equality Act, which deemed that any terms or agreements in place with a view to preventing discussion of pay levels with trade union officials or with colleagues will not be enforceable. This enables individuals to openly discuss pay if they fit within the definition of being a relevant pay disclosure[72], and provides a route to determining differences in pay within a workplace. In order to ensure that such pay disclosure discussions are protected s.77(4) provides that seeking or making such a pay disclosure, or receiving information about a pay disclosure will be considered a protected act for the purposes of a victimisation claim. In other words, if being involved in a relevant pay disclosure leads to a person being subjected to a detriment, this detrimental treatment will be deemed victimisation.[73] This seeks to free up workers to gather pay information from colleagues and other potential suitable comparators when determining whether they may have an equal pay claim.

There is also provision within the Equality Act, under s.78, for the Secretary of State to introduce regulations which would require some businesses and employers to publish information concerning the pay levels of their workforce with the purpose of highlighting any pay differences between genders. Although this section is limited to larger employers (those

---

[70] This is supported by the ECJ decision of *Commission v France* [1988] ECR 3559, paragraph 27. (Case 318/86)

[71] Paragraph 16.

[72] Section 77(3) provides that: A disclosure is a relevant pay disclosure if made for the purpose of enabling the person who makes it, or the person to whom it is made, to find out whether or to what extent there is, in relation to the work in question, a connection between pay and having (or not having) a particular protected characteristic.

[73] See **Chapter 4.6** for a discussion of victimisation.

employing fewer than 250 employees and public sector organisations are excluded) it appears to be a useful tool that could further assist in tackling the gender pay gap. However, it is unclear what information would have to be published as this detail was left to be prescribed within any such regulations. Despite, *prima facie*, looking like a useful tool, the provision is currently redundant given that the Coalition government, when in power, opted not to bring it in to force. However, this is will all change in spring 2016 (hopefully) following a late amendment to the Small Business, Enterprise and Employment Act 2015, which inserted s.147:

> (1) The Secretary of State must, as soon as possible and no later than 12 months after the passing of this Act, make regulations under section 78 of the Equality Act 2010 (gender pay gap information) for the purpose of requiring the publication of information showing whether there are differences in the pay of males and females.
>
> (2) The Secretary of State must consult such persons as the Secretary of State thinks appropriate on the details of such regulations prior to publication.

Given that the Small Business, Enterprise and Employment Act 2015 received Royal Assent on 26 March 2015 then we can expect regulations given effect to s.78 of the Equality Act being introduced by March 2016 at the very latest. In the meantime, the voluntary system that was introduced by the Coalition Government in lieu of enacting legislation will continue to operate in this area. Employers should also be aware that Employment Tribunals are empowered to require an employer to conduct an equal pay audit when it is found in breach of equal pays or has discriminated on the grounds of sex in non-contractual pay matters.[74]

10.7.2. Obtaining Information

There is also s.138 of the Equality Act, which is of further use for workers seeking to obtain information which may shed light on their respective pay position vis-a-vis a comparable worker. This provision enables an individual who believes that they are not receiving equal pay to that of their chosen comparator can write to their employer asking for information that will help to establish whether this is the case and if so, the reasons for the pay difference. If the employer fails to answer the questions within eight weeks or chooses to answer the request in an evasive or equivocal way, an Employment Tribunal can draw an inference, including an inference that the employer is in breach of the equal pay provisions.

---

[74] This is under EqA s.139A, which was inserted into the Act following the Equality Act 2010 (Equal Pay Audits) Regulations 2014, SI 2014/2559.

10.8. Remedying Equal Pay Claims

An equal pay claim is merely a breach of a contractual term that has been modified by the implied equality clause.[75] Consequently, the remedies for equal pay claims reflect the damages that are available for a breach of contract claim.[76] In addition to compensation the tribunal may 'make a declaration as to the rights of the parties in relation to the matters to which the proceedings relate'[77] If the equality clause has acted to modify a contractual term that relates to wages within ERA s.27, then a claim may be brought in accordance with those provisions as an unauthorised deduction of wages. , then a claim may be brought in accordance with those provisions as an unauthorised deduction of wages.

It is important to first note that an equal pay claim is in effect a claim that reflects basic contract claims, as this has an impact upon the time limits that may apply, and also the award of compensation.

10.8.1. Time Limits

The Equality Act s.129 expresses limitation in the following table:

Case	Qualifying period
A standard case	The period of six months beginning with the last day of the employment or appointment.
A stable work case (but not if it is also a concealment or incapacity case (or both))	The period of six months beginning with the day on which the stable working relationship ended.
A concealment case (but not if it is also an incapacity case)	The period of six months beginning with the day on which the worker discovered (or could with reasonable diligence have discovered) the qualifying fact.
An incapacity case (but not if it is also a concealment case)	The period of six months beginning with the day on which the worker ceased to have the incapacity.
A case which is a concealment case and an incapacity case.	The period of six months beginning with the later of the days on which the period would begin if the case were merely a concealment or incapacity case.

---

[75] EqA s.66.

[76] EqA s.132(2)(b).

[77] The declaration as remedial action is considered fully at chapter 9.3.

The standard position in relation to limitation for equal pay claims is six months from the last day of employment.[78] However, there are exceptions to this rule.[79] Most notably is the extension of the limitation period where there is a case of concealment. This acts so as to protect the claim in circumstances where the employer, or other responsible person, has sought to obstruct a worker from discovering, or hide from a worker, the fact that they have received unequal pay. This is useful given the difficulty an individual may have in gathering the required evidence. However, this does not enable a complainant simply to hide their head in the sand, given that the employer can defend against the extension of time by submitting that with reasonable diligence the worker could have discovered the fact of unequal pay.

Even where the claim is out of time or at least outside of the limitation periods prescribed within s.129, *Abdullah v Birmingham City Council*.[OBJ]80of whom were outside of the strict six month tribunal time limit, and so instead sought to bring a claim in the ordinary civil courts based on a breach of a contractual term, that being the implied term of pay equality. The question that was ultimately heard by the Supreme Court was whether such an alternative course was allowed. If this route was available the claim would be subject to the longer limitation period of six years, which applies to ordinary breach of contract claims. The case itself centered on EqPA s.2[OBJ]"could more conveniently be disposed of separately by an employment tribunal". [OBJ]They were successful at first instance, with both the Court of Appeal and Supreme Court confirming the decision on appeal. In considering this matter Lord Wilson, giving the majority judgment of the Supreme Court, held that it would never be more convenient to strike out an equal pay claim brought in time in the ordinary courts when it would be time barred in an employment tribunal. [OBJ].

Something worth bearing in mind if considering bringing an equal pay claim before the ordinary civil courts is the different costs system that is in place, a matter which was highlighted by Lord Wilson in *Abdullah*. Convincing an employment tribunal to award costs at the conclusion of a hearing is notoriously difficult and is rarely awarded outside of an exceptional case, whereas before the civil courts cost orders against the losing party are relatively frequent. This opens up the possibility of

---

[78] However, each of these periods are extended to nine months where the complaint concerns the terms of service in the armed forces (EqA s.129(4)).

[79] EqA s.130 provides further explanation of what concealment and incapacity cases are.

[80] *Abdullah v Birmingham City Council* [2012] UKSC 47

economic sanctions against a complainant should they opt to bring a claim before the civil courts and not succeed; this is a risk that will need to be weighed up before advancing such a claim.

10.8.2. Compensatory Awards

The tribunal is unable to award compensation in circumstances where it is solely considered that differences in pay is an unfair practice. However, where it has been established that there are differences in pay related to gender between a complainant and a suitable comparable worker who is undertaking like work, work rated as equivalent or work of equal value then a compensatory award is likely to follow. The order for compensation generally reflects the amount that the complainant would have received had the inequality of conditions not taken place.

As originally enacted under the EqPA, there was a two year limit placed on arears that could be compensated. In other words, even had the evidenced gender pay discrimination been going on for 50 years the complainant would not be awarded full reparation of this damage, but would be limited to compensation that reflected the two year period that immediately preceded the commencement of proceedings. This limitation on compensation was challenged under European law before the ECJ in *Levez v. T H Jennings (Harlow Pools)*.[81] The ECJ, although stating that the EU principle of effectiveness was not infringed, raised the question of whether the principle of equivalence had been infringed, a question which was returned to be answered by the national court. In considering the matter the EAT[82] held that such a two year limit on arrears was not equivalent to what could be awarded under other domestic breach of contract claims, which was six years, and as such the principle was infringed. This led to the limitation being disapplied. The EqPA was amended to reflect this position, with reference to the six year limit in damages now being found at s.132(4) of the Equality Act; although this only applies to standard cases as explained below.

The Equality Act does make a distinction between a 'standard' case, a 'concealment' case and an 'incapacity' case when considering the position of damages, which appears to potentially introduce a huge difference in the level of compensation:

---

[81] *Levez v. T H Jennings (Harlow Pools)* [1999] IRLR 36.

[82] *Levez v. T H Jennings (Harlow Pools) (No.2)* [1999] IRLR 764

- A standard case is deemed to be a case that is none of the other four types of cases.[83] In such cases compensation may be awarded for the six years of losses suffered before the day on which proceedings were instituted.[84]

- In a concealment or incapacity or concealment and incapacity case the calculation of damages does not appear to have a temporal limit placed upon it, but is calculated through consideration of all losses from the day on which the breach first occurred.

- However, this is not the case where the claim is based upon work rated as equivalent following a job evaluation study ('JES'). Where such a claim is based on this route alone the compensation can only be backdated to the date on which the JES came into effect.[85]

An interesting point on compensation arose in *Enderby v. Frenchay Health Authority*,[86] with the question surrounding pay increments. It must first be acknowledged that Ms Enderby succeeded in her equal pay claim, using the route of work of equal value with a suitable comparator. A crucial difference between Ms Enderby and the comparable worker was that she had been employed with the Health Authority for some six years, whereas the comparator had only been employed for one year. When it came to compensation, it was submitted on Ms Enderby's behalf that she ought to be awarded compensation based on what the pay that the comparator would have been on had he been employed for the same period of time that she had: in other words the compensation should have been calculated using the pay the comparator would have been on had he worked for the employer for six years and consequently seen his pay increase due to annual increments over that period. The Court of Appeal rejected this argument as the equal pay provisions operated to merely award an equalisation of pay. Although unsuccessful this case highlights the importance of selecting the correct comparator, especially in pay systems that operate on an incremental basis.

Unlike compensatory awards under the ordinary discrimination principles contained within the Equality Act, claims for equal pay are limited to

---

[83] EqA s.130(2).

[84] EqA s.132(4). Although this is reduced to five years where the claim is in Scotland (EqA s.132(5)).

[85] *Bainbridge v. Redcar & Cleveland Borough Council (No.2)* [2007] IRLR 494.

[86] *Enderby v. Frenchay Health Authority* [2000] IRLR 257.

pecuniary losses only; this again reflects the contractual nature of the claim. There is no compensation for injury to feelings.[87]

As with other forms of compensation, an award is free from income tax up to £30,000.[88] The Sex Discrimination and Equal Pay (Remedies) Regulations 1993[OBJ] of the Equality Act.

10.9. Conclusions on Equal Pay

There is much to be applauded in the approach adopted in the context of equal pay protection. The system in place appears to be broad in application, and attempts to ensure that it is given a wide scope. Of particular note is the approach to the requirement of comparator, which has seen a number of purposive approaches, including: allowing the use of predecessors, enabling multiple comparators to be used to equalise different terms, and adopting a broad interpretation to the concept of 'common terms and conditions'.

However, there are weaknesses in the equal pay system that detract from the equality protection that it seeks to ensure. Most notably is the acceptance of market forces as a legitimate aim that may justify pay differences. This has great potential to cause great detriment to the protections. A further criticism lies with the system remaining wholly negative and reactive: there is very little within the equal pay provisions that moves it away from a simple formal approach to equality, and nothing that places positive obligations onto employers to truly investigate and transform their systems to ensure equality is achieved.

The relative success of the equal pay protections can be seen by the narrowing gender pay gap. However, the fact that there still remains a gender pay gap suggests that its success has been limited.

---

[87] See *City of Newcastle upon Tyne v Allen* [1995] CLY 3664.

[88] ITEPA ss.401 and 403.

11. Family Friendly Policy

11.1. Introduction

It has long been recognised that the less flexible a person is perceived to be with regards work then the less attractive they are to employers; often this translates to an offer of employment on lesser terms and conditions or even no offer at all. This negative attitude has the greatest impact on females, given that they often (although not exclusively) have the greatest role to play in family life, which can act to limit the number of hours and times that such person may be willing to work, or will make themselves available for work. Furthermore, adding to this negative position adopted by some employers, pregnancy and child birth may also have an impact upon the flexibility of a female worker. However, this has the further factor of additional associated costs, which are generally as a consequence of having to fund a replacement to cover work that a pregnant worker is no longer able to fulfil.[1] All of these different factors can impact upon the position of a female worker in the workplace, often to their detriment. The impact is further exacerbated when one considers that some employers may act in a manner to ensure that they are not 'inconvenienced' by family responsibilities or childbirth by simply having a preference towards male workers, or those that have given the impression of not desiring a family. It is often the preconceived idea that a female worker will be inflexible because of family life commitments, whether a particular worker is or not, that leads to the disadvantageous position that they find themselves in.

The UK has developed a number of family friendly policies that are aimed at ensuring that certain periods of time away from the workplace and certain responsibilities that are consequential to family life and pregnancy do not lead to unequal treatment. These policies can be considered methods aimed at attaining substantial equality as they appreciate the different needs and characteristics of particular groups (in the main females) and try to take account of these differences when considering their treatment. There is a range of different policies that fall within the category of family friendly policies. This chapter will consider the operation of:

- maternity rights, alongside shared maternity rights
- paternity rights
- parental leave rights, and
- flexible working rights.

---

[1] For example, a pregnant worker's role may be limited on health and safety grounds, or may be away from the work place for antenatal classes or may have recently given birth.

Each of these different areas of family friendly policy has an important role to play in ensuring that there is a balance between family life and work life, which is not to the detriment of an individual's career. It tries to ensure that individuals are not marginalised in the workplace for having commitments elsewhere. This in effect tries to safeguard women who are having a child, have had a child, or may have a child from being treated less favourably as a result.

Importantly, family friendly policies are not solely about women in the workplace, but offer protection to men too. Furthermore, developments which strengthen and assist in supporting the role that men play within the family can also be viewed as a means of attacking the perception that family life is the exclusive domain of women, which is often the underlying basis from which less favourable treatment stems. In this respect the introduction of shared parental leave may have some cause for celebration in that it acknowledges the primary role of both parents in the upbringing of a child in the formative year(s), or during the initial year of placement, but it also shares the 'burden', meaning that employer's may no longer be able to point to one particular sex as the bearer of additional costs and inconvenience. In theory, male workers will be equally likely to take up to 50 weeks leave, or at least it will be a distinct possibility. Whether shared parental leave is capable of impacting upon this perception will be wholly dependent on the success of these regulations.

It is important to note that this is one area of UK employment law in which Europe plays a key role, in particular through decisions relating to the Pregnant Workers Directive. It is therefore important not just to know about developments in the UK, but developments on a European level are also vital.

This chapter now turns to consider each of these important areas of protection, discussing how each works alongside their relative strengths and weaknesses.

11.2.   Right to Request Flexible Working

Given the move towards a flexible workplace being evident across the UK and Europe in the 1990s it was of little surprise when a new right to request flexible working was introduced through the Employment Act 2002, which inserted ss.80F-80I into the ERA. However, it is worth making clear from the outset that these new provisions have not given anybody a right to adopt a flexible working arrangement, but merely the right, in certain circumstances, to request that their current contract of employment be altered.

The right to make the request was initially limited in some respect, and was only available to:

- employees who have parental responsibility for a child under the age of 17, or 18 where the child is disabled or where the employee has caring responsibilities for a near relative or somebody who lives at the same address as the employee who is over the age of 18; and
- those employees who have worked continuously for their employer for at least 26 weeks at the time that the request is made.

However, as from 30 June 2014, this right to make a request was extended to all employees through the Children and Families Act 2014, extending the right considerably. The application itself needs to be in writing and it needs to provide information on the type of change requested, when any such change would come into effect, as well as detailing the effect that the change may have on the employer's business alongside any solutions.

There is one important time period that both the employer and employee will need to be aware of during this process and that is whether the employer agrees to the variation or not the employee must be informed of the decision within what is termed the 'decision period'[2].

It still appears there is a need to hold some form of meeting with the employee to discuss an employee's application application for flexible working, as there is reference to the application being deemed to be withdrawn where "the employee without good reason has failed to attend both the first meeting arranged by the employer to discuss the application and the next meeting arranged for that purpose"[3]. However, confusion is caused by the relevant provisions of ERA s.80G having been repealed by Children and Families Act 2014 s.132. Due to this a prudent employer would be unlikely to breach their obligation by simply complying with the time limits that were set down in ERA s.80G before amendments were introduced, and these are as follows:before amendments were introduced, and these are as follows:

- If the employer is not in agreement with the written request then he is obliged to hold a meeting with the employee within 28 days of the request in order to discuss the matter further.

---

[2] ERA s.80G(1)(aa), with the decision period being the three month period that begins on the date that the application is made, or a longer period if the two parties agree to extend it: s.80G(1B).

[3] ERA s.80G(1D)(a).

- Following the meeting the employer has 14 days in which to notify the requesting employee of their decision.

- An acceptance leads to a variation of the contract, whereas a refusal must be provided with reasons.

Key behind this right is that there is a statutory obligation that once flexible working is requested by an eligible employee then the employer is duty bound to consider the application, with a right of appeal should the request not be acceded to. If the employee elects to appeal a refused request then the employer must hold the appeal meeting within 14 days of the decision being received, with a requirement to provide the employee with the outcome of the appeal within 14 days of the appeal meeting. The employee is entitled to be accompanied by a fellow employee at the appeal meeting. As one can appreciate the whole process is kept within a narrow time period.

There are no boundaries as to what flexible working entails. It is a matter of negotiation between employer and employee as to what type of arrangement is needed and what type of arrangement is possible within the business structure. In the majority of cases this will focus on the place of work (maybe allowing the employee to work from home at particular times), reduction of working hours, allowing a flexitime arrangement or enabling a role to become a job-share. It is important to note that if an agreement is reached then the change becomes a permanent change to the contract of employment, and as such both the employee and employer must think carefully before agreeing to arrangement. It would be more prudent when reaching an agreement to agree that the flexible working arrangement is on a trial period initially, which would then enable a move back to the original contractual position should the flexible arrangement not satisfy the employee's needs.

ERA s.80Gmakes it clear that employers must deal with the application in a reasonable manner[OBJ][4] it considers that one or more of the following grounds applies:

    (i)   the burden of additional costs,
    (ii) detrimental effect on ability to meet customer demand,
    (iii) inability to re-organise work among existing staff,
    (iv) inability to recruit additional staff,
    (v) detrimental impact on quality,
    (vi) detrimental impact on performance,

---

[4] This is the new ERA s.80G(1)(a) which was introduced following the Children and Families Act 2014.

(vii) insufficiency of work during the periods the employee proposes to work,

(viii) planned structural changes, and

(ix) such other grounds as the Secretary of State may specify by regulations.

As one can appreciate from the wording of section 80G this is an exhaustive list of reasons that can justify a decision to refuse a request. However, the ambit of the reasons as a collective is such that it leaves the employer with an awful lot of discretion in deciding whether to grant or reject a request. Further tipping the decision making process into the hands of the employer is that the employer need only find that one of the grounds listed above apply. Given the range of the reasons and the need to only find that one of them apply in order to justify refusing an application could lead to a decision being made by an employer before then searching for the reason that justifies it.

If a request is rejected and any subsequent appeal unsuccessful, the employee loses the right to make a statutory request for a period of 12 months. However, simply not being able to do so under statute does not preclude any informal application being made. As with much of the employment arrangement, the employer and employee can reach a suitable private arrangement between them, with a view to agreeing to change to their contract. Simply not having the right does not mean that an employer will not try to accommodate any such requests.

A failure by the employer in their duty, or where there is an unreasonable rejection of the request for flexible work, the employee can present a claim before the employment tribunal within three months of the failings. If the tribunal finds in favour of the employee it can make a declaration to that effect and order the employer to reconsider the application, as well award compensation that is just and equitable in the circumstances. This compensation is capped at a maximum of eight weeks wages of the employee. An additional two weeks compensation may be awarded if the employer refuses the employee's request to be accompanied at either the meetings where the application is discussed or any subsequent appeal meeting.

This will be replaced by a duty to consider all requests in a reasonable manner, with refusals being based on business grounds.

In effect these changes will not only widen the access to this right but it will also require the employer to provide fully developed business reasons behind any refusal, rather than simply being able to rely on a pre-set statutory reason.

11.3.   Maternity, Paternity and Adoption Rights

11.3.1. Maternity Rights

There are a number of rights that fall under the overarching maternity rights protection, the most recognisable being maternity leave; however, the rights do extend beyond this to include certain health and safety protections as well as periods of time away from the workplace pre-birth. It is important to note that rights in relation to maternity are only provided to those persons that have actually been pregnant and given birth, and thus do not extend to those who become a mother through a surrogacy arrangement.[5] This chapter will first turn to consider the 'other protections' that are provided to those employees that are pregnant before turning to the well-recognised right of maternity leave that is provided following birth.

Health and Safety Protection

When the Pregnant Worker Directive was introduced at European level the key underlying aim was to provide protection to pregnant workers on health and safety grounds. Although on the face of it it appears to be a form of social protection or even an equality instrument, the reality is that it was primarily introduced to ensure both mother and unborn child was offered a level of protection against harm at a period of time when they were vulnerable, and where such harm if incurred could be devastating.

As a consequence of the Pregnant Worker Directive the UK introduced a requirement under the Management of Health and Safety at Work Regulations 1999 (MHSWR) that the employer carried out a suitable risk assessment which had to assess risks to the health and safety at work of new or expectant mothers. This covers a range of individuals from those who are currently pregnant, who have given birth within the previous six months or who are currently breastfeeding.

There are particular circumstances where the risk assessment is of upmost importance, with the most notable, and given specific reference to under the regulations, is where the workforce has women of childbearing age who are involved in work which could involve risk to the health and safety to a new or expectant mother, or to that of her baby, from any processes or

---

[5] The CJEU in considering this matter in *CD v ST* [2014] ECR I-000, (C-167/12) held that an employer's refusal to provide maternity leave to a commissioning mother would not be considered an act of sex discrimination contrary to the Equal Treatment Directive; interestingly, this is in contrast to the Opinion of Advocate General Kokott.

working conditions, or from physical, biological or chemical agents[6] then the employer shall carry out a risk assessment.[7] It is important to note the use of the word 'shall' rather than 'may'. This requirement to carry out a risk assessment is thus, on the face of it, obligatory. A failure to comply with this requirement could amount to direct sex discrimination[8] or even a repudiatory breach of the employment contract which would enable constructive dismissal[9].

The obligation to undertake a second risk assessment (in addition to the general risk assessment for the entire workforce where some are female and of child bearing age, noted above) arises the moment the employer has knowledge that a particular employee is pregnant. Knowledge is an obvious prerequisite that starts this process. This risk assessment needs to focus solely on the pregnant employee in question, and needs to identify any such risks as well as any measures that can be taken in order to reduce that risk. The risk to employee can come in any form from prolonged standing, to long hours to physical risks of harm. If measures can be taken that avoid the risk then these must be adopted. However, if measures are not available that avoid the recognised risk then the pregnant employee should be offered alternative employment or put on a period of paid leave[10]. The duty to avoid risks is not a duty placed on the employer to completely eliminate all risks to the pregnant employee, as this simply would not be possible. Instead the requirement is to reduce the risk to the lowest acceptable level[11].

The obligation on the employer, from a health and safety perspective, becomes more explicit when the work involved is night work, with the requirement to suspend the employee on maternity grounds coming into

---

[6] A list of agents that need specific attention are listed in Annexes I and II of the Directive 92/85/EEC. Also important to be aware of is the biological agents that are contained within the Biological Agents Directive (90/679/EEC).

[7] Regulation 16 MHSWR.

[8] *Hardman v. Mallon* [2002] IRLR 516. However, in *O'Neill v Buckinghamshire County Council* [2010] IRLR 384 the EAT qualified this somewhat by deciding that the requirement to carry out a risk assessment for pregnant workers is only obligatory where there is some evidence to suggest that the work involves a risk to the health and safety of the expectant mother.

[9] *Bunning v GT Bunning & Sons Ltd* EAT/0136/03.

[10] ERA s.67 and Reg 16(3) Maternity etc Regs.

[11] *New Southern Railway Ltd v. Quinn* [2006] IRLR 266. However, this can be contrasted with the explicit position contained within the Pregnant Workers Directive which contains an absolute prohibition of exposure to certain risks.

effect if a certificate from a medical practitioner or registered midwife specifies that night work would be detrimental to the employee's health or safety if carried out during a prescribed period.[12] Before suspension, as above, the employer ought to first consider any suitable alternative employment that she can be offered. A point of not for employers who seek to transfer a pregnant employee to alternative work: if the alternative work is employment on terms that are considerably less favourable than those that she was employed on previously then this may be viewed as subjecting a pregnant employee to a detriment contrary to ERA s.47C.

Maternity suspension pay is provided for under ERA s.68, which makes it clear that such pay should be paid at the same rate that the employee would have been paid had they remained working. In other words, the employee continues to receive the same weekly wage or hourly rate that they would have received had the maternity suspension not taken place.

It is easy to appreciate from the approach that the employer has to take, that the health and safety of a pregnant employee is prioritised over everything else, and certainly ensures that a female is not dissuaded from entering the workplace based on any perceived risks that they may face in the event of becoming pregnant.

Antenatal Classes

Section 55-57 of the ERA provides for time off for antenatal care, and offers protection to those who take such time off. An employee from day one of employment has the right no to be unreasonably refused time off work to attend antenatal care where it has been arranged on the advice of a registered medical practitioner, registered midwife or registered health visitor. An important point to note is that this right is only provided to employees.

There is a need to provide some documentary evidence of the antenatal appointment.

Such leave is paid at the same hourly rate that the pregnant employee would ordinarily be paid.[13] Unreasonable refusal on behalf of the employer, or if the employer fails to pay for the time taken off for antenatal purposes will provide the affected employee with a cause of action before the tribunal, which must be commenced within three months of the date of

---

[12] ERA s.66.

[13] ERA s.56.

the appointment affected.[14] The tribunal, if it finds that the employer has not complied with ERA ss.55, will make a declaration to that effect and award her compensation that reflects the remuneration wo which she was entitled.[15] ERA ERA s.57, it is not limited solely to remuneration that would have been received, but enables compensation to be awarded for injury to feelings.

Maternity Leave

Maternity leave is made up of three separate periods:

1. **Compulsory maternity leave.**[16] It is a criminal offence for an employer not to ensure that a pregnant worker is not working in the two weeks immediately after the childbirth.[17] This is increased to four weeks where the employee is a factory worker.[18]

2. **Ordinary maternity leave (OML).** All pregnant employees are entitled to take 26 weeks OML. There is no length of service qualification for this right.

3. **Additional maternity leave (AML).** All women workers are entitled to a further period of 26 weeks AML once they have come to the end of their OML period. There is no length of service qualification for this right.

Ordinary Maternity Leave and Additional Maternity Leave

The position with regards OML and AML is contained within the Maternity and Parental Leave etc Regulations 1999. Up until amendments in 2008 there was a practical distinction in relation to maintenance of terms and conditions depending on which period of leave an employee was on. However, there is little difference today, other than in relation to the right to return to work (which is discussed below) and in relation to accrual of pension rights. Aside from these two minor differences the two periods of leave operate in almost an identical manner.

---

[14] This time limit may be extended by the Tribunal.

[15] ERA s.57.

[16] Compulsory maternity leave is provided for at ERA s.72.

[17] Childbirth is defined as either the birth of a living child, or a living or dead child after 24 weeks of pregnancy. This requirement is contained at ERA s.72(5), which states that if an employer contravenes this subsection then they will be liable on summary conviction to a fine not exceeding level 2 on the standard scale.

[18] Public Health Act 1936, s.205; Factories Act 1961, Sch. 5. If an employer contravenes this requirement then they will be liable on summary conviction to a fine not exceeding level 1 on the standard scale.

Qualifying

All pregnant employees are entitled to 26 weeks OML and 26 weeks AML from the day their contract of employment commences. There is no distinction based on working time, and so part-time employees have the same entitlement, and similarly there is no distinction between permanent staff and fixed-term or limited term employees. However, it is clear from the Regulations that the individual seeking this right must be an employee. As such the individual will need to be engaged through a contract of service, and will need to satisfy the Ready Mixed Concrete multiple test, which is expressed by MacKenna J as being:

> A contract of service exists if the following three conditions are fulfilled:
> (i)   The servant agrees that in consideration of a wage or other remuneration he will provide his own work and skill in the performance of some service for his master.
> (ii) He agrees expressly or impliedly that in the performance of that service he will be subject to the other's control in sufficient degree to make that other master.
> (iii) The other provisions of the contract are consistent with its being a contract of service.[19]

Aside from the requirement of being an employee, and that the individual is not employed in a excluded category, which includes, the armed forces, shared fisherwomen and members of the constabulary, the only requirement that needs to be satisfied to qualify for OML and AML concerns the giving of notice.

In order to comply with the notice requirements the employee is required to notify their employer at least 21 days before the date on which she intends to start OML, or where that is not reasonably practicable, as soon as is reasonably practicable.[20] The notice needs to inform the employer of three pieces of information: that she is pregnant, the expected week of childbirth, and the date on which she intends to start her OML.[21] There is

---

[19] Unfortunately this is far as this text can take the discussion concerning employee status. However, it suffices to say that satisfying this test is not as straightforward as it ought to be. In the majority of cases this will not cause a problem. For further understanding of how the test for employee status works see: Leighton, P. and Wynn, M. (2011), 'Classifying employment relationships- more sliding doors or a better regulatory framework?', *Industrial Law Journal*, Volume 40(1), pp. 5-44.

[20] Maternity and Parental Leave etc Regulations 1999 s.4(1)(a).

[21] The earliest OML can begin is from the date of the beginning of the eleventh week before the expected week of childbirth: Maternity and Parental Leave etc Regulations 1999 s.4(2)(b).

no requirement for the notice to be in writing, unless it requested to be so by the employer,[22] although ordinarily it would be wise to ensure that a written request is made just in case a dispute arises. Although not an automatic requirement, a pregnant employee will have to produce a certificate for inspection from either a registered medical practitioner or a registered midwife stating the expected week of childbirth if it requested by the employer.[23]

Although in most cases the OML will begin on the date stated within the notice given by the pregnant employee to her employer, there are three situations which may require this date to be changed. First, there may be an enforced variation to the date, which happens where an employee is absent from work wholly or partly because of pregnancy after the beginning of the sixth week before the expected week of childbirth[24]. Secondly, a variation of the start date of OML is also permitted where the employee gives her employer at least eight weeks' notice, or where it is not reasonably practicable to give such notice, as soon as is reasonably practicable. However, and an obvious point, this date cannot be varied to a date that is before the beginning of the eleventh week before the expected week of childbirth. Whereas the third situation provides for OML to commence where neither of the other two variations discussed above has taken place but childbirth occurs.[25] AML is much less complicated, as this is simply taken to commence on the day after the last day of OML.[26]

There is a notification requirement placed on to the employer once the employee complies with their notification obligation: the employer is required to inform the employee, within 28 days of receiving notice as described above, the date on which AML, if taken, will come to an end. An employee is protected against any detriment[27] or dismissal[28] action for returning late to work if the employer fails in this duty.

Once the notification requirements are complied with, a pregnant employee can be said to qualify for OML and AML. The importance of this is the protections that then follow. In particular, this comes in the form of

---

[22] Maternity and Parental Leave etc Regulations 1999 s.4(2)(a).

[23] Maternity and Parental Leave etc Regulations 1999 s.4(1)(b).

[24] Maternity and Parental Leave etc Regulations 1999 s.6(1)(b).

[25] Maternity and Parental Leave etc Regulations 1999 s.6(2).

[26] Maternity and Parental Leave etc Regulations 1999 s.6(2).

[27] Maternity and Parental Leave etc Regulations 1999 s.19.

[28] Maternity and Parental Leave etc Regulations 1999 s.20.

protection against a detriment or dismissal, and in some cases even preferential treatment, most notably in redundancy situations. However, there are also health and safety requirements that need to be considered, as there is a strict requirement to ensure that expectant and new mothers have their health and safety protected over and above the ordinary workforce.

Terms and conditions

When a pregnant employee is away from the workplace on OML or AML they are to be treated, in respect of their terms and conditions, as if they were not away on maternity leave. This in effect means that the contract of employment continues in the same way during maternity leave as it was during normal working conditions. The only exception to this normal operation of terms and conditions is with respect remuneration, which is discussed further below. What this means is that all terms and conditions, other than those relating to remuneration, must be maintained in the normal way. This means anything, such as medical insurance, company cars, gym memberships, or anything else that the pregnant employee was entitled to before going off on maternity leave must continue to be provided. Terms and conditions relating to bonuses and commissions are trickier, with anything that is described as remuneration not being maintained. However, if the bonus or commission is for a reason that falls outside of the concept of remuneration then this must also be maintained. One thing that is clear though, following the ECJ decision in *Lewen v. Denda*,[29] is that where maternity leave commences midway through a period in which a bonus is determined, the employee is entitled to a portion of the bonus, with a deduction made for the period spent away from the workplace.[30] There is also a restriction on taking paid holiday leave during maternity leave,[31] irrespective of how much leave a pregnant employee has accrued. This is fairly obvious given that paid holiday leave provides a period of rest with the maintenance of remuneration, whereas remuneration is not maintained during maternity leave, and furthermore maternity leave is not a holiday!

---

[29] *Lewen v. Denda* [2000] IRLR 67.

[30] Although this at first glance appears to be treating a pregnant employee less favourable, it was accepted as not being sex discrimination in *Hoyland v. Asda Stores Ltd* [2006] IRLR 468, since the deduction related to an aspect of remuneration. However, if the entirety of the bonus was removed due to maternity leave taking place at some point during a period in which a bonus was calculated then this would clearly be sex discrimination, as this would be reducing remuneration across a period where maternity leave had not commenced too.

[31] *Merino Gomez v Continental Industrias del Caucho* [2004] 2 CMLR 38 (Case C-342/01).

Regulation 17 of the Maternity and Parental Leave etc Regulations 1999 lays down the position in relation to terms and conditions during AML. This expresses that an employee on AML will still benefit from the implied duty of mutual trust and confidence placed on the employer, and will benefit from the terms and conditions of her employment which relate to notice periods, redundancy payments and disciplinary grievance procedures. The employee remains bound by the implied duty of good faith and she must comply with notice periods, confidentiality, terms and conditions relating to the acceptance of gifts or other benefits, or the participation in any other business.

Maternity Pay

There are in reality two different sources of maternity pay: contractual and statutory. As with most substantive employment rights employers are free to negotiate with their workforce a term in a contract of employment that deals with maternity pay.[32] So, often the first place to check with regards the provision of maternity pay is the contract of employment. If this provides for maternity pay then compliance with term is needed. However, there is a statutory fall-back position for circumstances where no such term has been negotiated.

Statutory maternity pay (SMP) was introduced by the Statutory Maternity Pay contributions. There are a number of qualifications that need to be satisfied in order to be eligible for SMP:national insurance contributions. There are a number of qualifications that need to be satisfied in order to be eligible for SMP:

- The employee must be an 'employed earner'. It is important to note that this is not referring to employee status, but covers those individuals whose earnings attract a liability for employer's Class 1 National Insurance contributions.
- There is a need to have been continuously employed for a minimum of 26 weeks before the 15th week before the expected week of confinement. This applies to all workers, with working hours not impacting upon this continuous service requirement.
- There is also an earnings threshold. She must earn at least equal to the lower earnings limit at which national insurance contributions are payable. The figure is updated annually, with the current lower earnings limit being £112 per week, as from April 2015.
- A medical certificate needs to be produced containing information on the expected week of confinement. This should also provide

---

[32] Although this must not be lower than the statutory scheme.

     information to the employer of the date when she expects maternity
     pay to become payable, and should provide at least 28 days' notice.
- The employee does not work during maternity leave.

If all of these qualifications are met then the employee is entitled to SMP. Interestingly, SMP is only payable for a portion of the potential 52 weeks that make up maternity leave (if one adds OML and AML together), with it being paid across the first 39 weeks of the leave. The amount of SMP differs across two periods of the maternity leave. The first period covers the initial six week of maternity leave. SMP during this period is directly related to the earnings of the employee, and will be paid at a rate equivalent to 90% of the employee's average weekly earnings. The second period of 33 weeks is paid at the statutory rate, which is currently set at £139.58 or at 90% of the employee's average weekly earnings if this is lower. The level of maternity pay was challenged in *Gillespie v. Northern Ireland Health and Social Board*[33], where Ms Gillespie submitted that 'but for' her pregnancy she would have continued to receive full pay rather than the lower statutory maternity pay, and thus to pay anything other than full pay during maternity leave would be discrimination because of pregnancy. The ECJ disagreed with Ms Gillespie and held that rates of maternity pay were a matter for national legislatures, so long as the level was not so low as to defeat the purposes of maternity leave. It is important to note that SMP is still pay for all purposes, and as such it will still be subject to tax and NI deductions as well as any other lawful deductions, which may include, for example, pension contributions.

Employers must also be vigilant in ensuring that the correct level of SMP is paid, especially in sectors where pay increments are an annual occurrence. It is not simply the case that SMP is calculated in advance of maternity leave being taken or at the beginning. Any changes to pay that would have taken place had the employee not been absent from work on maternity leave must also be taken into account[34]. Where there is a miscalculation in the award of SMP an employee has up to six years from the date in which the miscalculation took place in order to seek recovery before the courts.[35]

Maternity Allowance

Not all women will qualify for SMP: they may not be deemed an employed earner or they will not earn enough to satisfy the earnings threshold. In

---

[33] *Gillespie v. Northern Ireland Health and Social Board* [1996] IRLR 214, ECJ (Case C-342/93).

[34] Statutory Maternity Pay (General) Regulations Reg. 21(7)

[35] *Alabaster v. Woolwich Bank* [2005] IRLR 576.

such circumstances she will not receive SMP, but instead will receive a replacement form of remuneration in the shape of Maternity Allowance (MA), which is paid directly to the employee by the Department of Work and Pensions. In order to qualify for MA the employee must provide evidence to the DWP that:

- She is pregnant and has reached the beginning of the eleventh week prior to the expected week of confinement
- She has worked as either an employed earner but does not qualify for SMP, or works as a self-employed earner and pays Class 2 National Insurance contributions, for at least 26 weeks out of the 66 weeks that take place immediately before the expected week of confinement. There is no need to establish continuous service of any kind.
- She has had average weekly earnings that at least equal the MA threshold over any 13 week period selected from the 66 weeks before the expected week of confinement. The threshold is currently set at £30 a week.

If an employee is eligible for MA in accordance with the criteria above then she will receive MA for 39 weeks of either £139.58 per week (the figure as from April 2015) or 90 of her average weekly earnings, whichever is lowest.

There is a further category of MA for those individuals who do not qualify using the requirements listed above. There is also limited provision of MA of 14 weeks if for at least 26 weeks in the 66 weeks before her baby is due:

- she is married or in a civil partnership;
- she is not employed or self-employed;
- she takes part in the business of her self-employed spouse or civil partner;
- the work she does is for the business and unpaid;
- her spouse or civil partner is registered as self-employed with HM Revenue and Customs (HMRC) and pays Class 2 National Insurance;
- her spouse or civil partner is working as a self-employed person; and
- she is not eligible for Statutory Maternity Pay or the higher amount of Maternity Allowance (for the same pregnancy).

In these circumstances MA is paid at £27 per week for up to 14 weeks.

Reasonable contact and keep in touch days
Although in the norm an employee on OML or AML is effectively on leave from the workplace, there is provision for reasonable contact by the

employer with the employee during these periods.[36] The key term is obviously 'reasonable'. This can be used for a range of reasons, including:

- letting the employee know of training and promotion opportunities;
- giving workplace information that affects the employee; or
- discussing matters relating to her return to work.

In addition Regulation 12A enables the employee to agree to undertake up to ten working days during the statutory maternity period. This does not mean work in the purest sense, but can include relevant training or other activities that is useful for keeping the employee in touch with the workplace, so long as it can be viewed as something that the employee may do as part of their employment. In both cases, reasonable contact and keep in touch days, maternity leave continues as normal. It is also important to note that where the employee refuses contact during maternity leave they are protected against suffering a detriment.

Returning to work

As alluded to at the beginning of this section there is a distinction between returning to work following (or during) a period OML *or* AML.

On returning to work following OML the returning employee is entitled to return to her old job with seniority and pension accrual being as it would have been had she not taken a period of leave, and on terms and conditions which are not less favourable than those that she was on before she took OML. OML counts as continuous service for any rights or benefits that are dependent on length of service, and so will be included in any calculation for notice periods, unfair dismissal and redundancy rights, as well as contractual benefits such as pay increments. If the employer refuses to employ a returning employee in the same job that they occupied before OML then this may be considered to be an unfair dismissal, as well as being an act of direct discrimination. There are two exceptions to this general position:

1. If the employee has two or more consecutive periods of statutory leave,[37] each of which lasts more than four week, then in the event of the same job not being available for her to return to, and there has not been a redundancy situation, then the returning employee ought to be offered a suitable alternative role.

---

[36] Maternity and Parental Leave etc Regulations 1999 s.12A.

[37] Statutory leave includes OML, AML, ordinary adoption leave, additional adoption leave and parental leave.

2. If there is a redundancy situation during maternity leave (this is also the case following AML), and it is not practicable to continue to employ the employee on maternity leave on her existing contract, she ought to be offered a suitable alternative role on a contract that is not substantially less favourable,[38] with this contract taking effect immediately on the ending of the previous contract. It will be deemed automatically unfair dismissal if an employer in these circumstances fails to offer a suitable vacancy to an employee on maternity leave.[39] The ordinary rules concerning redundancy exist, as such if a suitable alternative role is offered to the employee and this is unreasonably refused then she will lose her right to redundancy payment.[40]

The position following AML is similar to that described above in relation to returning to work following OML. The employee is also entitled to return to work in the same role that she occupied before she took leave, and her seniority amongst other things again must be maintained as if she had not been absence, and likewise she must be engaged on terms and conditions that are not less favourable to those which she was engage don before she took maternity leave. Another similarity is that the period of AML, as with OML, will count towards her continuous service, and thus will form the calculation for rights and benefits that have a continuous service requirement. However, there are two exceptions to this rule:

1. Pension accrual is suspended during AML. During AML the employee will not accrue pension under an employment-related benefit scheme. Instead this whole period will be discounted, with her pension being calculated simply as if this period did not exist. In other words, the period before AML and the period after AML are pushed together and treated as if they were a continuous period of time.

2. Outside of a redundancy situation, if it is not reasonably practicable for an employee to return to her previous role following AML, then she ought to be offered a suitable and appropriate alternative role.

One key point worth highlighting, which reiterates a point made above, is that where a redundancy situation does arise and this impacts upon an employee on maternity leave (either OML or AML) then the duty placed on the employer to offer suitable alternative employment is an absolute one. There is a need to give preference to the woman on maternity leave over other affected employees. This is irrespective of whether the employee has

---

[38] Maternity and Parental Leave etc Regulations 1999 Reg.18(4) and Reg.10.

[39] See ERA s.99 and Maternity and Parental Leave etc Regulations 1999 Reg. 20(1)(b).

[40] ERA s.141.

returned from maternity leave at the point of redundancy or not. Obviously, if a role exists and the employer considers this not to be suitable for the employee then it will not need to be offered to her.[41] However, given that if the tribunal disagrees with the conclusion reached by the employer then it is likely to lead to a finding of an unfair dismissal by reason of redundancy, discussing potential roles with the employee would be the safest option. Such a defensive tactic is further supported by the decision in *Visa International Services Association v. Paul*[42], where it was held that if there is a suitable vacancy which the employer fails to inform an employee on maternity leave of, then the tribunal will readily find such action to be a fundamental breach of the implied term of trust and confidence, which as a repudiatory breach will enable the employee to resign from their position and claim it to be a constructive dismissal.

The date on which the employee will return to work from maternity leave is contained within the notice that the employer gives to the employee within 28 days of having received the employee's notice, as already noted above. This date can be brought forward by the employee giving eight weeks' notice that she intends to return earlier. If it is not possible to give this period of notice then this then becomes subject to agreement by the employer, who can reasonably require the employee to wait until the end of the eight week period before her return.[43]

Although the date contained within the employer notice, or an early return date where sufficient notice has been given, is taken to indicate the precise date on which the employee will return to work, there are circumstances where this may not happen:
1. if the employer does not provide the required notice of the date of return in circumstances where she reasonably considers that the maternity leave has not end;[44]
2. where she takes other leave periods, which can include accrued holiday leave or parental leave; or
3. where she is ill at the end of the maternity period, in which case she will be absent from work in the same manner as any other ill worker would be.

---

[41] *Simpson v. Endsleigh Insurance Services* [2011] ICR 75

[42] *Visa International Services Association v. Paul* [2004] IRLR 42.

[43] Although this delay cannot be used to extend maternity leave beyond the 26 weeks OML or 52 weeks AML.

[44] Maternity and Parental Leave etc Regulations 1999 Regs. 19(2)- 20(3).

EQUALITY AND ANTI-DISCRIMINATION LAW

Where the return date has been confirmed, and this passes without the employee returning to work then this will be deemed to be an unauthorised absence, and as a consequence she will be subjected to the same disciplinary processes that any other worker who is taking an unauthorised absence would be.

Remedies

An employee who is pregnant, given birth, was suspended from work on maternity grounds, or took a period of OML or AML is protected from detriment[45] or dismissal for that reason.[46] However, this protection only extends for treatment in relation to one of these matters and does not extend beyond the period of maternity leave; it will not extend to matters that arise during the pregnancy or maternity leave that continue to impact upon the worker beyond this protected period. So, for example, even if an illness is wholly as a consequence of a pregnancy the protection will not extend to cover the period of time that the illness covers outside of OML or AML.[47]

An important right provided to a pregnant employee who is dismissed whilst still pregnant or during maternity leave is that she is automatically entitled to be given a written statement of reasons that explains in plain English the reasons behind her dismissals.[48] Such statement needs to be provided to the dismissed employee within 14 days of the dismissal.

Adoption Leave

An equivalent right to that discussed above in relation to maternity leave is available to employees who decide to adopt, with an employee qualifying for ordinary adoption leave if the employee:

(a) is the child's adopter;

(b) has been continuously employed for a period of not less than 26 weeks ending with the week in which he was notified of having been matched with the child, and

---

[45] ERA s.47C.

[46] If a dismissal is because of one of those reasons mentioned then it will be deemed to be an automatically unfair dismissal: ERA s.99 and Maternity and Parental Leave etc Regulations 1999 Reg. 20.

[47] This was the decision in a number of ECJ decisions, including *Handels-og v. Dansk Handel* (Case C-400/95).

[48] ERA s.92.

(c) has notified the agency that he agrees that the child should be placed with him and on the date of placement.[49]

As with OML, ordinary adoption leave lasts for 26 weeks, with an employee automatically being entitled to a further period of 26 weeks additional adoption leave on the conclusion of the ordinary adoption leave.

During both ordinary and additional adoption leave the employee is protected and afforded the same rights as those afforded to employees taking OML and AML. Similarly, as the position during OML and AML, the employer can maintain reasonable contact with the adoptive parent(s), and likewise the adoptive parent can take up to ten "keep in touch" working days during their leave. The same rights exist for adoptive periods in relation to returning to work after a period of adoption leave as that noted above for females returning from either OML or AML.

Statutory adoption pay (SAP) is provided, as with SMP, for a maximum of 39 weeks. In order to qualify for SAP, the adopter must:
- have been an employed earner in continuous employment for at least 26 weeks;
- satisfy an earnings threshold which is equal to or higher than the lower limit for the payment of national insurance contributions, during a reference period of eight weeks ending with the week in which the adopter is notified of an adoption match; and
- elect to receive SAP as opposed to Statutory Paternity Pay.

SAP is at the lower rate of either 90% of the employee's normal weekly earnings or the statutory rate, which is currently set at £139.58 (as from April 2015).

Where a couple is jointly adopting a child then the couple can decide which of the two take adoption leave.

Where a father shares responsibility for bringing up a child, which includes adopting a child, and where the employee is the biological father of the child or is the mother's husband or partner then, subject to satisfying the continuous service requirement of 26 weeks ending with the 15th week before the baby is due, or the end of the week in which the employee is notified of being matched for adoption, there is a right to paternity leave.

Paternity Leave

The father[50] of a child is entitled to take paternity leave so long as he is an employee with 26 weeks continuous service before the beginning of the

---

[49] Paternity and Adoption Leave Regulations 2002 s.15(2).

week that is 14 weeks before the expected week of childbirth.[51] If this is the case then paternity leave can either be taken as either a one week block of leave or two weeks, and must be taken within the first 56 days of the actual date of birth. This is to be taken in an unbroken block, with it not being possible to break up the paternity period.

As with most of these rights there is a notice requirement, with the employee being required to notify his employer that he intends to take paternity leave, along with the dates of leave, and the length of absence. The employer may request that the employee provides a signed declaration that states that they are taking the leave for the purposes of taking care of a child or supporting the child's mother and that he is the father of the child or mother's partner and will expect to have responsibility for the upbringing of the child.

Paternity pay is paid at the lower of Statutory Paternity Pay (SPP), which currently stands at £139.58 (from April 2015), or 90% of the employee's average weekly earnings. However, to receive SPP there are again conditions that need to be satisfied, which are very similar to that highlighted for SMP:

- The employee must have 26 weeks continuous employment by the beginning of the 14th week before the expected week of childbirth, or by the date on which an adoptive child has been matched.
- The employee's normal weekly earnings over a period of eight weeks before the relevant week must have been equal or higher to the lower earnings limit for the payment of NI contributions. This currently stands at £112 per week.

The employee's terms and conditions, except for remuneration, are protected during the paternity leave period. Likewise the employee on leave will be entitled to any enhanced terms that he would have received had he not been absent on paternity leave. The same protection from being subject to a detriment,[52] and a dismissal for a reason connected to paternity

---

[50] Although the norm is that this leave will be taken by a male father there are exceptions to this: where the partner of a birth mother or adoptive mother is female then she is entitled to take paternity leave, or where the adoptive father is the one who elects to take adoptive leave then the adoptive mother has this entitlement.

[51] To qualify for paternity leave in respect of an adoption the time at which 26 weeks continuous service must have been satisfied is the week in which the child's adopter is notified that they have been matched with a child.

[52] ERA s.47C

leave will be automatically unfair, apply to offer protection to employees who opt to take up this statutory right.

11.3.2. Parental Leave

In addition to the maternity, paternity and adoption rights that one has, there is additional parental leave that may be taken on top of these rights. In order to qualify for this right then an employee must have completed at least one year's continuous service with their employer,[53] and have (or expects to have) parental responsibility for the child. Once these hurdles are satisfied an employee has the right to take up to 18 weeks unpaid leave (this was increased to 18 weeks from 13 weeks on 8 March 2013) for each child born or adopted up until the child is five years old, or five years after placement where the child has been adopted; this is extended to allow parental leave to be taken up until the child's 18th birthday where the child has a disability.

Parental responsibility is a key central concept of the right.[54] The following will be deemed to have parental responsibility for this purpose:

- The birth mother is automatically considered to have parental responsibility.
- The father, if either he is married to the birth mother, or if he is not married to her then if he registers the birth jointly with her.
- Those deemed to have parental responsibility by court order.
- Those identified as having parental responsibility in a formal agreement with the child's birth mother.

In order to take parental leave the employee is required to give at least 21 days' notice before the start of the leave to their employer. There is no strict requirement for this to be in writing, but good practice would be to do so. When taking parental leave it is to be taken in blocks of one week, and any part week will be treated as a full week for the purposes of parental leave.[55] The employee is restricted to taking a maximum of four weeks in any given year.

---

[53] Although Parental Leave (Maternity and Parental Leave Regulations s.13A does allow, in some circumstances, periods of employment with previous employers to be taken into account in the calculation of the one year continuous service requirement where the child concerned has a disability.

[54] It is defined in the Children Act 1989 s.3, as amended by the Adoption and Children Act 2002, or Children (Scotland) Act 1995 s.1(3).

[55] *South Central Trains v. Rodway* [2004] IRLR 777.

The employer can request that the parental leave is postponed for up to six months, so long as they can establish a good business reason for doing so.

Unlike maternity leave or adoption leave or paternity leave there is no obligation to pay an employee during parental leave. As with other pay rights this will be dependent on the contract, but in this case, where the contract does not provide for pay during parental leave then any leave taken is likely to be unpaid.

The same protections with regards to terms and conditions and returning to the same position that was occupied before the period of leave that apply for maternity leave and adoption leave likewise apply here. In other words, the employee's terms and conditions are maintained, they continue to be protected by the implied term of trust and confidence, they receive enhanced terms where these would have been given had leave not been taken, and the employee is protected in terms of the role that they return to on completion of the leave period.

Similar to the other periods of leave if notice is given for parental leave and the employer unreasonably refuses the request then the affected employee may present a complaint to the employment tribunal, which if it makes a finding of unreasonable delay, will make a declaration to that effect an award compensation at a level that is considered just and equitable in the circumstances. Equally, the employee is protected from suffering a detriment as a result of taking parental leave[56], with any dismissal that takes place because an employee requested to take or did take parental leave will be automatically unfair[57].

11.3.3. Shared Parental Leave

A new initiative introduced as part of the family friendly policies enables parents to share the leave period following either the birth or the adoption of their child. This idea of Shared Parental Leave (SPL) was introduced as of 5 April 2015. This enables parents, if certain eligibility criteria are satisfied, to share up to 50 weeks of leave; it reflects the same period of time that a mother receives as maternity leave (OML + AML) minus the first two weeks compulsory leave that a mother must take following giving birth.

There are some qualifications attached to the right to take SPL:

- The applicant must have shared responsibility for the child with:

---

[56] ERA s.47C

[57] ERA s.99

- - their husband, wife, civil partner or joint adopter;
  - the child's other parent; or
  - their partner (if they live together with the child.
- Either of the two individuals who have responsibility must be eligible for either maternity leave and pay, adoption leave and pay or maternity allowance
- There is a continuous employment requirement, with SPL only available to an individual who has been continuously employed for at least 26 weeks by the end of the 15th week before the expected week of childbirth, or by the date on which an adoptive child has been matched.
- There is a requirement to remain with the same employer whilst the SPL period is taken.

In addition there is a need to establish that during the 66 weeks prior to the expected week of childbirth that the partner of the individual applying for SPL has been working for at least 26 weeks (although this does not have to be continuously), and must have earned at least £390 in total over the an 13 weeks in that 66 week period.

If these qualifications are met then any remaining period of maternity leave can be exchanged for SPL, which can then be shared between parents during the child's first year (either of birth or from being placed with their adoptive parents). In order to transfer to the SPL system a mother (or adoptive parent) will need to give a minimum of eight weeks' notice with their decision to shorten their maternity or adoption leave with a view to SPL. In addition, which in reality is around the same time, both parents will need to submit a notice of entitlement stating their intention to take SPL. There is a cool-off period of six weeks, during which if there is a change of mind in respect of SPL then the request to exchange maternity or adoption leave can be reversed.

This gives parents great flexibility, especially when one considers that there is no requirement that any periods of leave must be taken independently. Parents are thus given a choice how to use this leave, and could opt to double up in effect by taking leave at the same time, so long as the cumulative number of weeks across both parents does not exceed the period of leave that has been provided.

Further flexibility in the system is provided by there being no need to take SPL all in one go. A parent is able to book up to three separate blocks of

SPL[58] of at least one week each, so long as they take place within that first year of the child being with the parents and they give their employer at least eight weeks' notice. However, there is a distinction between periods of leave that are continuous and those that are not: if the leave is continuous then the employer cannot refuse the request, whereas where the leave is discontinuous the employer does have an element of discretion.

As with the majority of these policies there is pay that may accompany the period of leave in the form of Statutory Shared Parental Pay (ShPP), with this being provided to those who are eligible for SMP or SAP, or if an individual is eligible for SPP with their partner eligible for SMP, MA or SAP. ShPP is paid at the same rate as SMP, and as such is the lower of £139.58 a week or 90 of an employee's average weekly earnings. ShPP does not cover the entire period of SPL, but as with SMP is limited to a maximum of 39 weeks. However, this 39 weeks starts to run from when maternity pay is received. In other words, ShPP is paid for a period that covers 39 weeks minus any weeks where maternity pay, maternity allowance or adoption pay is received.

SPL does not impact upon a person's eligibility to paternity leave. However, it has wholly replaced the previous system of additional paternity leave.

11.4. Conclusions on family friendly policies

The UK has introduced a number of useful initiatives in an attempt to ensure that family life, of which the burden often disproportionately rests with the mother, does not impact upon an individual's partipicipation in the labour market. In particular, it ensures that expectant mothers are protected in a number of ways, with a view to preserving the employment relationship: this can be seen through time off for antenatal classes, maternity leave and protection of the worker on health and safety grounds. Having a child should not be something that is balanced or offset against having a career. Furthermore, enabling an individual who has a caring responsibility the right to request flexible working, to try to remove situations where there is a choice to be made between family or a career, can again be viewed as a means of ensuring that a career is not given up in favour of a family life; the two are not mutually exclusive. The most clear impact of such protections is the retention of females in the workplace: not only are initiatives in place to ensure that such workers feel they can

---

[58] This can be increased by agreement with the employer.

continue to work, but it also precludes less favourable treatment against them.

However, there are also other useful initaives that have great potential. Involving other persons who have parental responsibility, either through paternity leave, shared maternity leave or other means has the potential to shift the presumption that a new family only affects the role of a woman at work; this potential to change attitudes may eventually equalise treatment and ensure that family life is not used as a reason to subject a female worker to a detriment.

Althought the protections discussed do appear to have use in establishing equality, they do not offer complete protections, and as such have their limitations. The right to request flexible working is just that, it is merely the right to request, with an obligation merely to consider. Furthermore, many of the rights have quite rigid qualification requirements, which not all can satisfy. But the biggest limitation in respect of the family friendly policies is that of remuneration: the low replacement remuneration involved makes it difficult for such rights to be invoked. This is particularly likely to reduce the number of working fathers who will choose to take shared maternity leave, just as there is one more mouth to feed.

12.   Atypical Worker Protection

12.1.   Introduction

This chapter will focus on the non-standard forms of work of part-time work and fixed-term employment – both of which are deemed to be atypical work arrangements. As this chapter will identify it is usually particular categories of individuals that take up part-time work, and as such any negative treatment towards these positions will have a disproportionate impact on those particular categories. Furthermore, this chapter will identify the rationale behind why UK employment law was focussed to offer protection for full-time and permanent workers, before relying on statistics to identify that 'atypical' work is no longer atypical to the extent of not needing regulated, and ought to be treated fairly and comparably with other contractual arrangements. As a consequence the atypical worker protection forms part of the vast equality landscape in the UK.

Moving away from protected characteristics, which is so often the focus when one considers equality and non-discrimination in the UK, protection of part-time and fixed-term workers fits in with the broader idea of equality: especially when one considers that ordinarily individuals will be undertaking like roles, and completing similar duties, irrespective of whether they are employed on a permanent full-time contract as opposed to a part-time or fixed-term arrangement. If equality between the types of contract is not achieved then in effect the UK would have a two tier labour market: the gold plated typical employment, and the lesser class atypical employment.

Atypical working relationships started to become much more popular as a working arrangement throughout the 1990s, with this trend continuing to this day. The popularity of these arrangements came through a desire to mix flexible working arrangements with job security (the popular term being flexicurity), which forms the dual objectives of the UK labour market. It must be noted from the outset that 'atypical work' is a collective term that is attached to work that is not deemed typical.

Many of the social rights that make up the regulatory labour systems across Europe, and in the UK, were introduced to supress perceived threats to the established social order, and as such were focussed in particular on unionised, skilled manual workers who ordinarily worked full-time hours. The consequence of this focus during the developmental stage of social and labour protection was that it was only the workforce that were deemed typical and the norm that were covered, with other marginal categories being ignored, leaving atypical workers simply falling outside of the protections. This in effect led to a regulatory gap in protection when one compares the position of the full time, permanent typical employee with those engaged on a different type of contract, including part-time workers and those on fixed-term contracts.

However, the labour market landscape has changed somewhat. According to the August 2015 ONS labour market statistics,[1] out of the 31.03 million people in work there are now 8.27 million part-time jobs, and as such part-time work made up 26.7% of the UK workforce, with 74% of these positions being filled by women. When one considers that over a quarter of those in work are now employed part-time then this in itself explains why equal treatment between full-time and part-time work ought to be a labour market aim. However, this is further supported by the fact that any less favourable treatment of part-time workers is likely to equate to less favourable treatment of female workers, given that the majority of par time work is filled by women. Statistics on incidence of fixed-term work is not quite as easy to find. However, Eurostat produces annual employment statistics, which considers the different forms of atypical work. This study suggests that in 2014 6.3% of the UK workforce were employed on fixed-term or limited duration contracts.[2]

It is clear from such statistics that what we deem to be atypical arrangements are no longer atypical to the same extent that they were previously, with a number of employers making use of such arrangements to a greater degree in the modern labour market. There are a number of forces that may explain this gradual shift:

- Manual skilled work is no longer as dominant in the UK economy as it once was, with there being a significant growth in the services industry. One of the key requirements for the service industry is flexibility, which appears to be better achieved through less rigid contractual engagements.[3]

- In a global market, such as the one that UK businesses are now competing, there is a need for businesses to operate in an efficient and

---

[1] The August ONS Labour Market publication can be accessed at: www.ons.gov.uk/ons/rel/lms/labour-market-statistics/august-2015/statistical-bulletin.html#tab-1--Employment [last accessed on 31.08.2015].

[2] The breakdown of the employment statistics relating to fixed term contracts can be seen at http://appsso.eurostat.ec.europa.eu/nui/show.do [last accessed 31.08.2015]

[3] Reference to flexicurity!!! [ADD]

cost effective way. Atypical working arrangements are often viewed as having the greatest cost efficiency potential.

- The supply and demand of labour no longer favours the supplier of labour, at least not the way it previously did. Employers, now being in a much stronger bargaining position, are now to insist on positions being occupied by atypical arrangements in order to maximise their efficiencies to the detriment of typical arrangements.

- The position of women in the workplace has changed dramatically, with women being valued and accepted members of the workforce; however, there is still the perception and the practice (to some extent) of females maintaining a work life balance, and having greater family responsibilities. This can lead to a desire for alternative, more flexible working arrangements being sought.

Increased regulation of both part-time workers and fixed-term workers was introduced in the early 2000s as a result of European developments, with the protection of agency workers being introduced through national legislation in 2010. Each of these will be considered respectively below.

12.2. Part-Time Worker Protection

Part-time work in the UK has traditionally had no statutory definition, but it has been generally accepted that this covers working arrangements that involve working less than 30 hours per week. The rights of workers that were deemed to be part-time workers varied depending on the position that the individual was in, with certain rights being subject to qualification periods or in some instances simply not being awarded. Some of the most notable exceptions include the preclusion of part-time workers from unfair dismissal and notice periods where the employee worked less than eight hours per week, although this is no longer the case.

In order to transpose Directive 97/81/EC[4] Part-Time Workers (Prevention of Less Favourable Treatment) Regulations 2000[OBJ], with a view to ensuring[5] *'that part-timers are no longer discriminated against'.*[OBJ][6] any of the provisions of the Regulations mirror verbatim those contained within the Directive, with the UK electing not to depart too far from its express wording. In essence, the UK has introduced the bare minimum needed to ensure that

---

[4] Which was extended to cover the UK by Directive 98/23/EC.

[5] The Regulations into force on 1 July 2000, and were passed under of the Employment Relations Act 1999 s.19.

[6] As declared by Stephen Byers, the then Secretary of State for Trade and Industry, on the unveiling of the Regulations; whether the UK Regulations achieve such.

they are compliant with their European obligations. In essence, the UK has introduced the bare minimum needed to ensure that they are compliant with their European obligations.

The bare minimum approach, as suggested by Kilpatrick and Freedland,[7] can be witnessed throughout the 2000 Regulations. For example, the definitions attached to both part-time and full-time employees contained within Regulation 2 mirror exactly that contained within Clause 3 of the Directive. Regulation 2 effectively identifies a full-time worker as an individual who can be identified as a full-time worker, having regard to the custom and practice of the employer, whereas a part-time worker is not identified in these circumstances as a full-time worker. This moves away from the commonly accepted notion that a part-time worker is anybody who works 30 hours or less, and moves the focus on to the custom and practice of the employer. This means that determining whether an individual is a full-time or part-time worker will always require consideration of the entire workforce of the establishment at which they are employed. This reinforces the idea of 'typical employment', but places this into the specific context of individual workplaces. The issue of a full-time worker and part-time worker will not cause too many problems in practice. However, two illustrative cases that suggest that the exercise will not always be straightforward. These are the *O'Brien*[8] case, where the Supreme Court found part-time judicial office-holders were part-time workers within the Regulations, and the *Hudson*[9] case, where the Court of Appeal found that a full-time job was in fact two separate part-time positions.

The core of the Regulations can be read at Regulation 5, which introduces the non-discrimination principle:

Less favourable treatment of part-time workers
5(1) A part-time worker has the right not to be treated by his employer less favourably than the employer treats a comparable full-time worker—
(a) as regards the terms of his contract; or
(b) by being subjected to any other detriment by any act, or deliberate failure to act, of his employer.

---

[7] Kilpatrick, C., and Freedland, M. (2004), *"The UK: how is EU governance transformative?"*, Ch. 10 in Employment Policy and the Regulation of Part-Time Work in the European Union – a comparative analysis, Sciarra, Davies and Freedland (eds.), Cambridge University Press: Cambridge.

[8] *Ministry of Justice v. O'Brien* [2013] I WLR 522.

[9] *Hudson v University of Oxford* [2007] EWCA Civ 336.

(2) The right conferred by paragraph (1) applies only if—

    (a) the treatment is on the ground that the worker is a part-time worker, and

    (b) the treatment is not justified on objective grounds.

In essence Regulation 5 attempts to ensure that there is equal treatment between those employed on part-time work with those who are suitable comparable full-time workers. However, there is the notable inclusion of the objective justification, which enables the employer to establish that there was good reason for treating the part-time worker less favourably when compared to those on a full-time contract. As with that discussed under the Equality Act (see **Chapter 4.3.1**), less favourable treatment requires consideration of whether there is some detriment present. This is a broad concept, and has been held to include a variety of different treatments, including lesser holiday entitlements being given to part-time workers[10] and lack of access to an occupational pension scheme that was open to full-time workers, or where access is given a different level of worker contribution.[11] There are the obvious inclusions too. Regulation 5(3) gives some substance to the principle, although not much, through requiring pro rata treatment to be applied 'where appropriate'.

As the Regulations are expressed in the terms of less favourable treatment, this automatically suggests the need for a comparison between a full-time worker and a part-time worker. Helpfully regulation 2(4) defines who will be a suitable comparable worker for the purposes of the Regulations:

A full-time worker is a comparable full-time worker in relation to a part-time worker if, at the time when the treatment that is alleged to be less favourable to the part-time worker takes place—

    (a) both workers are—

        (i) employed by the same employer under the same type of contract, and

        (ii) engaged in the same or broadly similar work having regard, where relevant, to whether they have a similar level of qualification, skills and experience; and

    (b) the full-time worker works or is based at the same establishment as the part-time worker or, where there is no full-time worker working or based at that establishment who satisfies the requirements of sub-paragraph (a), works or is

---

[10] *Zentralbetriebsrat der Landeskrankenhäuser Tirols v Land Tirol* [2010] IRLR 631 (Case C-486/08).

[11] *INPS v Bruno* [2010] IRLR 890.

> based at a different establishment and satisfies those requirements.

What is clear is that the concept has been defined quite narrowly. In particular, the concept is restricted through the need for both the full-time worker and the part-time worker to be employed by the same employer under the same type of contract. This can cause some difficulties especially when on the face of it a part-time role can look to involve broadly similar work to a full-time role, but may involve a different type of contract.[12] For example, if an individual is engaged to undertake part-time work under a *contract for servicescontract of service*. Irrespective of whether the two individuals have the same duties or work obligations they will not be suitable comparators on a strict reading of the Regulation 2(4). This ease of evading the scope of the Regulations is reinforced by Regulation 2(3), which provides a list of situations that will be regarded as being employed under different types of contract, these being:

(a) employees employed under a contract that is neither for a fixed term nor a contract of apprenticeship;

(b) employees employed under a contract for a fixed term that is not a contract of apprenticeship;

(c) employees employed under a contract of apprenticeship;

(d) workers who are neither employees nor employed under a contract for a fixed term;

(e) workers who are not employees but are employed under a contract for a fixed term;

(f) other description of worker that it is reasonable for the employer to treat differently from other workers on the ground that workers of that description have a different type of contract.

Categories (a) – (e) provide employers with a means of compartmentalizing their workforce with the consequence of avoiding the reach of the Regulations, should they wish to introduce full-time workers and part-time workers on different sets of terms and conditions. Furthermore, category (f) introduces an open-ended category, which will likewise disapply the non-discrimination principle of the Regulations. The breadth of Regulation 2(3) can only be viewed as damaging to the operation of this protection from a part-time worker perspective, although employer's will argue that it is a necessary compromise built into the Regulations, otherwise soaring costs would be incurred which would stifle part-time work creation.

Furthermore, there is reference to a need to work or be based at the same establishment yet there does not appear to be any guidance on the concept

---

[12] See *Matthews v Kent & Medway Towns Fire Authority* [2006] UKHL 8.

of 'establishment' for the purposes of part-time worker protection. However, given that this has come directly from the Directive, it is supposed that European jurisprudence will offer some light on the matter. Unfortunately, from a social protection point of view, it appears that the CJEU appears to favour a narrow concept of establishment, if the recent *Woolworths*[13] decision is anything to go by.[14] This would restrict consideration of comparable workers to those that are employed within the unit, rather than the business as a whole, in which any complainant is employed, which further narrows the concept.

Given that finding a suitable comparator is central to the operation of the protections then this narrow definition is clearly going to have an impact on the scope of the benefits that are derived from them. The requirement of such a comparator as a limitation is put into perspective when one considers that at the time the Regulations were introduced it was estimated that only one sixth of all part-time workers in the UK would be able to identify a suitable comparator.

There are two exceptions to the need for a comparator, covering a narrow range of situations: where there is a transfer to part-time work from full-time work or where the employee has returned after an absence of less than a year 'to the same job or to a job on the same level' (Regulation 3 and 4).

A useful right given to part-time workers is that they can request a written statement of reasons for less favourable treatment. This is supposed to explain in plain English why there are differences between the full-time staff and part-time staff. Unsurprisingly there is a three month time limit that applies for bringing a claim under the Regulations.[15]

The Regulations are not the most detailed, and as a consequence the Government issued 'guidance notes' and a 'programme of information' which was to add flesh to the bones and explain the practical application of the protection. These additional documents mostly provide very basic guidance. For example, it suggests that the Regulations require an equalization of hourly rate of pay and overtime pay where hours are

---

[13] *USDAW & Wilson v Woolworths & Ors* [2015] (Case C-182/13).

[14] Although this may be questioned given that this was decided in the context of collective redundancies under the Collective Redundancy Directive.

[15] Unsurprising in the sense that a three month time limit appears to be the norm in relation to employment law matters.

worked in excess of normal full-time hours.[16] Other areas that are mentioned where there is a need for equal treatment include contractual sick pay, maternity pay, access to occupational pension schemes, selection for redundancy, promotion and training. Although introducing practical guidance can only be a good thing, it is limited to consideration of matters that are fairly obvious.

12.3. Fixed-Term Workers

Fixed-term contract workers can be viewed through the UK's traditional approach to contractual relations, that parties were free to enter any contract that they so choose. In other words, fixed-term contracts were not subject to any significant restriction, either in their use, their duration or when a decision was to be made with respect renewals. Similarly, there were no provisions in UK law that would convert a fixed-term contract into a permanent one,[17] which in some senses could leave the worker in a long-term precarious position. Other than the limited duration of the contract the engagement operated in a fairly similar way to any other employment contract.[18] However, there was one major difference between fixed-term contracts when compared to a permanent contract, with the parties to a fixed-term contract being capable of agreeing to waive unfair dismissal rights where the dismissal was due to non-renewal,[19] whereas this was not possible for permanent employees.

The protection for those employed on fixed-term working contracts is derived from the Fixed-Term Employees (Prevention of Less Favourable Treatment) Regulations 2002 'FTER'), which transposed in to UK law Council Directive 1999/70/EC (the Part Time Worker Directive), the UK adopted a minimalist approach to satisfying their European obligations. Similar to the approach under the PTWR the FTER primarily offers

---

[16] This could be subject to criticism in that a part time worker would have to work a lot more hours over their contractual hours in order to attract pay at an overtime rate: a more suitable approach would have been to ensure parity of pay in circumstances where a worker workers over and above their ordinary working hours. The current approach does not offer the same incentive to a part time worker to work over their contracted hours as it does to full time workers. This is a clear example of ensuring formal equality rather than substantive equality.

[17] Although there was possibility of arguing that implicit conversion had taken place if a fixed term contract overruns the limited nature of it.

[18] For example, working time rights and termination rights operated in a very similar way.

[19] Non-renewal of a fixed term contract is deemed to be a form of dismissal for unfair dismissal purposes under ERA s.95.

protection through utilising the non-discrimination principle[20][OBJ] providing protection on non-discrimination grounds in relation to the terms and conditions of work ,[21] any other detriment by any act, or deliberate failure to act, of his employer'. There is express reference to periods of service qualification, training opportunities, and access to available permanent positions within the establishment,[OBJ] which require equal treatment. However, equally relevant to the FTER, as was present in the operation of the PTWR and in general equality law, is the principle of objective justification, with the Regulation 3(3) providing that the FTER will not be breached where the employer can establish that the less[22] treatment based on being a fixed-term employee was 'justified on objective grounds'.

In a shift in approach from that adopted under the equal pay provisions, Regulation 4 FTER enables the fixed-term contract to be viewed as a whole, rather than requiring a term-by-term comparison. In other words, less favourable treatment in relation to one term can be compensated for with more favourable treatment elsewhere within the contract. However, this introduces a difficult analytical exercise, as it is impossible to determine whether one term is sufficient to compensate for the less favourable treatment of another. This introduces an element of uncertainty, and provides the employer with easy submissions that may act to reduce the impact of the FTER.

A clear positive measure that has been introduced through the FTER is the removal of contractual waivers to unfair dismissal protection and redundancy rights.[23] This ensures that employers cannot use the unequal bargaining power present within such contracts to remove these key rights. In this respect, the FTER have had a positive impact, and ensure that such

---

[20] Arguably the UK has introduced protection that falls below that required by the EU, given that it has opted to restrict the 2002 Regulations to those who are defined as an employee, rather than the wider concept of worker, which the Directive appears to require.

[21] Regulation 3 FTER

[22] The protection in relation to permanent positions within the establishment is not limited to simply having access, but Regulation 3(6) FTER imposes an obligation on to the employer to inform any fixed-term employees working within the establishment of permanent positions that have been made available. Although there is no obligation to give priority to such workers, there is a clear requirement to provide the necessary information to enable them to make an application.

[23] These were removed by the Employment Relations Act 1999.

employees receive equal statutory protection in this respect with their permanent counterparts.

It is within Regulation 8 that we can view the attempts to regulate the 'abuse' of fixed-term contracts. Regulation 8 provides that any contractual term to the effect that an employee's contract is for a fixed term shall be of no effect if the contract has previously been renewed or the employee previously employed on a fixed-term contract, if

(a) the employee has been continuously employed for four years or more;[24] and

(b) the employment of the employee under a fixed-term contract was not justified on objective grounds.

Regulation 8(5) allows for a collective agreement to modify the maximum period, or the maximum number of renewals, or 'objective grounds justifying the renewal of fixed-term contracts, or the engagement' of employees under successive fixed-term contracts. This protection against abuse of fixed-term contracts, which if allowed could have seen employees being retained on such precarious contracts for significant periods of time with no long term security, is clearly key to the FTER. However, this is again subject to the defence of objective justification, which, depending on how this is applied, may reduce this protective provision.

One point in relation to the abuse of fixed-term contracts is worth noting, and that is that the protection against successive fixed-term contracts only applies once the cumulative extent of contracts goes beyond four years. Should the relationship never extend beyond four years then the employer is free to make use of fixed-term contracts. Even in circumstances where the multiple contracts eventually go beyond this time period, conversion to a permanent contract is not an automatic consequence, given that retaining the employee on such a limited term contract is still possible where it is justified by objective reasons. In other words, even where the four-year period is completed the employee may need to go to great expense, both in time and money, to bring an employer before tribunal in order to gain their rights under Regulation 8 of the FTER, and even in these circumstances it will be a matter for the tribunal as to whether they find for the employee or for the employer. At no point is such a conversion a foregone conclusion. It is quite clear when one considers the FTER that it is unlikely that they will have a major impact upon the protections of such workers.

---

[24] Continuity being measured from a date on or after 10 July 2002.

12.4. Conclusions

It is easy to make a case for increased protection and equal treatment for individuals who are engaged under a contract that is either lacking in permanency or is subject to less working time than the norm. Some of this rationale is based upon the type of individual who often accepts such work, most notably working mothers, with whom flexibility of working hours or reduced working hours are desirable. However, there are other clear justifications: most notably being that the historic labour market conditions that led to the development of labour regulation such as to focus on full time, permanent employment no longer exists. Indeed there is a strong case now to suggest that the UK labour market is diverse, and constitutes of individuals on a number of different forms of contracts, including part-time and fixed-term contracts. The growing incidence of such contracts suggests that the regulatory framework needed to change to take account of such growth, and ensure that individuals who are engaged under such contracts are not treated as if they were second class employees.

In order to ensure that equality across typical and atypical contracts exists the EU took the lead, and required each Member State to introduce protections to give effect to Directive 97/81/EC on part-time worker protection and Directive 99/70/EC on fixed-term worker protection. The UK purported to satisfy their obligations in both respects through the Part-Time Workers (Prevention of Less Favourable Treatment) Regulations 2000 and the Fixed-Term Employees (Prevention of Less Favourable Treatment) Regulations 2002 respectively.

There are clear weaknesses present within the two sets of regulations that have been introduced which, to some extent restrict the protections that they seek to introduce. Of particular note is the restricted approach to a comparable worker under the PTWR, and the restriction of the FTER to employees. Each of these has the potential to curb the success of these statutory instruments. Even if these restrictions are overcome, much of the success of each set of the protections will ultimately depend on the approach taken by the courts to objective justification. There is little guidance on this matter as yet in this specific context. However, should the approach mirror that adopted under equal pay and indirect effect then the employer will not be held to a high standard of proof, and the protection of both part-time workers and fixed-term employees will suffer.

Despite the negative tone adopted above in relation to both the PTWR and the FTER, there are some positive aspects of each of the regulations:

- they introduce some protection into a previously unregulated area, and ensure that employers bargain and maintain part-time and fixed-term relationships in the shadow of these protective instruments; and
- they have acted to remove the idea that the type of contract one is engaged under can determine the level of employment protections, with both part-time workers and fixed-term employees not being stripped of basic employment law rights.

This is best seen through the application of unfair dismissal protection and redundancy protection to such contracts.

13. Concluding Remarks

The principle of equality is not a simple concept to understand, given that it is an umbrella term that covers a variety of different approaches, one of which is key concept of 'non-discrimination'; the term that is often associated as the primary facet of equality. This makes an evaluation of equality laws in the UK extremely difficult as the standard differs depending on the strand of equality that underpins the protection in question. One thing that is evident is that the equality protections of the UK have developed away from the simplistic approach of direct comparisons between individuals to ensure that like is treated alike, with greater focus on equality of opportunity through removing aspects of the labour market that impede participation. This development can be clearly identified throught the Equality Act 2010, and is one to be applauded given its greater focus on dealing with systemic and perpetuating issues with a view to removing the problem at its core, rather than considering the matter solely from the perspective of an individual complainant.

Equality and non-discrimination law is legally complex and a difficult subject to keep abreast of, which is where I hope this book has been of great use. Case law and statutory developments are fast moving in this area, given that political agendas, the economy and societal needs are not static, and often require the scope of such protections to be reconsidered in light of these. Further complexity is introduced by the fact that this area is not the domain of a single entity, but witnesses the divergence of three separate legal systems into it: namely national law, EU law and the law of the ECHR. Consequently there is a need to understand the co-operation and inter-dependence that exists between these three systems, but also introduces other sources of development.

The UK's approach to equality has developed rapidly since the first sources of such non-discrimination protection existed. Focus was initially extremely limited, with a focus on race and sex, before expanding dramatically, which was mainly due to EU developments in this area.

Despite some 50 years in the making there are still some questionable approaches to equality and non-discrimination protection evident in the UK, which can be suggested to weaken or undermine the UK's system.

A central weakness is that despite advancements toward substantive and transformative equality, the UK still develops such protection on the principle of formal equality. This is most evident in the protections that have developed outside of (and before) the Equality Act 2010, such as the atypical worker protections. Even those developments within the Equality

Act that appear to offer equality on a different footing may be criticised for their approach: the Public Sector Equality Duty, for example, on the face of it, has great potential. However, it is limited in real use through only having a requirement to have 'due regard' to equality issues rather than imposing a more substantial obligation.

Other sources of criticism can easily be identified such as the decision not to introduce s.14 of the Equality Act 2010, which would have offered combined discrimination protection. Or the need to identify an actual comparator for equal pay protection, despite developments in the use of hypothetical comparators outside of equal pay (although this is understandable given equal pay is about discriminatory conduct in contracts, and in any event s.71 of the Equality Act 2010 allows hypothetical comparators through the back door where no actual comparator exists for equal pay purposes).

An area that may need to be tightened up on is that of objective justification. This appears too easy to utilise, especially in equal pay situations or where it is being considered in a direct age discrimination complaint. The use of market forces to justify differences in pay makes it a system that is fairly easy to evade, whereas the acceptance of intergenerational workforces as a legitimate aim has the same consequence in the context of direct age discrimination.

A final point of critism that I would like to raise briefly is in relation to family friendly policies: this appears to witness the giving of rights with one hand, but the taking away with the other. The family friendly policies as a whole look fairly generous, and offer some useful rights and protections; however, their take up was inevitably going to be difficult given that pay was restricted to what appears to be a deterent level.

Despite there being weaknesses evident within the system, it is not all doom and gloom. And there have been developments over the past decade or so that have enhanced the journey towards equality in the UK. Notable developments include the use of broad and inclusive interpretations of key concepts where possible. This has led to various welcome developments, including protection against both associative and perceptive discrimination, a definition of disability that covers a wide range of impairments, as well as extensions across harassment protection.

A key development in the progress of equality protection is the reversed burden of proof. This is significant. Placing the evidential burden on the perpetrator once a prima facie case is established by the complainant is quite possibly the greatest advancement in this area. Given that it is usually the person who causes discrimination that is in the best position to explain and evidence the reasons behind an action, and that such person is often in the better financial position, it makes sense from a practical and evidential point of view to adopt such an approach. Alleviating such an evidential burden from the complainant in situations where it would be difficult for them to compile the requisite evidence acts to ensure that complaints do not fail simply due to the employer acting covertly in the decision-making process.

Other useful developments include the wide range of remedial action, which includes the discretion to award unlimited compensation (a huge deterrent) as well as the discretion to order various recommendations of change to an employer's practices ensure that not only will a victim be sufficiently compensated but that the root cause of the discrimination can be remedied too. The atypical worker protections also have unique and useful approaches evident, including placing obligations on employers to justify non-renewal of fixed term contracts, and the removal of the need for statistical evidence in bringing complaints of part-time worker discrimination (this is in comparison to the previous approach where female part-time workers would rely on indirect sex discrimination to bring a claim). Such developments go some way to advancing equality of treatment. The family friendly policies also have positive aspects to them: of particular note is the focus that these have in changing perception. By retaining talented mothers it widens the skills pool for selection, but also evidences to employers that becoming a mother is not a barrier to success. Furthermore, by giving more opportunity for a father to be involved in the raising and caring of a child there is potential that the long held view that mothers have the caring responsibility in the family, which can have the consequence of negative perceptions, may be changed over time; although such a change in view is likely to be a long process, this is at least a start.

As one can appreciate every system has its relative strengths and weaknesses. One point that we need always to bear in mind is that no law is perfect, and many of the protections that we introduce are the result of compromise following parliamentary debates and with a view to retaining sufficient support from both members of the public and from business. Pushing the protections (or lack thereof) too far in one direction will alienate a key portion of political support, which could have inevitable consequences come the next general election. Consequently, the laws of the UK, evident to those who have equality at their heart, are a compromise. Furthermore, even with the system being far from perfect, one thing is clear, the protections that have been introduced are incrementally developing, and it is always better to have some protection with weaknesses, rather than none at all!

Index

INDEX